Ambivalent *Macbeth*

First published in 2018 by Sydney University Press
© R.S. White 2018
© Sydney University Press 2018

Parts of this work originally appeared in *Shakespeare's Macbeth*, part of the Horizon Studies in Literature series, published by Sydney University Press in association with Oxford University Press, 1995.

Reproduction and communication for other purposes
Except as permitted under the Act, no part of this edition may be reproduced, stored in a retrieval system, or communicated in any form or by any means without prior written permission. All requests for reproduction or communication should be made to Sydney University Press at the address below:

Sydney University Press
Fisher Library F03
University of Sydney NSW 2006
AUSTRALIA
sup.info@sydney.edu.au
sydney.edu.au/sup

This catalogue record for this book is available from the National Library of Australia.

ISBN 9781743325483 paperback
ISBN 9781743325490 epub
ISBN 9781743325506 mobi
ISBN 9781743325513 pdf

Cover image: *Macbeth*, c. 1820, by John Martin (1789–1854), oil on canvas, reproduced by permission of the National Galleries of Scotland. Photograph by Antonia Reeve.
Cover design by Miguel Yamin.

Ambivalent *Macbeth*

R.S. White

SYDNEY UNIVERSITY PRESS

Contents

Preface and Acknowledgements — vii

Prologue: Sinners as Heroes — 1
1. Contexts of Ambiguity: Text, Sources, History — 13
2. "Fair is foul and foul is fair": The Radical Ambivalence of *Macbeth* — 33
3. "Nothing is but what is not": Emotional Worlds of Characters in *Macbeth* — 59
4. "The seeds of time" and the Macbeths — 101
5. "Palter with us in a double sense": Leading Ideas – Temptation, Equivocation, Evil — 117
6. "This is the very painting of your fear": Imagery and the Emotional World of *Macbeth* — 143
7. *Macbeth* on Stage and Screen — 167

Bibliography — 199
Index — 209

Preface and Acknowledgements

The "first coming" of this book was in 1995, when a very much briefer version appeared in the Horizon Studies in Literature series published by Sydney University Press in association with Oxford University Press, with a strict word limit on each volume to suit the series. The aim of that admirable collection of short critical studies was "to refresh students' and teachers' readings of these books, by offering detailed close analysis allied to an overview informed by recent trends in criticism and scholarship". The decision to reissue this one in a form completely revised and substantially expanded (three times the length) has been made for three main reasons. First, the original book sold out very quickly and has not been revived, while records show that in educational libraries it has consistently been borrowed on an annual basis, suggesting there is a continuing readership. Secondly, the general editor's preface, written by Penny Gay, suggested:

> Literary criticism is never static; what seemed important to say about a work twenty or fifty years ago will seem glaringly obvious, or irrelevant, to us today. This is because our own perspective or way of viewing the world limits and defines our reading, especially our reading of the past (even the recent past).

This is the case in my re-readings of Shakespeare, and since it is now over twenty years since I recorded my impressions of *Macbeth*, it is inevitable they have changed, explaining and perhaps justifying the longer length and a wider perspective. The main theme concentrating on ambivalence remains, but the "horizon" of consideration has widened to incorporate new material and ideas. Thirdly, the restriction on the previous publication was that its audience was conceived as students, whereas here I have tried to address in more detail some of the scholarly issues, hoping to make suggestions which other scholars might take up, widening the potential readership while not losing touch with student needs and interests. I have also tried to write in a way that will interest the wider play-going public. One ghostly trace remains in that now and then key quotations will recur in the new chapters since they can be used to exemplify different points when placed in different contexts and seen from different angles. This is also at times a function of the fact that each chapter is presented as to some extent a self-sufficient discussion of an aspect of a single play, so there will be inevitable overlaps here and there.

Most obviously, there have been many more staged performances and movies of *Macbeth* since 1995, which have opened new and different perspectives and further demonstrate the play's plurality of readings, so the final chapter needed updating. In addition, this edition presents several completely new chapters on ideas or themes driving the play, which now seem to me to be important in understanding the play's substructure. The most prominent change has taken place in myself. In particular, my involvement since 2011 in the Australian Research Council Centre for Excellence in the History of Emotions 1100–1800 has provided an opportunity to focus on the primacy of emotions in history, literature and beyond. The concept of "emotional worlds" is advanced as a loose but suggestive way of expressing new insights into characterisation in an old and familiar text. At every level of understanding of *Macbeth*, from the text itself to performance on stage and screen and to analysis of ideas, characters and imagery, emotions will be involved as driving forces behind interpretation. Fundamentally, the aim remains the same as the original Horizons series' philosophy to be "liberating" in the hope that scholars and students will find "new information about the writer's world (both historical and imaginative)", and that readers of Shakespeare will be directed to explore "techniques of critical reading that they may not yet have encountered ... to expand the reader's horizon". But the horizon of the book has expanded considerably.

I should like to thank Penny Gay, general editor of the Horizon Studies in English Series, for her inspirational efficiency and encouragement in seeing the former series into print. More recently, I am grateful to Ciara Rawnsley for reading the whole typescript and saving me from a host of errors of omission and commission (the remaining ones are mine), and Agata Mrva-Montoya and the Sydney University Press for giving me the opportunity to turn what was little more than a booklet into a book.

Prologue: Sinners as Heroes

Two Elizabethan dramatists became room-mates made in heaven, or more likely in hell. Christopher Marlowe and Thomas Kyd shared lodgings in 1591, with disastrous results for the latter. Two years later, and just before Marlowe's death, Kyd was imprisoned, interrogated and probably tortured by authorities keen to investigate Marlowe's notorious atheism, a transgression second only to treason in seriousness in a state where religion was commensurate with politics. Undoubtedly terrified under such compulsion, Kyd spilt the beans on his writing companion while trying to save his own reputation, confirming that Marlowe was an atheist and "blasphemous traitor" who also believed Jesus was homosexual. "That I should love or be familiar friend with one so irreligious, were very rare", he says, and he does his best to imply that although sharing a chamber seems an intimate affair, yet their association was little more than professional: "*Idem ex minimo vestigio artifex agnostic artificem*", or "an artist recognises an artist by the slightest trace" (Honan 2005: 243).

> It was his custom when I knew him first to jest at the divine scriptures, gibe at prayers, & strive at argument to frustrate and confute what hath been spoke or writ by prophets and such holy men ... He would so suddenly take slight occasion to slip out [a blasphemy]. (Honan 2005: 246)

Marlowe, Kyd attested, was wont also to argue that "things esteemed to be done by divine power might have as well been done by observation of men" (Honan 2005: 246), expressing at least blasphemy and a degree of scepticism close even to atheism. Most damagingly, there was found among Kyd's papers a tract described as containing "vile heretical conceits denying the eternal deity of Jesus Christ", which Kyd claimed had been owned by Marlowe ("C. Marley"). The impression Kyd gives of himself, or tried to give, was of one easily shocked and bland, whose sense of incompatibility with his erstwhile room-mate had finally driven him to separate from the accommodation arrangement. We must remember that he was in a difficult situation under interrogation, eager literally to save his own skin, and that too much evidence against Marlowe might well have resulted in incriminating himself. He was eventually released, but even so lost his patronage and could never escape the cloud of suspicion. Certainly the glimpses Kyd gives of a turbulent and troubling shared domicile are intriguing, since both were major and controversial playwrights in their time, dominating the theatrical landscape in fact, and their "chamber" seems to have held, in terms of sheer writing power, "infinite riches in a little room" (Marlowe's phrase in *The Jew of Malta*; Marlowe 1969: V.1.37).

These two dramatists, at about the same time (somewhere between 1588 and 1591), each wrote a play which was in its own way seminal, and which taken together were two of the most revolutionary, popular and enduring works on the Elizabethan stage right through to the 1630s. They are claimants to having ushered in and sustained the great age of English drama, and for significantly influencing and inspiring the young Shakespeare. Moreover, their paradigm-shifting plays shared in common the kind of double vision – simultaneous but contradictory world views – which was steadily to become Shakespeare's practice. To be specific, Kyd is often credited with having written a virtually mythical, now lost play alluded to during the period, which goes under the name "Ur-*Hamlet*". No prizes for guessing that this unicorn has been hailed as the source for the most famous play of all time, Shakespeare's own *Hamlet* (1600), but it is even more wraith-like than *Hamlet*'s Ghost, leaving no more than a few references in the 1590s hinting at its existence without proving it (Wells 2006: 73). However, Kyd's play *The Spanish Tragedy* was certainly as large as life on stage, probably the single most popular play in the entire period, and it has been described as "perhaps the single most *influential* play" in the period (Semenza 2010: 153). It certainly influenced and perhaps helped to inspire the whole enterprise of Shakespeare's *Hamlet*. The fundamental premise of the play is that tragedy need not portray "the fall of kings" or the great man brought down by a fatal flaw, but it can occur to a relatively ordinary person, even a nonentity (Hieronimo is initially a minor character in a play that steadily becomes his), faced with an appalling situation not of his own making – the hero as victim. Imitating the favoured genre of the classical dramatist Seneca, Kyd single-handedly invented the English version of revenge tragedy, and the character Revenge is onstage throughout and acts as a chorus. The revenge play held the stage well into the 1630s and inspired a whole tribe of other famous plays throughout the period, from Shakespeare's early *Titus Andronicus* through to Jacobean works by Marston, Tourneur, Middleton, Webster and others. *The Spanish Tragedy* was reprinted an astonishing (for a play) ten times between 1592 and 1633 (Wells 2006: 75). At the heart of the genre was a fundamental sense of grievance on the part of the protagonist, who faces an impossible moral and legal predicament: he is initially wronged (Hieronimo in *The Spanish Tragedy* suffers the murder of his son Horatio, as Hamlet of his father) but in a situation which renders public justice unattainable because the justice system is corrupted at its centre. This creates the quandary in a seemingly Christian society in which personal vendettas were discouraged and certainly illegal if they were to lead to another murder. The Biblical injunction in *Romans* 12:19-20 was "Dearly beloved, avenge not yourselves, but rather give place unto wrath: for it is written, Vengeance is mine; I will repay, saith the Lord", suggesting that righting a wrong must be left in the hands of the law and failing that, of God alone. Francis Bacon, in condemning revenge as "a kind of wild justice", added,

> the first wrong, it doth but offend the law; but the revenge of that wrong, putteth the Law out of Office. Certainly, in taking revenge, a man is but even with his Enemy. But in passing it over, he is Superior: For it is a prince's part to Pardon. (Bacon 1625: 19)

The problematical status of revenge, however motivated and justified, in a Christian society is one of the things on the mind of a scrupulous philosophy student named Hamlet, who wishes not to rush into retribution, who feels the need to corroborate the Ghost's story of the murder, and who recognises that legal redress is impossible if indeed it is the reigning monarch who committed the murder. Kyd's play also makes the point that in the Christian system, private revenge is ethically questionable, but public justice may not be available – the kind of double bind not entirely addressed in its full force by Bacon, no matter how noble is his advice to forgive. Such plays, then, are based on a clash of incompatible world views, the pagan and Christian, secular and spiritual, which tear the unfortunate protagonist in two different directions, leading either to personal incrimination and even damnation, or to an overwhelming sense of perpetual grievance. Hieronimo, like Hamlet, faces the agonising choice whether to be a sinner or a victim. No wonder most of these protagonists go mad in their respective plays, understandably unable as they are to tolerate such extremes of ambivalence. *The Spanish Tragedy* was subtitled "or Hieronimo is mad again", a phrase that became almost proverbial for the regular revivals of the play; there are "mad" scenes in other Jacobean revenge plays like Middleton's *The Revenger's Tragedy*, and a debate over whether Hamlet's madness is feigned or real is central to Shakespeare's play.

The stakes are even higher in Marlowe's equally celebrated and more notorious play *The Tragical History of Doctor Faustus* (Bevington and Rasmussen 1993), for which there is ample evidence of heavy state censorship because of its controversial theological and political content (Clare 1999: 125–31). Mark Thornton Burnett has written, "At a number of levels, and in a variety of ways, *Doctor Faustus* can be said to disturb, if not assault, the sensibilities of its audience" (Burnett 2010: 163), and given the facts of Marlowe's life and death this intimidating effect seems a part of his own image. He has been associated with shadowy figures like the Italian mathematician Giordano Bruno, who defied the church in his speculations that the universe is infinite and is not earth-centred, and that the stars are distant suns – for which heterodoxies he was burned at the stake. It was rumoured in the 1590s that there was a "School of Atheism" centred on Raleigh, Marlowe, Bruno and others, and some modern scholars have speculated about this group as "The School of Night".

Prologue: Sinners as Heroes

Critics invariably ask a series of questions about *Doctor Faustus* such as the following: "Is Marlowe challenging conventional Christian perspectives on hell and heaven, or does his play ultimately conform with them? Is Faustus a tragic hero or misguided sinner?" (Healy 2004: 174). The answer offered here is "both". Paradoxically, the sinner *is* hero, and *also* victim. This play too has close connections with *Hamlet*, not least the references to Wittenberg University in both (White 2015: 32-5), but here its central relevance to *Macbeth* will be asserted. Based on a translation of the German *Faust Book* (Wootton 2005: 67-153), Marlowe's play tells the tale of Doctor Faustus, the most learned and best-read scholar in the world, reputed to have been attached to Wittenberg in the early sixteenth century. Driven by curiosity he finds himself at the outermost limits of human knowledge in all fields, such as religion, history, law, medicine and magic, yearning to know more, like any self-respecting scholar and academic dedicated to advancing human knowledge. Like Adam and Eve in the Christian myth of origins, however, he finds himself at an impasse since God himself, or at least the church, forbids him going further. As John Milton was to put it in *Paradise Lost* about fifty years later, in the Christian cosmology such aspiring people are warned "O yet happiest if ye seek / No happier state, and know to know no more" (Milton 1966: IV. 775) lest they risk falling from grace and into eternal damnation. Milton had been a young theatregoer when he attended the Fortune Theatre in 1612, and may well have seen there one of the frequent revivals of *Doctor Faustus*. Adam and Eve are tempted by Satan in the figure of a serpent, but Faustus finds within himself the fatal temptation to call on the devil. He signs away his soul in blood and embarks on a journey which does not really deliver the omniscience and power he had craved, but rather presents episodes of trivial, comic manipulation of others, and one moment of apparent sublimity in seeing and kissing an image of Helen of Troy (who is actually a *succubus* or female devil who sucks the souls from unwitting men during sexual intercourse). Most enlightening but still inadequate to Faustus' mind is an ongoing tutorial with Mephostophiles, who explains some of the mysteries in touchingly self-aware terms – "Why, this is hell, nor am I out of it ... for where we are is hell, / And where hell is, must we ever be" (Ormerod and Wortham 1985: ll. 318, 569-70) – suggesting that hell is an eternal state of mind and a psychological experience rather than a place (Logan 2007: 201-03). Macbeth discovers something similar, though in his case a living hell of mental torture. In his desire to "feel now / The future in the instant" (1.5.57-8), one critic points out that "Macbeth trades a present freedom for the knowledge of a future that in the nature of things must enslave him; yet he never ceases to believe in his own freedom to act". (Wilks 1990: 128), a fate partly enjoined on him when the Witches give him a glimpse of that future. Faustus signs away his soul in blood, and given the frequency of blood imagery in Shakespeare's play, Macbeth does similarly though with the blood of others rather than his own. Marlowe's play ends with Faustus' final anguished moments, neither explicitly repenting nor reifying his actions – simply terrified out of his wits before being ushered offstage by Mephostophiles. Macbeth's mood in his "To-morrow, and to-morrow, and to-morrow ..." speech is more dispirited and resigned but equally rooted in the knowledge that time is running out, and in each case the dramatist exploits the device of dramatic monologue to convey intense inner suffering as the play approaches its end. Both soliloquies in their different ways focus on the centrality of time in the play, and the emotional panic conveyed in another play by Shakespeare, "I wasted time and now doth time waste me" (*Richard II*, 5.5.59). In *Faustus*, neither Lucifer nor God appears in person, but the former is represented by Mephostophiles, an eloquent spokesman, and by sundry diabolical apparitions. The actual existence of God is not called into question so the play is not strictly speaking "atheistic", although it could be accused of veiled blasphemy in implying a cruel and unjust deity determined to keep humanity in a state of ignorance.

But not according to the pious Chorus who begins and ends the play in simplistic, sermon-like pronouncements. At the outset this character issues a dire warning to the audience about Faustus' fate which they will witness from its ominous inception as he studies forbidden necromancy:

> Till, swoll'n with cunning of a self-conceit,
> His waxen wings did mount above his reach,
> And, melting, heavens conspired his overthrow.
> For, falling to a devilish exercise,

Prologue: Sinners as Heroes

> And glutted more with learning's golden gifts,
> He surfeits upon cursed necromancy.
> (Wootton 2005: Prologue 21-6)

And at the end the Chorus reappears to emphasise the lesson we should learn:

> Faustus is gone: regard his hellish fall,
> Whose fiendful fortune may exhort the wise
> Only to wonder at unlawful things,
> Whose deepness doth entice such forward wits
> To practise more than heavenly power permits.
> (Wootton 2005: Epilogue 1513-17)

The problem with accepting such a neat and apparently inconvertible moral is that, drama being drama and theatre being theatre, our sympathies are tugged in more perverse and even perverted ways, away from doctrinaire platitudes into an emotional complicity and sometimes identification with the sinner, who becomes the more a victim as his status becomes more heroically that of everyman. The crucial determinant of our sympathies lies in the sheer thrill and power of dramatic poetry fuelled by what Ben Jonson called "Marlowe's mighty line" – blank (unrhymed) verse in iambic pentameters, which Marlowe made into the staple of Elizabethan dramatic utterance and which Shakespeare followed memorably. There is something both dismayed and defiant in Faustus' declarations:

> Lucifer and Mephastophilis! Ah, gentlemen, I gave them my soul for my cunning.
> ALL: God forbid!
> FAUSTUS: God forbade it indeed, but Faustus hath done it (5.2.33-6)

The result of an overt moral pasted onto a covert emotional appeal through poetry is a form of divided consciousness in apprehending the play in all its intellectual and emotional complexity. Faustus' desire to "Resolve me of all ambiguities" in his quest for ultimate knowledge is not delivered by the play itself, since we cannot make firm judgements, or pass a verdict so harsh and moralistic as the Chorus', on a man who begins with an apparently benign and laudable aspiration for knowledge and understanding which are incomprehensibly forbidden to human beings. After all his trials, Faustus learns little more than he has been told by Mephostophiles, that "the wages of sin is death", which he would already have known from his Bible. Even after we, like Faustus, have been coached in understanding the ways of hell, yet we still cannot tell fully what Faustus will experience in the world of the damned beyond the mortal's grave – "the undiscovered country from which no traveller returns" as Hamlet puts it, even if both Marlowe and Shakespeare do bring revenants back to tell their tales.

Even putting aside the textual doubleness of a play existing in two published versions (known as "A" and "B" [Ormerod and Wortham 1985]), "ambiguities" abound in *Doctor Faustus*, as most critics who have studied the play in detail conclude. Editors point out that the play splices two different traditions of drama which are not necessarily compatible, in drawing on the English morality tradition on the one hand and the post-Reformation depiction of inner spiritual conflict on the other, as well as breaking Aristotelian dramatic unities by mingling kings and clowns and representing a far longer time span than the single day in classical drama – twenty-four years in the case of Faustus (and by comparison, theoretically seventeen years of Macbeth's reign). It opposes a Good Angel with an Evil Angel giving discrepant advice. Nicholas Brooke opened up the play to two quite different readings which are hard to unify, by arguing for "a constant bitter irony" that "the power of God is to have made man desiring a greatness he cannot achieve" (Brooke 1952: 686). Andrew Duxfield, following Brooke's lead, has more recently argued that unified knowledge, both in Faustus' world and the play-world, is unattainable because of the "persistently ambivalent world" depicted, rendering a "problematic nature … to a perplexing extent", and presenting "concepts and structures which are fundamentally incompatible" (Duxfield 2007: 1 and throughout). Even the kind of theological beliefs Marlowe is challenging is subject to debate. It is certainly a post-Reformation cosmos, and Elizabethan audiences would have lapped up the comic sight of the Pope himself being boxed around the ears, drawing more sympathy to Faustus as an anti-papist. But the exact shade of Protestant thought depicted is not at all clear, some arguing that it builds upon the apparently harsh Calvinist doctrine of predestination where man has no true free will and is damned or saved from the outset, or belief in the innate natural law favoured by Luther and later by Milton and Bunyan, in which human beings have a direct link with God through their consciences, and are free to choose either virtue or vice in the face of temptations. The latter could place even more intolerable pressures on the lonely, alienated individual wrestling with his soul, unable to have his transgressions absolved in the Catholic confessional or by the church's official litanies. Even if the insoluble questions of a range of theological concepts could be somehow negotiated, the matter is further problematised when we ask whether Marlowe is condoning any particular stream of thinking available in the religious views of his day, or cursing all families of Christians alike. If nothing else, the play builds ambivalence upon ambivalence, and at every level of morality, theology and even genre (containing farce as well as tragedy) is more challenging in its outlook than the doctrinaire Chorus can conceive.

In this book I shall be arguing that similar layers of ambivalence and ambiguities are the hallmarks of *Macbeth*, another play resting on issues of temptation and fall, reprobates and penitents, the sinner as hero or, in Honigmann's formulation of *Macbeth*, "the criminal as hero", predestination and free will, good and evil counsellors, apparitions, equivocations, and meditations on hell and heaven. If *Hamlet* had been to some extent an homage to Kyd's evergreen play *The Spanish Tragedy* (or even a redoing of his mysterious "Ur-*Hamlet*"), then *Macbeth* may have been written in the wake of Marlowe's *Tragical History of Doctor Faustus*. Both works arguably require a need to suspend our sense of uncertainty and embrace with non-judgemental empathy a dismayingly plural universe. In both plays the sheer emotional desolation of the endings, when judged in orthodox terms of good and evil, itself raises ambiguous answers to the question of why accomplished dramatists wrote them in the first place: if for nothing else than to show us little more profound than that evil actions will be punished, what is the point of that? There is surely some residual sense of angry resistance pointing to ways in which the constricting world of ideas and politics around Faustus and Macbeth may legitimately be challenged for placing such exhilaratingly poetic "sinners as heroes" in predicaments not entirely of their own making. Logan speaks of how "Marlowe's description of rebellious figures [in all his plays] in an unidealized political world is more congenial to Shakespeare's perceptions later rather than early in his career" (Logan 2007: 205), which, we can add, may be as much a reflection of the constant restagings of *Faustus* in new, Jacobean times, as exemplifying the abiding, lifelong influence of Marlowe on Shakespeare. In fact one of the strongest recollections of *Faustus* comes at the very end of Shakespeare's career in *The Tempest*, almost two decades after Marlowe's death, where a "white" but flawed *magus* is the bookend to Marlowe's "black" but sympathetically treated magician. Macbeth may then be seen as a companion to the Marlovian "overreacher", as several critics have noticed over the years:

> The ambivalent response has the effect, as Robert Ornstein observes, of denying to the play the "tragic acceptance" that we find in other Renaissance dramatists. Death is for Marlowe a metaphysical outrage which annihilates the meaning of existence, and so the Marlovian hero, who begins as a lover of the world he would re-make, ends in nihilism and despair. (Bevington and Rasmussen 1993: 32, paraphrasing Ornstein)

With some modification, the same can be said of Macbeth. Not that ambivalence has always been conceded as part of the effect of *Macbeth*. Nick Moschovakis has traced through both criticism and performances over at least three centuries until the late twentieth century a dominant "dualistic and pro-monarchical approach", which asserts that *Macbeth* portrays a conventional moral struggle between good and evil and assumes that regicide is unthinkable (Moschovakis 2008: 1-72). Movement towards a "problematical" approach came with the publication of Jan Kott's book *Shakespeare Our Contemporary*, in which he turns the spotlight on "the system" of monarchy which turns history into a "murder-cycle" (Kott 1962: 87) and at least explains if not absolves Macbeth's actions. Since then, dualistic and problematical versions have both been advanced in about equal measure (Moschovakis 2008: 49-55). My book, as its title suggests, sees ambivalence as saturating all levels of *Macbeth*, as the play's defining aspect.

Prologue: Sinners as Heroes

One more theatrical fact links *Faustus* and *Macbeth*, and it is perhaps the strangest of all. Both plays offer evidence of what has come to be known as audience contagion, by which spectators collectively "catch" moods generated by a play as it unfolds (Helm 2016). We find a description of what must have been a moment of alarming audience contagion when John Melton in 1620 recorded the following terrifying spectacle:

> Men go to the Fortune in Golding Lane, to see the Tragedy of *Doctor Faustus*. There indeed a man may behold shag-haired devils run roaring over the stage with squibs in their mouths, while drummers make thunder in the tiring house, and the twelvepenny hirelings make artificial lightning in their heavens. (Quoted in Bevington and Rasmussen 1995: 51)

In another account of a performance, written in 1632, William Prynne describes how real devils came onto the stage "to the great amazement both of the Actors and Spectators", who were "distracted [mad] with that fearfull sight" (quoted in Hopkins 2008: 51). However, we need to be aware that Prynne, as a Puritan preacher who thought all theatre was sinful, had an axe to grind and was not averse to creating fictions to suit his prejudice. Even if such stories are apocryphal, including Aubrey's later description of the agitated actor Edward Alleyn wearing a cross each time he played Faustus, and being so guilt-stricken that he retired into helping charitable institutions, they at least attest to the possibility of audience involvement at a visceral level. Likewise, the legends which gathered rapidly around ill-omened and unlucky productions of "The Scottish Play" have persisted down to the present day, blurring the line between stage and reality and suggesting that these two plays in particular by depicting evil have stirred, then and now, strong emotional responses in their audiences. As a result, companies routinely take out higher than average insurance for rehearsals of *Macbeth* because it has been claimed to be historically associated with sometimes bizarre accidents. By entering the theatre when these plays are being performed, we run risks, and anything can happen.

1
Contexts of Ambiguity: Text, Sources, History

Editing *Macbeth* is, at least in one regard, a less complex task than editing some other major tragedies by Shakespeare. For this play there is only one version to take into account. This is the one printed in the First Folio, a near "complete works" collected in 1623, seven years after Shakespeare's death, by his professional colleagues, John Heminges and Richard Condell. In the cases of *Hamlet*, *King Lear* and *Othello*, the textual situation is complicated by the existence of one or more Quarto editions published in Shakespeare's lifetime but not necessarily authorised or approved by him, and each differs significantly from the respective Folio text. This is not to say the text of *Macbeth* is without its share of problems, as we shall see, including ones of authorship, but for good or ill there is no other textual evidence to take into account than the Folio.

The brevity of *Macbeth* in comparison with the other tragedies mentioned has often been presumed to suggest a problem, as though something has been lost. But since there are no glaring, major loose ends which could be tied up with more scenes, and because it is coherent as a narrative in its own right, this hardly seems crying out for explanation. Censorship was always a danger when a play dealt with sensitive political issues (in this case the part of the English king Edward the Confessor, and the fact that parts of one of the indirect sources, Buchanan's *History of Scotland*, had been banned). But as Janet

Clare concludes, "Shakespeare's circumspect redaction of his sources and the play's silence on those ideological issues which were anathema to James may well have sprung from judicious self-censorship" (Clare 1999: 159). In the theatre at least, the sense of breathless urgency ("almost dead for breath" [1.5.35] in the Messenger's phrase) is an undoubted aim of the dramatist, since the action is tight and tense, and gains dramaturgically from its speed of execution. The compression enhances the play's narrative strength and emotional impact, since the prophecies by the Witches set up immediate expectations of what is to come, and it is important that Macbeth should be plunged rapidly into his dilemma so that he does not have much time to ruminate before King Duncan leaves. His moral reflection and resolution not to murder Duncan is a serious factor in interpreting the play, but it is rapidly overturned when he speaks to his wife. Precipitate haste is at least a subjective and emotionally driven compulsion for Macbeth, who realises that timing and seizing opportunities are key to success, though as he himself realises the plans can be compromised by a failure to consider future consequences of his actions. After all, he is a soldier whose world view is unlike that of Hamlet, who is a university student of philosophy who constantly considers the consequences of his actions. Time itself, as well as Macbeth's apprehension of his vocation or "office", will turn out to be a thematic issue throughout the play, as we shall see in the chapter on "Ideas".

Other suspected problems are probably more apparent to editors, who need to explicate every word and line, and who have time to consider details, than to audiences and readers who are swept along by the forward momentum of the action. There are a few minor things not fully explained in the otherwise carefully planned chronology of the play. Shakespeare could have filled in more of the background as to why Macdonwald and the Thane of Cawdor are rebelling against Duncan, the broader reasons for civil war, and why "Sweno, the Norways' king" (1.1.59) is invading Scotland, but lingering on these would have delayed and diluted the central conflicts in the play. The play is often performed without an interval, again for these theatrical and atmospheric reasons rather than simple lack of text. Bradley comments that "our experience in traversing it is so crowded and intense that it leaves an impression not of brevity but of speed. It is the most vehement, the most concentrated,

1 Contexts of Ambiguity: Text, Sources, History

perhaps the most tremendous, of the tragedies" (Bradley 1904: 333). Furthermore, as a "short" play, *Macbeth*, at 2477 lines, is not really so unusual, if we look beyond the tragedies. It is longer, for example, than *The Comedy of Errors* (1786), *A Midsummer Night's Dream* (2165) and *The Tempest* (2275), which are themselves among the most complete and self-sufficient plays in Shakespeare's canon yet have never been questioned on the score of incompleteness.

The other "problem" raised by scholars relates to authorial integrity, and arguments have been proposed (most insistently by Gary Taylor) that the text we have was either a combined effort written with Thomas Middleton, or at least a later revision of Shakespeare's text by Middleton himself. Neither suggestion is completely unlikely, since the writing of plays in Elizabethan and Jacobean times was routinely collaborative – it is certain, for example, that *Pericles* (a play perhaps tellingly not included in the Folio) was begun by George Wilkins and picked up in the middle by Shakespeare – but in the case of *Macbeth* the fairly indisputably non-Shakespearean parts are minor in terms of the play as a whole. Judging from the different poetic style, it does look likely that the two scenes with Hecate lecturing the Witches (3.5 and 4.1) were written by another hand, probably Middleton's in preparation for his own later play *The Witch* (1611) which itself echoes *Macbeth*. The appearances of Hecate, which add little or nothing to the narrative of *Macbeth* and tend to tame the force of the Witches, are often cut in performances. Without more evidence than this, there is hardly a strong argument of comprehensive collaboration. Since other plays that we know were written by more hands than Shakespeare's alone do not appear in the Folio (*The Two Noble Kinsmen* with John Fletcher, as well as *Pericles* and some others), and since there is no raging argument about authorship of those plays which *are* included in this volume, there seems a *prima facie* case that the editors included only plays where Shakespeare was the single or major author. This would be appropriate for such a *Festschrift* volume and consistent with Ben Jonson's earlier Folio.

By common scholarly consent, the writing and first performances of *Macbeth* are dated 1605–06 in the earliest years of the reign of King James I of England, VI of Scotland. Since James wrote books on both kingship and demonology, *Macbeth* seems angled to appeal to his interests, if not always his opinions. There was also a claim that James could trace his ancestry back to Fleance and Banquo. However, although it is plausible that Shakespeare may have written a play about Scottish history partly to ingratiate his acting group with the new king, yet the choice also would have led him into dangerous waters if he were not careful. Any play depicting volatile political issues such as usurpation, assassination of a monarch, tyranny and succession, not to mention depicting apparent witches and alluding to the topical act of terrorism known as the Gunpowder Plot, would have attracted close and critical scrutiny from the Privy Council and the office of the Master of the Revels, which had the power to censor or ban a play and even imprison the perpetrators. The possible connection between Banquo and James would also have been double-edged, since in the *Chronicles* on which the play is based there is at least a suggestion that Banquo is in knowledgeable collusion with Macbeth and a party to the killing of Duncan. Given the treacherous gauntlet he had to run through such controversial material, Shakespeare must have been politically adroit himself in handling it. Placing the action in the distant past and geography of eleventh-century Scotland gave him some cover, allowing him to claim a fictional licence, even though his sources were official Tudor history. He also renders equivocal the depiction of witches by variously calling them "weird sisters" and leaving unexplained the nature of their influence on the action, and largely (though not entirely, as we shall see later) removing any possible suspicion over Banquo's actions.

There is no evidence of whether the play was first produced in the outdoors Globe playhouse or an indoor space (as it later was revived, at Blackfriars). Some, like Iain Wright, have implicitly supported the indoors venue by suggesting some of the apparitional effects, including the "floating" dagger, could have been achieved in the age of masques by using candles and mirrors (Wright 2005). However, the verbal art of Shakespeare is capable of conjuring illusions for audiences even in broad daylight. Even though much of the play is set at night this would pose no problem for audiences, since many plays by Shakespeare had nocturnal scenes, including *Richard III*, *A Midsummer Night's Dream*, *Romeo and Juliet*, *Much Ado About Nothing*, *Julius Caesar*, *Henry V*, *King Lear*, *Othello* and *Cymbeline*. Shakespeare's visual poetry on the

1 Contexts of Ambiguity: Text, Sources, History

bare, open stage could transcend physical limitations with ease, for reasons partially explained in Chapter 6.

We do uniquely have an invaluable contemporary description by an eyewitness who saw a later performance at the Globe in 1610 or 1611, so the play was definitely revived on the public stage, if not necessarily written for it. Simon Forman kept a diary and wrote his thoughts on seeing *Macbeth*, his words transcribed in modern English from the Bodleian Library's manuscript copy:

> In Macbeth at the Globe 1610 the 20 of April, Saturday
>
> There was to be observed first how Macbeth and Banquo, 2 noblemen of Scotland, riding through a wood, there stood before them 3 women fairies or nymphs, and saluted Macbeth, saying 3 times unto him, "Hail Macbeth, king of Codon [thane of Cawdor], for thou shall be a king but shall beget no kings," etc. Then said Banquo, "What, all to Macbeth, and nothing to me?" There said the nymphs, "Hail to thee, Banquo, thou shall beget kings, yet be no king." And so they departed and came to the court of Scotland to Duncan, king of Scots, and it was in the days of Edward the Confessor, and Duncan bade them both kindly welcome, and made Macbeth forthwith Prince of Northumberland, and sent him home to his own castle and appointed Macbeth to provide for him for he would sup with him the next day at night. And did so. And Macbeth contrived to kill Duncan, and through the persuasion of his wife did that night murder the king in his own castle being his guest. And there were many prodigies seen that night and the day before. And when Macbeth had murdered the king, the blood on his hands could not be washed off by any means, nor from his wife's hands which handled the bloody daggers in hiding them. By which means they became both much amazed and affronted. The murder being known, Duncan's 2 sons fled, the one to England, the [other to] Wales to save themselves. They being fled they were supposed guilty of the murder of their father, which was nothing so. Then was Macbeth crowned king, and then he, for fear of Banquo, his old companion, that he should beget kings but be no king himself, he contrived the death of Banquo and caused him to be murdered on the way as he rode. The next night being at supper with his noblemen, whom he had bid to

a feast (to the which also Banquo should have come), he began to speak of noble Banquo and to wish that he were there. And as he thus did, standing up to drink a carouse to him, the ghost of Banquo came and sat down in his chair behind him. And he turning about to sit down again saw the ghost of Banquo which fronted him so that he fell into a great passion of fear and fury, uttering many words about his murder, by which when they heard that Banquo was murdered they suspected Macbeth.

Then Macduff fled to England to the king's son, and so they raised an army and came into Scotland, and at Dunsinane overthrew Macbeth. In the meantime, while Macduff was in England, Macbeth slew Macduff's wife and children, and after, in the battle, Macduff slew Macbeth. Observe also how Macbeth's queen did rise in the night in her sleep and walk and talked and confessed all, and the doctor noted her words. (Bodleian Library copy)

Apparently writing from memory, Forman gets some of his facts wrong (for example, muddling up the English dukedom of Northumberland and the Scottish Cumberland), but nonetheless this is a fascinating account for its thoroughness in describing the action, and because so few of its kind have survived. It provides insight into the ways Elizabethan plays struck their audiences as emotionally loaded – "they became both much amazed and affronted"; "a great passion of fear and fury". Some critics have argued "hypothetically" (Benecke 2014: 253) that the differences between the text we have and Forman's description suggest that there were variant texts available at the time, but this is not a necessary deduction since we can assume Forman's account reflects his own interests and what he remembered (and forgot, or did not notice). Furthermore, it was customary, and probably necessary, for a company to shorten and adapt a script for particular performances in ways that we can rarely recreate because of the paucity of evidence. The overarching context was that the whole script had to be read and approved by the Master of the Revels, and after that players were at liberty to shorten the play in performance, but not to add anything more. Moreover, we do not know the exact status of the Folio text of *Macbeth*, whether it represents the play in its totality or is itself a shortened version for performance. Forman's phrase "3 women fairies

1 Contexts of Ambiguity: Text, Sources, History

or nymphs" is an interesting description of the Sisters, oddly innocent, quite unlike the descriptions offered by Macbeth and Banquo of the figures as "So wither'd and so wild in their attire", "secret, black and midnight hags" (4.1.48), whose "beards" belie their apparent female gender. On the contrary, "3 women fairies or nymphs" suggests that in Forman's mind they are without any connection with the devil's business, perhaps strengthening the suggestion that Shakespeare was careful in not being explicit about their status, which Macbeth in his letter to his wife sees somewhat neutrally as "fate or metaphysical aid" (1.5.29-30). Forman slightly misheard but in a revealing way, "Then said Banquo, 'What, all to Macbeth, and nothing to me?'" This again raises some questions about this character, implying an audience's impression at least that Banquo was ambitious himself, justifying Macbeth's wariness of him, which leads to his murder. Forman's words, "through the persuasion of his wife did that night murder the king", attribute clear agency to Lady Macbeth, and we get some hints of how the banquet scene was staged from his description: "the ghost of Banquo came and sat down in his chair behind him. And he turning about to sit down again saw the ghost of Banquo". All these issues have been debated by critics, and Forman's comments, while not being based on more than an impressionistic memory, are revealing of a contemporary auditor's impressions. He emphasises ways in which the action is driven by emotions and plausible motivations, rather than supernatural intervention.

The questions which might vex an editor within the text itself are some puzzling verbal *cruces*, lines which are difficult to interpret as they stand, while one large issue is left unexplained and does indeed have critical significance. This is encapsulated in the title of an appendix to A.C. Bradley's monumental book on Shakespearean tragedy, phrased as "How many children had Lady Macbeth?", a question which was addressed a generation later by L.C. Knights, who objected that the literalism of the question and its suggested answers were inappropriately asked of a dramatic text (Knights 1946). However, it does matter at least to ask the question, even if we cannot offer a conclusive answer, since succession through a line of children is crucial to the politics and family dynamics in the play, explaining why Macbeth is obsessed with killing Fleance and Macduff's children (although in this case he intended to kill Macduff himself), for example, adding force to the series of apparitions in 4.1 including a "bloody child" (4.1.93) and "a child crowned, a tree in his hand" (4.1.102), and it relates also to the riddle of Macduff as a man "not of woman born" (4.1.96). The evidence is fragmentary at best, since the Macbeths clearly have no potential heirs at the time of the play and yet Lady Macbeth categorically states, "I have given suck" (1.4.54ff). However, even if this is all there is, it is not necessarily contradictory but simply unexplained, and there is no special dramatic reason why we need to know all the details, beyond the assumption that Macbeth has no heir to succeed him. It is a part of the general argument that I will be proposing, that the play builds in a pattern of radical ambivalence leaving some questions open, and this is not a threat to interpretation but a contribution to a play whose genre we might now describe as a "thriller". There are other niggling questions, such as why there are two men interviewed by Macbeth for the job of hired killers yet three actually murder Banquo, but they are minor when compared with the many unsolved questions left dangling in the much longer *Hamlet*.

Sources and Historical Background

The editors of the First Folio at the beginning of the volume divide the plays into three groups, providing a table of contents as "A Catalogue of the severall Comedies, Histories, and Tragedies contained in this Volume". *Macbeth* is listed under the tragedies, and clearly its structure is that of a tragedy. However, like others on the list, it could well have been classified as a history play because of its sources. As a corollary, *Richard II* and *Richard III* are classified as histories but they are structured similarly to tragedies. These, including *Macbeth*, are based on historical accounts available in Shakespeare's day, the *Chronicles of England, Scotland and Ireland* (1577 and 1588), assembled mainly by a team under the editorship of Raphael Holinshed. In the material on Scottish history, which provides the source for *Macbeth*, Holinshed in turn based his story partly on historical accounts of Scotland written by Hector Boece (1527) and George Buchanan (1582), both of whom, unlike the Englishman Holinshed, wrote with direct access to Scottish

1 Contexts of Ambiguity: Text, Sources, History

traditions and with considerable national sympathy for them. Extracts from both Holinshed and Buchanan are conveniently reproduced as appendices to Kenneth Muir's earlier Arden edition of *Macbeth*, and more detail is provided in Geoffrey Bullough's study of Shakespeare's sources. Muir believes it is likely Shakespeare read Buchanan's account in Latin, since the description of Macbeth there, as "a man of penetrating genius, a high spirit, unbounded ambition" but too severe and cruel for his own good, is arguably more like Shakespeare's than the one in Holinshed, and gave Shakespeare some character complexity to work on (Muir 1962: xxxix, all quotations in modern spelling). One detail is crucial to interpreting the play, since it is Buchanan, who obviously knew his Scottish law better than the Englishman Holinshed, who wrote that "the command of Cumberland was always considered the next step to the crown" (Muir 1962: xxxix) – just as today the Prince of Wales is next in line to the crown of Britain. This explains Macbeth's otherwise puzzling aside, when Duncan appoints his son Malcolm to the position, "The Prince of Cumberland – that is a step / On which I must fall down, or else o'erleap, / For in my way it lies" (1.4.48-50). The significance of this crucial moment will be considered later.

All these aspects of Shakespeare's use of his sources give fascinating insights into his own creative process of synthesising and reshaping a host of details in order to create a concise play where the *Chronicles* had been more confusing and prolix. Scholarly editors have found multiple opportunistic sources for passages and *sententiae*, ranging through classical writers such as Seneca, contemporary foreign works in translation such as essays by Montaigne, and otherwise ephemeral pamphlets (Clark and Mason 2015: 82-97). One other borrowing shows more of his genius in "the quick forge and working house of thought" (*Henry V*, Prologue). The all-important relationship between Macbeth and his wife splices several details from the *Chronicles*, and includes a substantial component from a completely different historical couple. Another figure called Donwald murdered King Duff and he is said in Holinshed to have done so "through setting on of his wife, who bare no less malice in hir heart towards the king". She appears to be the principal plotter, giving her husband "the meanes wherby he might soonest accomplish it". Donwald is extremely reluctant but bribes the servants to commit the murder "through instigation of his wife".

Macbeth's wife, in Holinshed's account, "lay sore upon him to attempt the thing, as she was verie ambitious, burning in unquenchable desire to have the name of a queene" (Muir 1962: 179). Shakespeare merged the two accounts by building Donwald's scruples into the figure of Macbeth and dramatising Lady Macbeth's ruthlessness, though he appears to stress that her motivation is more for her husband's advancement than her own. By doing so, Shakespeare thus provides some possible mitigating considerations to explain, if not absolve, the actions of both partners, another way in which different explanations are incorporated in the play, providing some openness for different interpretations and staging possibilities.

Not only was Holinshed writing at second hand from Scottish historical sources, but he also had a political purpose. Like Shakespeare, he was addressing the English Queen Elizabeth I before England and Scotland were united under James I (James VI in Scotland) in 1603-04, and his great enterprise could be seen as part of a Tudor-inspired burst of proud nationalism at a time when England was at war with Spain. The *Chronicles* were more propaganda than history in our sense, and the compilers had to be careful in their portrayal of Elizabeth's own ancestors. For example, Holinshed, and in his turn Shakespeare, eulogised the English King Edward the Confessor as almost mystical in his saintly powers of healing (4.3.141-59), and the flight of Malcolm and Macduff to England would have been seen by Shakespeare's London audience as a flight away from barbarism and towards civilisation and safety. Donalbain's defection to Ireland may have been regarded more ambiguously. Then, as now, the English had many prejudices against people in other countries, and particularly their Celtic neighbours, Scotland and Ireland. However, since Shakespeare was writing under the auspices of the new King James, he had to be careful not to antagonise his company's patron by including too much of Holinshed's attitudes, which had been based on Queen Elizabeth's conflict with her Scottish relatives. It was a tightrope for the dramatist to tread between several subtly different readings of Britain's history.

Scottish readers, and their own Chronicler Buchanan (on whose work Holinshed drew), saw things very differently. England was Scotland's traditional enemy, and the flight south would be seen as at least "equivocal" and more like the act of traitors. Macbeth, on the other hand, was regarded north of the border as the last "pure" Celtic king, and therefore a figure who could be regarded with admiration. Buchanan was a Scottish republican, with an innate suspicion of the kind of hereditary monarchy which prevailed in England. Not surprisingly, for the Scots, Macbeth was a much more sympathetic and comprehensible figure than Shakespeare's depiction of him, which generally follows and even amplifies the negative picture in Holinshed, although even Holinshed concedes that Macbeth ruled peaceably for many years, before becoming a paranoid tyrant as a response to threats to his position. Shakespeare also suppresses the fact that Banquo collaborated actively with Macbeth in the regicide, but on the other hand he picks up Holinshed's hint to implicate and strengthen the relationship between the Macbeths as man and wife. Other details of their plot are taken from a different episode in Holinshed's account. What we have in Shakespeare's play, apart from a masterclass in adaptation and condensation of many strands into a unity, is historically biased and anglophile in the ways that Holinshed's enterprise is but with other perspectives woven in. Awareness of this can enhance our understanding of the play, since some of the more radical material keeps peeping through. Unlike Richard III in Shakespeare's presentation, Macbeth is far from being a completely unsympathetic serial killer, and the play genuinely probes his doubts and hesitations, while presenting him as a tragically flawed but potentially admirable protagonist. We detect in the various historical strata lying behind the play a strain of radical ambivalence in its presentation of the institution of kingship, which will become significant in this book's argument.

By incorporating in our view a more Scottish attitude (some elements of which are admitted by Holinshed) we find sharpened our understanding of how Shakespeare has shaped his own dominant narrative along ideological lines while also holding in suspension a potentially more subversive reading. He has glossed over, but not entirely eliminated, the basic difference between the system of Celtic monarchy and the English of his own age. Buchanan makes clear that in Scotland the succession of monarchs was not automatically an hereditary matter of handing power down from father to son, as in England. Clark and Mason explain that "[i]n medieval Scotland the monarchy had been elective and largely governed according to the process of tanistry, whereby royal successors were named from a collateral rather than a direct branch of the family, kingship passing not from father to son but from brother to brother, uncle to nephew or cousin to cousin" (Clark and Mason 2015: 35). A range of people could by kinship be "eligible" (electable) to be king, including not only Malcolm and Donalbain but also Macbeth through his mother's line and as cousin to Duncan. Arguably, Macbeth's claim is strongest (Norbrook 1987: 86; Lemon 2006: 99). O.R. Baker disagrees with the suggestion that Macbeth may have some claim to legitimacy (Baker 2016: 123), but Baker's own reading may be coloured by a general assumption that Shakespeare would not depict anything that King James might object to (which never really deterred Shakespeare on other occasions). On the contrary, it does seem crucial to take Macbeth's claim seriously that "chance" may crown him and also it is impossible to exaggerate how seriously he takes Duncan's nomination of Malcolm as his successor – it is the moment when Macbeth is given a plausible motive, without which the play would be woodenly moralistic. On the other hand, primogeniture or succession of the eldest son would have been the familiar and may even have been regarded as the "natural" way, to an English audience, and it did prevail from Malcolm onwards in Scottish history, thus making Duncan the one to set a new precedent for the future. In a kind of tragic irony, according to the rules of elective tanistry, Macbeth may have been ultimately right in his hypothesis, "If chance will have me king, why, chance may crown me, / Without my stir" (1.3.142-3). The time-honoured processes of election might well have declared unconstitutional Duncan's nomination of Malcolm as his successor, without pre-emptive "stir" from *Macbeth*. Shakespeare knew this, since Holinshed raises the possibility of any future claim by Malcolm being that of a "pretender", and emphasising that character's minority of age when his father dies. In at least a fictional way in Shakespeare's scheme, Banquo also seems to have some claim. He was not a historical figure but one invented by Boece as the founder of the Stuart dynasty which led to the King James of Shakespeare's time, and in this sense he is presented by the dramatist as possibly legitimate in the longer term. Holinshed, writing before James Stuart's accession to the English

1 Contexts of Ambiguity: Text, Sources, History

throne, introduced Banquo as the man "of whom the house of the Stewards [Stuarts] is descended, the which by order of lineage hath now for a long time enjoyed the crown of Scotland, even till these our days" (Muir 1962: 174). Historically, the person who emerged as Prince of Cumberland and therefore king-apparent had to undergo something like elective processes between the different branches of the "royal family" – processes which Shakespeare's Duncan bypasses by declaring Malcolm as next in the royal line. At the same time, succession was not always orderly and constitutional but often proceeded by factional struggle, civil war and assassinations, just as did the English Wars of the Roses between the houses of York and Lancaster, as Shakespeare shows in his series of history plays. Here very clear traces of political controversies are made visible by Shakespeare, although he does his best to suppress or at least mute them by shifting the location from England to Scotland and relying on his London audience holding prejudices that the Scots were a violent and unruly race. No wonder Macbeth holds potential for various different readings, since it was built on diverse historical accounts skilfully but not entirely seamlessly incorporated into the action.

Furthermore, these traces would have had strong, recent associations even for the English audience. Throughout Queen Elizabeth's reign, and increasingly towards its end, speculation and advice circulated feverishly concerning who would be her own "legitimate" successor since she had not married and lacked offspring. Shakespeare's English history plays no doubt contributed to the "media speculation" at the time. It was expected that Elizabeth would announce a name, and so she eventually did. The chosen one was, to the surprise of many, the Scottish James VI, Elizabeth's nephew and son of Mary Queen of Scots, whom Elizabeth had executed for papist treason. James had pre-emptively attempted to eliminate the possibility of doubt ever occurring again, first by converting to Protestantism and later by writing a treatise entitled *Basilikon Doron* (1599), framed as a letter to his son, destined to be a future king. It emphasises the twin doctrines of primogeniture and divine right of kings (the king proclaimed himself ordained by God directly and, therefore, could do no wrong). In another book, *The True Law of Free Monarchies* (published 1598), James strongly reiterated the second point, which interestingly was contrary to the published view of Buchanan, James' own tutor, that the king in Scotland should accept a contract with the people limiting his powers, and that if he did not he could be removed from office. In England, Parliament also did not, without reservations, agree to follow James' preferred way, and the Civil War was to be fought in the 1640s over such issues of the king's powers. Buchanan's view was cited among the reasons for the usurpation and execution of Charles I. Shakespeare, like any knowledgeable subject, would have been aware of such political tensions and debates, and it is unsurprising to find them reflected in his play, though in writing for James as his patron he had to be politically adroit in a volatile and complex political situation. In an excellent new book by historian Peter Lake, though it does not mention *Macbeth* as a history play, we find plenty of evidence for Shakespeare's extraordinary skill in avoiding political trouble while dealing centrally with topical and inflammatory problems in his plays (Lake 2016). Moreover, there was another twist which made his task even trickier. James' mother Mary had been executed not only because of the dynastic threat she posed to Elizabeth, but also because she was Catholic and her long-term plan was to return Protestant England to the Church of Rome. James himself had converted to Protestantism, but to English eyes there was always a question mark over his allegiances, which Shakespeare's audience would have been aware of. Even apart from any such uncertainty, the evidence of the Gunpowder Plot in 1605 to blow up the Houses of Parliament and to kill the king showed that organised Catholic groups were actively plotting a coup (or conversely, as some have argued, that the plot was a conspiracy by Protestant forces to force James to stick to his anti-Catholic policy). It was a tense time, and Shakespeare's company were taking some risks in staging a play which raised some of the most contentious issues of the period. Shakespeare's audience would have been attuned to comprehending the underlying conflict between different forms of governance, inherited monarchy on one hand and a proto-parliamentary kind of elective monarchy on the other.

The playwright felt it necessary, in the interests of giving his characters plausible motivations and driving emotions, to offer some explanation for Macbeth's actions without condoning them, and for this he borrowed from history. Historically and in Shakespeare's play, Duncan made a decisive attempt to change the old system so that his

1 Contexts of Ambiguity: Text, Sources, History

own son Malcolm would inherit the crown directly; in other words, to change to what became James' own preferred system of primogeniture. Many nobles in medieval Scotland resisted Duncan's move and preferred the old, elective system, just as emerging Protestant republicans in Stuart England were advocating parliamentary controls on the monarch's power. Macbeth had legitimate claims to the throne himself as Duncan hints: "I have begun to plant thee, and will labour / To make thee full of growing" (1.4.28-9). There is another reason why Macbeth could be understandably optimistic, beyond the Witches' prophecy, namely the fact that Malcolm historically was a minor at the time of the events. Even the unsympathetic Holinshed says that "by the old laws of the realm, the ordinance was, that if he that should succeed [Malcolm] were not of able age to take the charge upon himself, he that was next of blood unto him should be admitted" (Muir 1962: 179), and Holinshed tacitly accepts that such a claim could be made by Duncan's cousin, Macbeth. Buchanan, who was more sympathetic to Macbeth than Holinshed, says that Duncan "made Malcolm, while yet a boy, governor of Cumberland. This appointment highly incensed Macbeth ..." (Muir 1962: 190). Shakespeare leaves Malcolm's age indeterminate, but as we shall later see he does present this character as untested, inexperienced and callow, by contrast with Macbeth, and potentially an even worse tyrant when his time should come. Historically, Macbeth also had some reasons to suspect that he could not trust vague promises made by Duncan, who, the *Chronicles* report, "did what in him lay to defraud [Macbeth] of all manner of title and claim", fearing that Macbeth "might in time to come, pretend unto the crown" (Muir 1962: 179). This seems to add weight to the suspicion that Duncan nominated Malcolm as his successor partly in order to block Macbeth's claims. Macbeth was also critical of Duncan's "softness, and overmuch slackness in punishing offenders ..." (Muir 1962: 174-5), which he saw as fanning rebellion. In short, Macbeth had many rational and emotional reasons to realise that he faced a genuine dilemma between action and inaction, and in this sense the Witches are simply focusing his mind on the need to make a decision of some kind. Interestingly, Holinshed concedes that before seizing power himself, Macbeth trusted Banquo as co-leader of the loyalist forces against the rebels and a future co-ruler. Shakespeare in his dramatisation confirms this initial trust between the two, but establishes that it is undermined only when Macbeth realises that Banquo holds the dangerous knowledge of his crime as a tool of blackmail, and equally that the prophecy of future accession of his own bloodline provides a powerful motivation in the mind of Banquo, who remains inscrutable and non-committal, evidenced in his aside, "hush, no more":

> Thou hast it now: King, Cawdor, Glamis, all
> As the weird women promised; and I fear
> Thou play'dst most foully for't. Yet it was said
> It should not stand in thy posterity,
> But that myself should be the root and father
> Of many kings. If there come truth from them –
> As upon thee, Macbeth, their speeches shine –
> Why by the verities on thee made good
> May they not be my oracles as well,
> And set me up in hope? But hush, no more. (3.1.1-10)

For dramatic effect, Shakespeare has in other ways drastically foreshortened and slanted the historical record of Macbeth's own reign. In all the chronicles, including Holinshed's, Macbeth is reported to have ruled well for fourteen years, in particular reforming the system of justice and law, "and when he saw that no man went about to trouble him, he set his whole intention to maintain justice, and to punish all enormities and abuses, which had chanced through the feeble and slothful administration of Duncan" (Muir 1962: 179-80), "but a counterfeit equity shown by him, partly against his natural inclination to purchase thereby the favour of the people" (180); a calculated distortion of his own source, Buchanan, who imputed democratic leanings to Macbeth in his desire to win "the favour of the nobles by large gifts" (191). The historical Macbeth (or to give him his proper name, Mac Bethad mac Findláich) did in fact kill Duncan, not in his bed but in battle waged over a genuine dynastic claim. His subsequent marriage further strengthened his claim to legitimacy under the Celtic system. We shall soon see why. He then ruled for seventeen years (1040-57) and for the first fourteen was considered a capable, competent and even-handed king. The Scots saw him as a nationalist for his forays against the north of England. In the last three years, however, in Buchanan's

1 Contexts of Ambiguity: Text, Sources, History

and Holinshed's view, a haunted conscience made him fear would-be competitors who might do to him what he did to Duncan. This was by no means an idle fear, since medieval Scottish history, like England's for that matter in Shakespeare's depiction, was littered with men who became kings through regicide. In 1054, Siward, Earl of Northumbria (the English borderland), launched an attempted coup on behalf of Malcolm, Duncan's son, which Macbeth defeated. Under the pressure, Macbeth eventually showed signs of becoming a tyrant. Only then, at this late stage, did he kill Banquo (at least in Holinshed's account [Muir 1962: 180]) or more historically the pro-Malcolm Siward, "fearing that so powerful and active a chief, who had already dipt his hands in royal blood, might imitate the example which he himself had set" (Muir 1962: 192). However, in 1057, Malcolm himself challenged on his own behalf and killed Macbeth in battle, becoming King Malcolm III.

It is this strain of the play, incidentally, which might have given some cause for alarm to King James, for whom Shakespeare was writing in his tricky capacity as a member of "The King's Men". Under James' own doctrine of the "divine right of kings" there was no such right to overthrow and murder even a tyrant, let alone an anointed king. Therefore, Shakespeare had to create problems of Macbeth's dynastic legitimacy, and to minimise the debate about how kings were empowered in the Scottish system. He also had to turn Macbeth's rightful grievance into an emotional rather than a calculated motivation that could simply be described as personal ambition, supported and reinforced by love for his loyally determined wife. This is similar to Shakespeare's writing out altogether another historical fact: that Macbeth's historical stepson, who was his heir, was killed by Malcolm, thus doubling Macbeth's motivation for keeping him from the throne and placing him in the exact position of Macduff in the play. In turn and in the future, King Malcolm, like his father, tried to consolidate the system of primogeniture rather than clanship, aligning himself more and more with England, and he created many new titles along the English lines to buy support among the nobles. This is dramatised at the end of *Macbeth*, when Malcolm turns his thanes and kinsmen into earls, "the first that ever Scotland / In such an honour named" (5.11.29-30). It could have been a chilling moment for Scottish nationalists, betokening a capitulation to the system of their ancient enemy south of the border.

Significantly, when Malcolm died, the whole struggle began again, as his own son, yet another Duncan, was opposed and killed by Malcolm's brother Donalbain, who argued for the older, elective system of Celtic succession, which Macbeth had fought for. In this sense, it is significant even in Shakespeare's play that while Malcolm fled to England, Donalbain in going to Ireland, the other Celtic, anti-English nation, is perhaps set up as a future rival to his brother.

It is clear that Scottish history, and for that matter English history right up to the end of the Wars of the Roses, which Shakespeare depicted in his *Henry VI* plays, could be read equally as an unending cycle of monarchs being overthrown by others who in turn may become tyrants in office, are assassinated, and so on, a repetitive cycle stretching "to the crack of doom". Shakespeare may indeed be less explicit than his sources, which relentlessly harp on this pattern as a warning to kings, but it still inescapably exists in his play. When we read the *Chronicles* we realise that Shakespeare's Macbeth is a composite of figures before and after, and no matter how the dramatist tries to make him a unique, unrepeatable character, there remain many traces of the cyclical historical processes by which he is defined. He is in several senses the plaything of destiny, at the mercy of opportunity and temptation. As we see time and again as a part of the play's total vision, so long as there is a crown, however dented it may be, so there will be rival claimants, and there will be murderers and tyrants who kill for power. The radical ambivalence between pro- and anti-monarchical aspects of *Macbeth* reflects tensions in the sources upon which Shakespeare based his play.

If this account of Shakespeare's *Macbeth* considered alongside that of the chroniclers' has not centralised the supernatural element and the Witches, it is because these are in the sources given the attention befitting brief anecdotes and local colour. Holinshed writes of the meeting with the Weird Sisters:

> This was reputed at the first but some vain fantastical illusion by Macbeth and Banquo, insomuch that Banquo would call Macbeth in jest, king of Scotland; and Macbeth again would call him in sport likewise, the father of many kings. But afterwards the common opinion was, that these women were either the weird sisters, that is

(as ye would say) the goddesses of destiny, or else some nymphs or fairies, indued with knowledge of prophecy by their necromantical science, because every thing came to pass as they had spoken ... (Muir 1962: 178)

It will be seen that Shakespeare used this passage as his starting point, but by beginning with the women and thus giving them a position of collusion with the audience, and spellbinding rhyming verse akin to chanting, he brought into the foreground an atmosphere of mystery and magic that was only momentarily visible in the sources. In a sense this enabled him to mystify the political events with which he was dealing; but when we examine the politics at a more narrative level, we recognise that he is basically drawing upon the ideologically inflected and sometimes conflicting sources, and presenting as historical destiny two rival views of kingship which could apply as well, with variations, to the political debates emerging concerning monarchy and parliamentary rule in Stuart Britain, as to analogous conflicts in early Scotland.

2
"Fair is foul and foul is fair": The Radical Ambivalence of *Macbeth*

If literary interpretation has any point, it should lead an interested reader into greater understanding and appreciation of the work under discussion. At best it does not coerce, but rather encourages us individually to clarify, amplify, modify and articulate our own unique, individual impressions. With such an ideal in mind, this book aims to open up a range of possibilities for reading and staging *Macbeth* and to demonstrate how the play reveals a plurality of varying interpretations. The poet John Keats, whom many regard as Shakespeare's ideal reader, coined the phrase "negative capability" to describe the dramatist's openness to experience without holding fixed preconceptions, and his theory applies as much to readers as to writers in accepting many different points of view held in suspension: "The only means of strengthening one's intellect is to make up one's mind about nothing – to let the mind be a thoroughfare for all thoughts. Not a select party" (Keats 1958: vol. 2, 213). In outlining his view of the "poetical Character" of Shakespearean drama, Keats describes also an answerable "reading Character":

> it is not itself – it has no self – it is every thing and nothing – It has no character – it enjoys light and shade; it lives in gusto, be it foul or fair, high or low, rich or poor, mean or elevated – It has as much delight in conceiving an Iago as an Imogen. What shocks the virtuous

philosop[h]er, delights the camelion Poet. It does no harm from its relish of the dark side of things any more than from its taste for the bright one; because they both end in speculation ... (Keats 1958: vol. 1, 387)

"Speculation" is our end here, and this play lends itself to such a "Keatsian" reading since it revolves around a character who can be seen variously as murderer, victim and hero. We can take as much "delight" in a Macbeth or Lady Macbeth as in any other character, and build into our interpretation the light and shade of the play without compromising either. Indeed, one of the play's governing images turns on light and darkness, and in just these two of its characters we find both virtuous and evil impulses, while the actions of others are to a greater or lesser extent morally ambiguous.

A central aim of this book is to demonstrate that *Macbeth* as a play is multi-vocal and open to a range of interpretations – some contradictory – and that an important part of its overall significance is generated by paradoxes and discordances within its overall unity of atmosphere and emotional register. Other critics have found in the play elements of what I shall call "radical ambivalence", or "indefinition" in the term proposed by Stephen Booth (Booth 1983). Where my approach differs from those by Booth and others is that, while they locate the play's breaking of limits and of consistency as aesthetic matters relating to the play's artistic unity, I regard them as equally underpinning the play's treatment of political, psychological and moral content, presenting as problematic and ambiguous such issues as power, legitimacy, assassination and tyranny, which are clearly primary subjects of the play. The reasons for a character's moral confusions may not lie "within" the person, but may exist externally as part of the play's world, and, more comprehensively in some ways, our world.

Often critics seek to help readers by presenting one theme or argument very systematically. "Macbeth is a great man flawed by ambition"; "*Macbeth* is a Christian (or Catholic or Protestant) play"; "*Macbeth* was written to flatter King James"; "the Witches represent fate in a deterministic universe", and so on. Such arguments can enhance understanding, but their very appeal is built upon a tendency to exclude detail that does not support them, in the effort to present a unified experience. This book also pursues a specific theme, but it is one which incorporates diverse elements, and the kind of unity which emerges is more one of atmospheric intensity and rich emotional impact rather than a singular thematic line of enquiry. It follows in the footsteps of another honourable line of critics who have worked from the assumption that literary works may be highly ambiguous and not subject to a single mode of explanation. They use words such as "indeterminate", "problematical", "open", "inconclusive", "lacking thematic closure" and "ambivalent", and they attempt to find ways of explaining how these qualities operate within a complex structure. A moment's thought will confirm that the very skill of a dramatist like Shakespeare is to construct dramatic agents who voice conflicting and opposed points of view, each held with equal conviction, and to let these points of view challenge each other in fierce opposition. If they were not open to very different interpretations which change from generation to generation, then they would no longer hold the stage or the attention of readers in ways that *Macbeth* in particular clearly does. The whole is greater than the sum of the parts. The polyvocal range is in part a legacy of Shakespeare's humanist education, which was based on dialectical thinking and skills in advocacy, gleaned from classical writers like Aristotle, Cicero, and (in poetry) Ovid and Virgil. Elemental conflict between subject positions is also the stuff of drama and theatre, and it must, unless the dramatist is overtly didactic (and not always then), raise problems about where the audience's allegiances and sympathies lie at any moment, and how they shift and turn, swayed by implacably opposed but equally eloquent and passionate statements by characters. Even silence, or absence, or mere visual presence and images, can tacitly challenge the dominant voices, as we shall see in examining the role of women, children and birds in *Macbeth*. The ambivalence that reigns is, at least in *Macbeth*, radical, that is, existing at the conceptual roots of the play, in such a way that there is no consistent preference expressed that is unquestionably acceptable. This accounts for the myriad ways in which *Macbeth* can be performed, depending on which viewpoint a director, actors or reader choose to accept as the leading one.

Paradox and ambivalence have, of course, been espoused as critical tools by other critics, whether they write on *Macbeth* or other plays. As is often the case in literary theory, the origins lie in other disciplines, which readily show that a fusion of contradictions exists all around us. Physics and mathematics, for example, have joined forces to give at least two influential models of paradox at work in the physical world. Relativity, as analysed by Albert Einstein, gives a formulation which inescapably links perceiver and object perceived. Shifted from the world of physics to conceptual thought, no statement can be ultimately "true" since it is inevitably and always made in a way that is "relative" to other perceivers and to personal beliefs. This is not to deny objectivity, but simply to say that two observers, believing themselves to be equally "objective", will see two, sometimes incompatible but equally valid, versions of reality. This model has been pursued in the field of the social sciences especially, most notably in the work of Foucault on the history of prisons and of human views of sex. Equally, it has very clear and rich implications when applied to works of the literary imagination which give ample room for individual feelings and perceptions to operate and fluctuate.

The second model taken from physics is the discrepancy between descriptions of the phenomenon of light as simultaneously continuing and unbroken waves, and as self-sufficient packets ("quanta") of energy. These two explanations are mutually incompatible – it is literally impossible for them to co-exist – and yet the evidence of the properties of light itself necessitates that they must co-exist. Again, we find here a fertile metaphor for the complexity and warring elements in a Shakespearian play, whether we are reading or watching it. Norman Rabkin in *Shakespeare and the Common Understanding* argues that interpretation of a Shakespearean play is not a matter of "either/or" but "both/and", applying this approach to plays such as *A Midsummer Night's Dream* and *Henry V*, with fascinating results. More recently, Stephen Greenblatt has referred to the example of a sociologist of science, Helga Nowotny, who "uses 'the cunning of uncertainty' to characterise such fields as genetic engineering, big-data culturomics, economic modelling, and the like", but as Greenblatt suggests,

> it is a concept that perfectly characterises the fascination of Shakespeare and, specifically, the elusive and astonishing flexibility of the Shakespearean text. Each of his great plays is an adaptive, open system, complex, unfixed, and unpredictable. Shakespeare was the master of creative uncertainty and hence of ongoing, vital cultural mobility. (Greenblatt 2017)

2 "Fair is foul and foul is fair": The Radical Ambivalence of *Macbeth*

Art history and theory confirm in the world of representation the ambivalences found in the physical world. Some in this discipline, such as Ernst Gombrich, have found it useful to dwell on the phenomenon of visual representation that can be open to opposed and yet compatible interpretations. In some famous images he has used, you may see a duck or a rabbit, a vase or two faces looking at each other, but the strange thing is that you cannot see both at once. There is no way of asserting one over the other with absolute confidence. The image is both, and yet paradoxically it is not possible to see both at once. Two different "readings" are held in suspension, waiting for viewers either to prefer one or to remain in a state which can tolerate ambiguity. Some psychological theories (notably that called *Gestalt* theory) have found it useful to adopt this model of perception as an active choice or preference. This in turn has found its way into market research and the world of advertising, in which the stimulus of invoking "mixed emotions" in an image has been shown to be useful in selling products (White 2014).

Thirdly, linguists and philosophers have joined forces in questioning the very stability of what we all take for granted – language – arguing that words exist in a state of relativity too, and that they mean only what context allows them, and even this is not a single "meaning" but a plurality. Such a dizzying and dismaying recognition of indeterminism underpins recent theories such as deconstructionism, a discipline more or less synonymous with the name of the French philosopher Jacques Derrida. Again, the perception is not unitary but paradoxical: simultaneously it can be literally proved that language is unstable, that words are arbitrary sounds and not the things they signify, and yet our everyday experience shows that this is no barrier to effective communication. Pragmatists may not wish to accept the first premise, and deconstructionists may not wish to accept the second, and yet in some objective way both points of view can be proved to be defective in not tolerating this paradox. In the world of literary criticism, a monumental work published in 1930 by William Empson, *Seven Types of Ambiguity*, written long before deconstruction was named but in many ways its precursor, draws upon the theory of richly fertile linguistic ambiguity in order to demonstrate the multiple and complex structures of meaning in imaginative texts.

A.P. Rossiter seems to have been the critic who coined the term "radical ambivalence" when analysing Shakespeare's works, with reference not to *Macbeth* but to *Richard II*. In *Angel with Horns* (1961), he suggests that in the plays based on *Chronicle* sources, two dominant and mutually incompatible interpretations can co-exist, and our perceptions depend on where we locate our sympathies and assumptions. Since *Macbeth* is in terms of its source a history play, based as it is on historical records or chronicles that were available in Shakespeare's time, Rossiter's book is particularly pertinent and will repay a reading of more than just the chapter on *Macbeth*. His position is consistent with the Marxist's and feminist's respective analyses of human history as class-based or gender-based, allowing at least two conflicting but equally valid versions. New Historicism adopts a broadly similar model of history, arguing that at any time there is a dominant, prevailing ideology and its equal and necessary opposite. Stephen Greenblatt, for example, argues that works by Shakespeare and his contemporaries not only reflect, inscribe and comment upon these ideological tensions but also actively intervene to change them in the popular and politically charged forum of public theatre. Jonathan Goldberg pithily sums it up, "dominant discourses allow their own subversion" (Goldberg 1987: 244). Others have used different terms to describe the dualism, or rather multivision, that can be at work in imaginative literature. For example, Graham Bradshaw speaks of several interpretative "framing perspectives" being available at any point in a Shakespearean play (Bradshaw 1987: 50-80), and Neil Rhodes attributes to humanist training in rhetoric "the ability to see things from different points of view" (2004: 88), so that even the actors' perspective may differ from the audience's, and each individual spectator will hold a slightly or considerably different understanding from any other spectator. *Macbeth* exemplifies these principles by giving an array of character perspectives which change from time to time, and by allowing the audience to be privy to Macbeth's thoughts as he debates his agonising decision.

In this book on *Macbeth*, the play will be seen as radically ambivalent on many levels, and equally open to opposite lines of interpretation, which is one good reason why it has survived for so long as a performance script and text for study. Using Goldberg's words,

2 "Fair is foul and foul is fair": The Radical Ambivalence of *Macbeth*

"dominant discourses allow their own subversion", we might label two major lines of approach in shorthand, respectively the conservative and the subversive, although these are loose terms and are not used with particular precision. Their application to *Macbeth* takes us back to the two different ways of reading Marlowe's *Doctor Faustus* in the Prologue above. Because the conservative or orthodox view dominated criticism in the twentieth century, I shall simply sketch it very briefly, reserving detailed study for the subversive, radical approach which opens up newer lines of enquiry. A reading based on an assumption that monarchy provides national stability could see Malcolm's accession as solving all the problems and providing a decisive closure to the conflicts with no loose ends. Furthermore, a play about kingship that ended otherwise could simply not have been staged in 1606, without attracting charges of treason and without being censored. Even the question of overthrowing and killing an obvious tyrant like Macbeth, although countenanced by some writers, was by no means settled, if it could be argued that he was in some way enthroned by due process. If his authority was legal, then writers like Aquinas insisted that he could be removed only by God, which, the argument runs, in this case occurs through the human agency of Macduff. However, given the many shades of opinion in a volatile debate that eventually came to a head with the execution of Charles I in 1649 and deposition of Charles II in 1651, the evidence suggests a highly sophisticated and politically well-informed audience that could appreciate the skill with which a dramatist enfolds oppositional positions within an apparently bland overall framework acceptable to the authorities of the day. *Macbeth* and Marlowe's *Doctor Faustus* stand together in this dual vision which challenges orthodoxies, and it may be significant that both deal with evil, ambiguously locating its source not just in the realms of black magic and religion, but also, more materially, in power relations and politics. Both also locate the central issue as human aspiration, the one for power and the other for knowledge, and both can be read equally as, on the one hand, moralistic condemnations of such ambition, and on the other as anti-moralistic claims for the naturalness of ambition within human institutions that impose limitations on action and advancement. The two plays are capable of undermining positions presented as apparent certitudes. Besides, even the attribution of "ambition" itself is debatable in these plays. In the case of Faustus, curiosity and the pursuit of knowledge seem, as the character himself assumes, to be legitimate, even God-given rights, making any line arbitrary which claims to divide acceptable and "forbidden" knowledge. In Macbeth's case, despite assertions by many critics, the protagonist is not depicted as driven by ambition in an unqualified sense. His wife at least hesitates conditionally over the issue: "Thou wouldst be great, / Art not without ambition, but without / The illness should attend it", believing her husband to be "too full of the milk of human kindness / To catch the nearest way" (1.5.15-19), which is hardly an endorsement of a ruthless upstart. Macbeth concedes that the only reason for killing the king would be "vaulting ambition" (1.7.27), which he finds is less powerful in himself than his own conscience, and as Rossiter points out, "when he names it that [ambition], he rejects it: 'We will proceed no further'" (Rossiter 1961: 211).

The orthodox Christian reading of Marlowe's *Doctor Faustus* can be simply encapsulated in the words of the Chorus already quoted: "Faustus is gone: regard his hellish fall, / Whose fiendful fortune may exhort the wise, / Only to wonder at unlawful things". This straightforward, even glib and complacent moral does make perfect sense of the narrative in a play showing the fate of a man who sells his soul to the devil, but it renders very docile and tame the implicit intellectual challenge to Elizabethan Christianity as a religion, with a tyrannical god who will not allow humans to move beyond certain prescribed limits of knowledge. It is inconceivable that such a searching mind as Marlowe's would have been satisfied with this description of his action, even though he strategically begins and ends with the moral reading. What is lacking in such a moralistic account are the ebbs and flows of sympathies, and emotional volatility. In *Macbeth*, the equivalent orthodox message is voiced at the end by Macduff: "Behold where stands / Th'usurper's cursed head. The time is free" (5.11.20-1) – and Malcolm:

> What's more to do,
> Which would be planted newly with the time,
> As calling home our exiled friends abroad,
> That fled the snares of watchful tyranny,

2 "Fair is foul and foul is fair": The Radical Ambivalence of *Macbeth*

> Producing forth the cruel ministers
> Of this dead butcher, and his fiend-like Queen –
> Who, as 'tis thought, by self and violent hands
> Took off her life – this, and what needful else
> That calls upon us, by the grace of Grace
> We will perform in measure, time, and place. (5.11.30-9)

Such a reading would be built upon assumptions that Duncan was a saintly, wise and legitimate king of war-torn Scotland (not looking too closely at *why* Scotland is war-torn when there are rebels and invaders who seem to be challenging the king's authority), and that Malcolm is the only rightful heir to the throne. The orthodox conclusion would agree with Macduff and Malcolm that Macbeth's mental anguish and the fate of his wife are fully deserved, downplaying any audience implication in the presentation of these two powerful theatrical figures.

Winners, after all, rewrite history, and in this case their account is cogent. Macbeth, whether simply informed by, or motivated by, three apparently prophetic Witches, plays out a destiny which leads him to kill the good king to further his own personal ambitions, and in this he is encouraged by his even more ambitious wife. Malcolm, the rightful heir to the throne, authorised by Duncan before our very eyes early in the play, flees to England to meet up with the other saintly king, Edward the Confessor of England, and with Macduff, who flees Scotland in terror of his life, they return to overthrow the new tyrant. Because Macbeth's accession is illegally the result of murder, so his reign is destined to be bloody and beleaguered. He turns into a paranoid tyrant, killing all potential enemies such as Macduff's wife and children and Banquo, whose son Fleance escapes later, as predicted by the Witches, eventually to sire a line of kings which stretches down to Shakespeare's King James. The tyrant's "fiend-like queen" is racked during her sleep with the remorse of conscience, and in the end dies an unspecified death, rumoured to be suicide. Macbeth fears no human foe when resistance to him turns into military siege, until the twin prophecies of the Witches come about – trees from Birnam Wood "come" (are carried) to Dunsinane as camouflage for soldiers, and Macduff fulfils the Witches' riddle by revealing that he was as a baby delivered by Caesarean section rather than being "born of woman" in the usual manner. At this point Macbeth's power is at an end, and he is unceremoniously beheaded by Macduff. Malcolm returns to be crowned "by the grace of God" as legitimate king authorised to reinstate the peace, harmony and order which his father Duncan had stood for, before the savage disruption to history perpetrated by Macbeth. And, we are tempted to say, they all lived happily ever after in a state of God-ordained divinity of inherited kingship, leading, we assume through the line of Fleance, right down to King James who in his very person unified the traditional rivals Scotland and England, turning them into one peaceful nation. *Macbeth*, then, becomes a theatrical justification for the English form of monarchy, and a dire warning to all who would ambitiously reach above their station and dare to kill a king, just as *Doctor Faustus* provided a stern lesson to scholars who aspire to rise above the boundaries set by God on their knowledge. In rewriting the play for children in their influential *Tales from Shakespeare* (1807), Charles and Mary Lamb are unambiguously judgemental:

> With these frantic words [Macbeth] threw himself upon Macduff, who, after a severe struggle, in the end overcame him, and cutting off his head, made a present of it to the young and lawful king, Malcolm; who took upon him the government which, by the machinations of the usurper, he had so long been deprived of, and ascended the throne of Duncan the Meek, amid the acclamations of the nobles and the people.

The implicit value judgements made here ("frantic", "lawful", "machinations of the usurper", "the Meek", "acclamations") allow no other reading than the orthodox.

Like the Chorus' words in *Doctor Faustus*, this reading of Macbeth is coherent and explanatory, making complete sense of the action in ways that would please a God-fearing King James and his obedient subjects. Influential critics in the earlier twentieth century such as A.C. Bradley (1904), Lily B. Campbell (1930) and G. Wilson Knight (1930) give sophisticated and powerful presentations of this kind of argument, and are still well worth reading with respect. However, such orthodoxy can be sustained only by ignoring some questions that will be raised in this book, concerning, for example, the clear ineffectuality of Duncan as

2 "Fair is foul and foul is fair": The Radical Ambivalence of *Macbeth*

king, the dubious legality of Malcolm's claim to the throne in a Scottish system that did not favour primogeniture, alongside doubts about his own moral fitness for the post. Above all there is the emotional aspect of the audience's complex blend of understanding and even sympathy for Macbeth and his wife in their different ways. It is more difficult to judge them categorically when we see and even share the feeling states they undergo in their tragic course. There is also some uneasiness concerning what ethical system, whether Christian or pagan, prevails in the society represented. On the one hand, as we shall see later in Chapter 5, Christian references are prevalent. We note, for example, that Macbeth is disconcerted in an oddly poignant and childlike way by his inability to intone the word "amen" after he hears the grooms saying their prayers, a concern dismissed by his wife as insignificant:

> MACBETH
> One cried "God bless us" and "Amen" the other,
> As they had seen me with these hangman's hands.
> List'ning their fear, I could not say "Amen"
> When they did say "God bless us".
> LADY MACBETH
> Consider it not so deeply.
> MACBETH
> But wherefore could not I pronounce "Amen"?
> I had most need of blessing, and "Amen"
> Stuck in my throat.
> LADY MACBETH
> These deeds must not be thought
> After these ways. So, it will make us mad. (2.2.24-32)

On the other hand, there are signs that a pagan, pre-Christian world view is at least available in memory, when matters of right and wrong could be decisively settled by warriors in bloodshed, without scruples or recriminations. Macbeth recalls nostalgically and almost wistfully that in "olden days" men could get away with murder without fear of consequences, whereas for him the image of Banquo seems to have come back from the dead to accuse him, and will not leave him alone:

> Blood hath been shed ere now, i' th' olden time,
> Ere human statute purged the gentle weal;
> Ay, and since, too, murders have been performed
> Too terrible for the ear. The time has been
> That, when the brains were out, the man would die,
> And there an end. But now they rise again
> With twenty mortal murders on their crowns,
> And push us from our stools. This is more strange
> Than such a murder is. (3.4.74-82)

For the soldier used to killing, this form of "strange" accountability comes to Macbeth as a surprise. We might notice first the almost Freudian way in which the murdered "crowns" may rise again, recalling and anticipating the prophecy that Banquo's line will eventually "rise up" to create a line of kings stretching to the dawning crack of the Day of Judgement. But more broadly, Macbeth's words suggest almost blasphemously that Christianity is a debatable system created by men ("human statute") rather than stemming from divine authority, close to a fanatic's superstition creating false visions for gullible mankind. It is too easy to dismiss such questions as inappropriate or to explain them away by saying, as some have done, that we must have lost some of the text in transmission. The underlying problems of whether to place the play firmly in a Christian or pagan cosmos seem to be part of the design of the play, and meant to remain as unsettling doubts.

In the following chapters we examine the evidence for a range of resistant readings which pull against the grain of the orthodox, monarchist view offered above. We need to be alert to detail and ask some questions which may not have been systematically addressed before. For the sake of an orderly argument, we look in turn at the ways in which each principal agent is constructed in the scheme of the play, then at some leading concepts which underlie the debates conducted in the play, and then at clusters of imagery which enrich the atmosphere and texture of the play, and add an often subliminal set of associations which complicate, subvert and enrich our responses. The overall perspectivef offered, I hope, reveals layers of intellectual and emotional complexity which account for the power and unity of the effect of *Macbeth* on readers and audiences. First, I will now suggest, such plurality of readings was implicit in educational practices and literary theories of Shakespeare's time.

Rhetoric and Dialectic

One of the unsung heroes of literary history was Shakespeare's schoolmaster, who may or may not have been Thomas Jenkins as headmaster of the King Edward VI Grammar School in Stratford-upon-Avon in the mid-1570s. To him we obviously owe a huge debt. Shakespeare himself repaid it in his gently mocking but affectionate vignettes of teachers in *Love's Labour's Lost* and *The Merry Wives of Windsor*. Holofernes and Parson Evans in these plays may be pedantic, especially in their insistence on sound knowledge of Latin, but they are also conscientious, valued members of the community, and at least the former critically appreciates poetry and is happy to mount a play for the entertainment of the citizens. More than this personal but undocumented link, the young Shakespeare was also a fortunate beneficiary of a remarkable system of education which had been originated by humanists of the late fifteenth and early sixteenth centuries, John Colet, Desiderius Erasmus and Sir Thomas More. Indeed, humanism itself was in essence an educational program as well as being a more general way of viewing the world. Shakespeare, in his "petty" (*petit*) school and then grammar school, learned to read and write English and to translate and compose Latin and later Greek. After learning grammar and vocabulary he would have moved on to texts such as those by the Roman dramatists Terence (comedy) and Seneca (tragedy), the poets Ovid, Horace and Virgil, and the prose of Cicero (Simon 1966: 378). Of these, perhaps the most important conceptual training came from Cicero. His *De Officiis*, expounding how to be a good citizen, was one of the most influential works throughout Europe in the medieval and Renaissance periods, and *De Oratore* is a work in dialogue presenting principles for arguing a legal case as well as writing persuasively and eloquently, and his own orations offer examples of this forensic art. Meanwhile, Shakespeare's contemporary Sir Philip Sidney structured his *Defence of Poetry* (written about 1579-80) as though he is presenting a legal case, with the cardinal sections advocated by Cicero: Narration,

Divisions (distinctions), Examinations (analysis), Refutation (of the analysis) and Peroration (summing up and conclusion). Other classical writers such as the Roman rhetorician Quintilian and the Greek Aristotle laid down similar rules for composing works of literature, with comparable divisions: Invention, Arrangement, Style, Memory and Delivery. Educational writers of the sixteenth century including Sir Tomas Elyot, John Rainolds and Thomas Wilson introduced into English school syllabuses the aspects of *Art of Rhetorique* (Wilson's title) which were gleaned from the classical writers. Recently, Quentin Skinner in his book *Forensic Shakespeare* has provided sustained analysis of some of Shakespeare's works and passages, showing them to be assembled with a close knowledge of these classical theories of judicial rhetoric, and as a considered part of his creative labours.

At the heart of the rhetorical training learned and displayed by Shakespeare is a principle of dialectic. Another influential humanist from France, Petrus Ramus, wrote a whole book on logic as a way of strengthening the memory, called *Dialectica*, which found its way across Europe and especially into Protestant schools. It is a perennial requirement that lawyers in particular must develop the habit of mind of being able to understand, justify and defend any subject-position offered them. Something similar operates in drama and literature in general, with the added need to inform logic with feelings, not simply to argue with reason and logic but with imagination of alternative emotional states. In both forms of advocacy, the to-and-fro of arguments mounted, refuted and synthesised as in a court of law, whether presented in dialogue or monologue (such as in a poem or work of prose – or even Hamlet's soliloquies), take into account and assemble systematically different points of view, all of which need to be inspected and compared before a judgement can be made. In other words, we have the medium of drama – the play and interplay of different points of view, each presented sympathetically and voiced with commensurate persuasiveness by a range of characters in opposition or agreement. Macbeth in Act 1 Scene 7 argues with himself concerning the merits and morality of killing Duncan, using both logic and emotions, and in an exemplary consideration of the pros and cons he decides it is not the right course of action. However, when he then declares to his wife that "We will proceed no further in this business" (1.7.31) and gives his reasons for the conclusion, they then debate the issue together, and this time Lady Macbeth persuades him to change his mind, mainly through her decisive use of imagery that calls into question his masculinity and adds a layer of emotional logic he had not considered. Many other scenes are posed as similar dilemmas which are cogently reasoned in different ways – between Malcolm and Macduff, between Macduff and his wife when apart – all pitting logic against feelings. And here we have the basis for the possibility of the dramatist suspending judgement and leaving decisions up to actors and audiences as to how to stage and interpret these many conflicting expressions of opinion. Given the emotional consistency and intensity (or *ethos* in Aristotle's terminology) of any one of the competing angles, some conflicts, especially those based on respective feelings rather than reasoning, are simply incompatible and insoluble. The result, in the case of Shakespeare's practice in his plays, is a multiplicity of simultaneously available perspectives which allow for multiple interpretations, and in the process can generate the kind of double vision which is evident in *Macbeth*.

Another aspect of humanist literary training was the use of metaphor, imagery, and figurative language in general, and it is this which helps to provide *Macbeth* with its unique atmosphere. How it operates in the play will be analysed in Chapter 6, but its general importance in drama and literature can be established by referring again to Sidney's *Defence of Poetry*. At the heart of this brief but important work is an argument that literature or "poesy" differs from history (which we observed in considering the sources of *Macbeth*), which simply gives "the bare *was*" of the records without inviting us to feel the emotions of the characters in their situations. He also compares poetry with philosophy, which gives moral lessons in dry, prescriptive "learned definitions, be it of virtues or vices, be it of public policy or private government [rules of proper conduct]" which, Sidney says, "lie dark before the imaginative and judging power, if they be not illuminated or figured forth by the speaking picture of poesy". Imaginative literature does the work of both history (in representing past events) and philosophy (in teaching us about virtue and vice), but it does more, by providing a narrative which can move our feelings, and by embellishing, "delighting" and "enticing" us with the manner of telling:

Now, therein, of all sciences (I speak still of human, and according to the human conceit) is our poet the monarch. For he doth not only show the way, but giveth so sweet a prospect into the way, as will entice any man to enter into it. Nay, he doth, as if your journey should lie through a fair vineyard, at the first give you a cluster of grapes, that full of that taste, you may long to pass farther. He beginneth not with obscure definitions, which must blur the margin with interpretations, and load the memory with doubtfulness. But he cometh to you with words set in delightful proportion, either accompanied with, or prepared for, the well-enchanting skill of music; and with a tale forsooth he cometh unto you with a tale, which holdeth children from play, and old men from the chimney-corner. And, pretending no more, doth intend the winning of the mind from wickedness to virtue – even as the child is often brought to have a pleasant taste … (Sidney 1973: 91-2)

The poet provides us with a unified and inveigling story, clothed in the music of "words set in delightful proportion", and not couched in "obscure definitions" but visual images. The work of literature provides "to speak metaphorically, a speaking picture, with this end, to teach and delight", and the word "delight" signals the emotional content. Events are brought to life before us "allegorically and figuratively written" instead of as unadorned narration, using facts from history not for their own sake but "as an imaginative ground-plot of a profitable invention". In *Macbeth* we find history, but history embellished with imagination; and philosophy, but a philosophy that gives as much credence to the dangerous attraction of temptation to evil as to the virtues of inaction. This play is considerably more than a scholarly exercise in revived classical rhetoric. A wild and even primitive layer of meaning is genuinely a part of its composition, provided by compelling poetry and subtly imaginative imagery. But *Macbeth* is at least on one level the product of an historically aware author, steeped in literary precepts of composition learned from a humanist education.

Numbers

While a humanist education gave Shakespeare consummate skill with words, it was not so sophisticated in mathematics. There is evidence from the plays that he was not good with adding and subtraction, since the school system did not progress students beyond simple arithmetic. Shakespeare was, however, intrigued by the philosophical significance of numbers themselves, especially "zero" (*King Lear* turns on "nothing") and the curious way that adding "noughts" to a number increased rather than diminished its size (the Chorus in *Henry V* plays on this in saying that one actor can stand for 1000 troops in an army) (White 2013). In *Macbeth*, he clearly gives much thought to the numbers two and three, in their disconcerting habit of creating discordances when placed together – two is an "even" number and three is "odd" so they do not go well together. Ambivalence, given the prefix of the word's root (*ambi-* as "both" or "on both sides"), usually refers to a hovering choice between two positions. But the choice is further complicated when there are three possibilities available. By emphasising these numbers in his play, Shakespeare accentuates its multi-vocal and multiply ambiguous nature in a conspicuous and persistent manner.

Macbeth is unusually specific in its repetition of the numbers three and two. We need not attribute to these any mystical qualities to recognise that they provide a kind of anchoring structure to the plot, albeit one that shifts with currents between the two numbers, which are mathematically incommensurate with each other. There are three Weird Sisters, who appear three times and deliver to Macbeth and Banquo three prophecies, each of which comes true in front of our eyes. The Witches themselves harp on the number in their opening incantation:

> FIRST WITCH
> Thrice the brinded cat hath mew'd.
> SECOND WITCH
> Thrice and once the hedge-pig whined. (4.1.1-2)

They present events in threes as though this number represents a series which is endlessly repeatable once "the charm's wound up":

> ALL
> The weird sisters hand in hand,
> Posters of the sea and land,
> Thus do go about, about,
> Thrice to thine and thrice to mine,
> And thrice again to make up nine.
> Peace! the charm's wound up. (1.3.30-5)

Three "apparitions" appear before Macbeth. By the end of the play there have been three kings, Duncan, Macbeth and Malcolm. Three murderers turn up to murder Banquo and Fleance, to which the play enigmatically draws special attention since there were supposed only to be two:

> Enter three Murderers
> FIRST MURDERER (to *Third Murderer*)
> But who did bid thee join with us?
> THIRD MURDERER
> Macbeth.
> SECOND MURDERER (to First Murderer)
> He needs not our mistrust, since he delivers
> Our offices and what we have to do
> To the direction just.
> FIRST MURDERER (to *Third Murderer*)
> Then stand with us.
> The west yet glimmers with some streaks of day.
> Now spurs the lated traveller apace
> To gain the timely inn, and near approaches
> The subject of our watch. (3.3.1-8)

Critical speculation that the third is Macbeth himself seems unlikely since the latter is genuinely surprised and appalled when he hears later that Fleance has escaped. If he had been one of the group, he would know this. It looks more like the First Murderer guesses correctly that the third has been hired through "mistrust" to spy on the first two, and perhaps even murder them if they do not carry out their orders. By

2 "Fair is foul and foul is fair": The Radical Ambivalence of *Macbeth*

this stage of the play Macbeth is driven by paranoia, which has its own special logic, but it further reinforces the number three as though it is especially significant to the design of the play, and raises in an oddly physical way the proverbial saying, "two is company, three's a crowd", suggesting the third does not belong.

Following this last point, there is equal stress in *Macbeth* on the number two. The sergeant who reports the opening battle harps on "double":

> I must report they were
> As cannons overcharged with double cracks,
> So they doubly redoubled strokes upon the foe. (1.1.36-8)

In the same way Lady Macbeth assures Duncan that everything has been done twice in preparing hospitality for him:

> All our service
> In every point twice done, and then done double,
> Were poor and single business to contend
> Against those honours deep and broad wherewith
> Your majesty loads our house. (1.7.14-18)

Macbeth, pondering the wisdom of assassination, also focuses on a binary, a consideration of pros and cons, debits and credits:

> He's here in double trust:
> First, as I am his kinsman and his subject,
> Strong both against the deed; then, as his host,
> Who should against his murderer shut the door,
> Not bear the knife myself. (1.7.12-16)

When Macbeth arranges the seating at the table for the banquet he is careful to ensure that "Both sides are even" (3.4.9) while he sits "I'th'midst" (3.4.10), presumably at the head of the table, and his wife "keeps her state" (3.4.5), no doubt at the other end. However, the symmetry is broken when (to Macbeth's eyes only) Banquo appears.

Even the Witches vary their attention on threes by picking up the same word in their chorus: "Double, double, toil and trouble, / Fire burn, and cauldron bubble" (4.1.9-10). When Macbeth comes up against his nemesis Macduff, he recalls the Witches' words:

> And be these juggling fiends no more believed,
> That palter with us in a double sense,
> That keep the word of promise to our ear
> And break it to our hope. I'll not fight with thee. (5.11.19-23)

"Double" can raise doubts about truth and falsehood, while "treble" opens multiple possibilities to nine and beyond. And as number systems they are mutually incompatible – mathematically, and the same applies to all multiples of each given powers by being squared into infinity, 2 x 2 ("double double") will always give an even number while 3 x 3 ("thrice times thrice") will always give an odd number, and never the twain shall meet. Like parallel lines, they will continue forever apart. And if truth and falsehood are taken to be equally incompatible, then there is also a further ambiguity between existence and non-existence – is and is not – in what Macbeth alone sees, the dagger leading him on. The comparable vision of the spectre of Banquo at the feast leads Macbeth on to a more personal and existential doubt of his own existence: "To know my deed, 'twere best not know myself" (2.2.70). Paradoxes around "self" and "other" mount up. Predictions in themselves "Cannot be ill, cannot be good" (1.3.130), but if they are ill then they cannot be good, and if good they cannot be ill, creating a kind of semantic riddle. There is no way of knowing the morality of events until the future reveals itself, except through "imagination", which can be misleading:

> MACBETH
> [*Aside*] This supernatural soliciting
> Cannot be ill, cannot be good. If ill,
> Why hath it given me earnest of success,
> Commencing in a truth? I am Thane of Cawdor.
> If good, why do I yield to that suggestion

2 "Fair is foul and foul is fair": The Radical Ambivalence of *Macbeth*

> Whose horrid image doth unfix my hair
> And make my seated heart knock at my ribs
> Against the use of nature? Present fears
> Are less than horrible imaginings.
> My thought, whose murder yet is but fantastical,
> Shakes so my single state of man that function
> Is smothered in surmise, and nothing is
> But what is not.
> BANQUO [*to Ross and Angus*]
> Look, how our partner's rapt. (1.3.129-41)

Such moments of speculative "raptness" must face every high-ranking politician required to vote for or against some policy which may lead to a better future or an appalling catastrophe. Ever since George W. Bush decided to invade Iraq he has persuaded himself that there still can be no final pronouncement on the wisdom of the war, continuing to speak from an indeterminate present declaring, "time will tell". His comrade-in-arms, the British prime minister of the time, Tony Blair, still insists on a similar indeterminacy as though weirdly the event had not actually happened, still intoning helplessly time and again, "I did what I thought was right", as though this prior intention overrules later evidence that he was *not* right at all. The road to hell, we recall, is paved with good intentions. Both Bush and Blair faced their historical moments believing they were actors in literary works, respectively the hero of *Henry V* (Bush's favourite work) or *Ivanhoe* (Blair's), and they still seem not to comprehend that the most relevant narrative to the violent and ambitious "regime change" they carried out was *Macbeth*.

In terms of the play itself, by overlaying number series based on two and three, Shakespeare is drawing attention to different ways of conceptualising time, especially at significant turning points of decision in a person's life when the character stands on "this bank and shoal of time" (1.7.6) contemplating a course of action. Three is a series and implies a sequence from one to two, from two to three, which suggests a causation between the events amounting to an inevitability. If one and two happen as predicted, three must follow or the sequence is broken. Thane of Glamis leads to Thane of Cawdor, so king must be next by a temporal logic. There are so many equivalents that underlie the expectation: after the past comes the present and then the future; the present is a result of the past and prelude to the future; and fictional tales proverbially have three parts, beginning, middle and end, which Aristotle had decreed must have a close fit with each other or the narrative unity is destroyed and rendered random. Two, however, presupposes only an oscillation from one point back to the other. This or that? Here or there? Then and now? Or true or false, right or wrong? This formulation creates a limiting, binary valuation of time, as we stand anchored in the present, capable only of dividing time by looking back to the known past and forward to the unknown future. This implies not causative inevitability but an element of chance, and the need to make a decision here and now. In a nutshell, three is predetermined destiny, two is choice. Macbeth does recognise and articulate these two models of time, and he realises he must decide between them, debating their merits in the style of a humanist rhetorician: "If chance will have me king, why, chance may crown me, / Without my stir" (1.3.142), and he realises also that it is a matter of confronting time, present and future, actions and their consequences:

> If it were done when 'tis done, then 'twere well
> It were done quickly. If th'assassination
> Could trammel up the consequence, and catch
> With his surcease success: that but this blow
> Might be the be-all and the end-all, here,
> But here, upon this bank and shoal of time,
> We'd jump the life to come. (1.7.1-7)

If only the present could be the "be-all and the end-all", that we could leapfrog over the appalling event and face no future reckoning; if only the sequence were a narrative certainty of destiny, instead of a choice, then we could "vault" straight into a "happily ever after" time hereafter, without having to face the consequences of making the decision. This is the last moment when Macbeth can truly choose between two alternatives, but he is about to trust almost helplessly the logic of three as a destiny which requires no agency. He is about to relinquish choice and instead surrender himself to chance, which presents itself as destiny.

2 "Fair is foul and foul is fair": The Radical Ambivalence of Macbeth

There are two more instances in the play when Macbeth realises that the moment of binary choice is gone forever and he is locked tragically inside the pattern of threefold destiny, which in his case can have no happy ending. The first is when he acknowledges that his act of murdering Duncan has irreparably ruptured the past from his future, and the present offers no choice but to go forward:

> I am in blood
> Stepped in so far that, should I wade no more,
> Returning were as tedious as go o'er. (3.4.135-7)

The second is the most dismal threesome in the play, Macbeth's emotional state when he finally realises that the future is now completely known and must simply be played through to its bitter end:

> To-morrow, and to-morrow, and to-morrow
> Creeps in this petty pace from day to day
> To the last syllable of recorded time,
> And all our yesterdays have lighted fools
> The way to dusty death. (5.5.17-22)

Now that Macbeth's wife is dead, the reassuring company offered by two is gone, while the disappearance of the Witches removes any appeal to a destined future except his own "dusty death". He is himself alone, a solitary one, soon to be a cipher.

Power and Monarchy

There is another, more political implication to the primacy of the number two in this play and others by Shakespeare. When we inspect his history plays, including the Greco-Roman plays, it seems an apparent rule that wherever there is a ruling monarch there is also a shadow to him, either a pretender or a legitimate claimant, each of which is capable of resorting to assassination to press his legitimacy: Richard II and Bolingbroke; Henry IV and the Earl of Northumberland;

Hal and Hotspur. The Duke of Gloucester shadows and assassinates each claimant in turn to the throne until he is crowned; old Hamlet and Claudius, then Claudius and young Hamlet; the list goes on. In this Machiavellian world of *realpolitik*, legitimacy is conferred not by philosophical logic but by actual power. King James himself would have been only too aware of this gloomy fact: he hoped, and asserted in his book *Basilikon Doron*, that his own authority was conferred by God in the form of divine right, but the respective fates of his own mother and his son proved otherwise.

The logic that for every ruler there is a ruler-in-waiting, either legitimate or pretender, is not confined to the early modern political world, or to monarchies. The system of democracy is based on a contest between two major parties with two rival leaders, even if their policies may be indistinguishable and the result may be complicated by smaller groups. Irrespective of the particular incumbent, the existence of power as an institution itself attracts and perhaps necessitates the "shadow" or rival claimant. This pattern is replicated in any hierarchical organisation, which has led to plausible adaptations of Shakespeare's *Macbeth* into business corporations, restaurants, and other workplaces with management structures. The point can be generalised still further to apply to crime more widely: as power itself, whether wielded wisely or tyrannically, galvanises opposition which may be violent, so authority by its very existence attracts rebellion. So also, even in apparently neutral and even benign human environments like banks, the existence of potential profit makes crime likely and even inevitable, as evidenced in the invention of the internet and email, which have led to a vast and ever-increasing wave of "white collar crime".

The uncanny ability of Shakespeare to identify general processes behind unique events provides in the case of *Macbeth* a story which seems as simple as a fable while choosing to highlight specific human impulses and motivations that complicate the apparently easy moral with multiple, profound questions. These turn on ambiguities that allow us to see a man as villain or as victim; a king, whether good or bad, as trapped in the official role he holds, which makes him vulnerable; the disturbing of moral categories merging good and evil, fair and foul, truth and "equivocation" – historical processes that question the extent to which men are making free choices as agents of their own destiny, or are mere playthings of predetermined historical cycles and patterns, tumbling around the wheel of fortune. Men are tempted by power, and succumb, only to be replaced by others who are tempted and succumb. We may be led to sympathise with the individual or condemn him, or like the Weird Sisters simply to look on and make predictions. It is the existence of power itself which generates the apparently endless and self-destructive system, and it is to the individual emotions and motivations that sustain the struggle for power to which we now turn.

3
"Nothing is but what is not": Emotional Worlds of Characters in *Macbeth*

Quite a lot of evidence suggests that the study of character for its own sake is a relatively modern preoccupation. Before William Hazlitt, who perhaps provocatively at the time named his book *Characters of Shakespear's Plays* in 1817, the personages represented in a play seem to have been regarded as roles dictated by the plot and design of a play as a whole, rather than individuals with anything like the modern conception of an "inner life" or an existence beyond the words in the play. Hazlitt was primarily a theatre critic and reviewer, and his interest lies in the different ways that actors, depending on their own temperament and styles, can play a character. On the Elizabethan stage, actors would have been so busy in doubling and trebling the "parts" they played (since the company had only about a dozen personnel to represent many more figures), and attending to their cues for when to enter and exit, that they may not have had time to develop subtle, singular traits to separate each character from others at a psychological level, relying more on broad, differentiating effects. As we have partly seen, Shakespeare himself found hints of personal traits for each personage in the source he was using (in this case Holinshed's *Chronicles* and Buchanan's history of Scotland), since most of his plays adapt to the stage stories already authored by others and printed. He also drew to some extent on the medical model then current of "humours" in which body and mind were closely connected, and some figures show mental characteristics that stem from an imbalance in their physiology – Hamlet as a melancholic (too much black bile), for example (see Babb 1951; Arikha 2007; Schoenfeldt 1999; Paster 1993 and 2004). Macbeth seems to be "choleric", with an over-balance of blood, and in another category of early modern medicine he is also driven by a "passion" which amounts to an obsession, in his case arguably fear (Hobgood 2013).

Other character types came from different dramatic traditions, such as the classical device of giving masks to actors (Frow 2014: 253-65), Italian *commedia del arte*, or the use of "vice" figures from medieval drama. Shakespeare was also certainly aware of a minor literary genre called "The Character" dating back to the ancient Greek writer Theophrastus and used in the Renaissance by writers like John Earle in *Micro-cosmographie*, Bishop Hall's *Characters of Virtues and Vices*, and Sir Thomas Overbury's *New Characters (Drawne to the Life) of Several Persons in Several Qualities*. Here, distinctive delineations between people are drawn through stereotypical typologies based on occupations, or single-minded passions, and sometimes humours ("The Surly Man" [Theophrastus]; "A Discontented Man" and "A Poor Fiddler" [Earle]; "A vaine-glorious Coward in Command" and "A fayre and happy Milk-mayd" [Overbury]; "The Envious Man" [Hall]). Like the humoral approach, this also gives a model of people being functions partly of temperament and partly of their outer circumstances. Macbeth on this typology is defined as a soldier. Thus we can see the dramatist building up a character, layer by layer. Onto these techniques, Shakespeare grafted individualising notes like use of dialects and particular speech idiosyncrasies. He edged towards a notion that people "have that within that passeth show" (*Hamlet*) – emotional states which can be concealed and revealed at will, evident especially in his sonnets. However, this does not mean he thought of his characters as we do in our world informed by modern psychology. When characters like Falstaff and Cleopatra break out of types and act inconsistently, it is more likely a situational change to suit the plot rather than attributable to some deeper, inner principle stemming from a unified identity. Besides, Falstaff and Cleopatra are depicted as prone to lying and exaggerating, which intrinsically means they are not consistent truth-tellers, while Macbeth sees visions and ghosts, which equally distorts any sense of mental continuity in his perceptions, and makes him the sort of person who rapidly changes his mind and his moods according to circumstances. It is those circumstances and how he reacts to them which make the play what it is.

Nonetheless, despite bits and pieces of their origins taken from contemporary literary, dramatic and physiological constructs, the remarkable thing about Shakespeare's creations is that they have continued to be susceptible to analysis using later ways of modelling human mental processes, such as the novelistic and the psychological. It was the rise of the novel in the eighteenth and nineteenth centuries which encouraged readers, and therefore audiences, to think about fictional figures having plausible motivation, emotional consistency, and some kind of imputed "backstory" of the kind that we find in works by Dickens, George Eliot and Virginia Woolf. As her title suggests, Mary Cowden Clark's *The Girlhood of Shakespeare's Heroines*, published in the 1850s at the height of the Victorian novel's popularity, is a largely fictional construction along the lines of a novel, using Shakespeare's words as little more than a starting point for speculation about where these characters "came from". But a moment's thought tells us that novels and plays are different. In the former there is generally a narrator on hand, or an omniscient author, who subtly manipulates readers to make judgements about their characters and often describes their mental and emotional states, while in drama there is no authorial mouthpiece. All we have are the words, no more and sometimes less depending on cuts in performance. Sympathetic identification is possible but negotiable, depending on the director and actors who make their own choices about what is plausible behaviour. In the twentieth century there followed the rise of psychology as a study of the mind, especially of the Freudian kind, which imputed to individuals conscious and unconscious desires, ego and id. In the theatre, also in the early twentieth century, the famous Russian director Konstantin Stanislavski took a step further in training "method" actors to think in a self-searching and disciplined way of their roles in terms of characters having rounded personalities with emotions, motivations and subconscious desires, which can be represented in performance as justifying their actions. Actors were encouraged to "live" the role they happened to be playing, no doubt to the frustration of their families and friends outside the theatrical context.

Even if this psychologising is not the way Shakespeare would have conceived of his actors (whom he sometimes refers to as "shadows") representing different roles on the stage, it is nonetheless impossible nowadays to ignore a character-based approach, since so much in theatre and movies today hangs on casting or "star quality", and presupposes some degree of psychological realism and depth, while in teaching drama "characterisation" is a virtually obligatory tool of analysis. More enlightening in understanding Shakespeare's practice of "situational" characterisation, looking at the dramatic personages in detail is one way of revealing underlying patterns of dramatic design, as well as different ways of evaluating the action and making moral judgements about behaviour on stage – both important aspects of Elizabethan playwriting. An approach through character also opens up a dynamic experience changing from moment to moment since, at least in Shakespeare's practice, each personage brings to situations a set of emotional awarenesses and desires not shared by others. They do sometimes express their feelings, even when these are disguised, mixed or explicit. Malcolm urges Macduff to exercise stoicism on hearing that his wife and children have been slaughtered, but the latter replies that he must "feel it as a man" (4.3.221), one point where an unashamedly affective response is voiced as an understandable and valid reaction to appalling circumstances, and a moment when Shakespeare's unerring humanity intrudes to guide the audience. Each role represents a unique emotional world either in conflict or accord with those of others who interact, in an enactment of "discrepant emotional awarenesses" (White and Rawnsley 2015).

In this chapter we look at the circles of characters "around" the central ones, reserving consideration of the Macbeths themselves for the next. Initially, characters in *Macbeth* broadly might be seen as fitting into a threefold scheme (so much in *Macbeth* runs in threes, as we have seen) – the good, bad and indifferent. However, on closer inspection, the large qualification that the interpretation offered in this book argues is that the good are not all wholly good, the bad not wholly bad, and the indifferent are like the Weird Sisters, standing inscrutably apart and disinterested in human affairs, neither good nor bad. There will be an opportunity later to consider other structuring concepts and underlying, unifying patterns such as dominant themes, ideas, and trains of imagery, after looking at how the characters, each envisaged as an "emotional world" acting with and against others, may support or undermine general interpretations of the play. All are to some extent either victims or observers of "what happens", of the plot or action in which they are intertwined. It is this approach, acknowledging the primacy of plot, linked with a notion of each character being an emotional world capable of feelings that are sometimes inscrutable and sometimes barely articulated in language, which will be pursued in this chapter. We first turn our attention to others like Duncan, Banquo, Malcolm, Macduff, Lady Macduff, the Weird Sisters, and even children, whose more limited parts in the pattern show in microcosm aspects of the fuller picture given of *Macbeth* as a play in which nothing is certain, and where events and people often seem what they are not. Each may be seen as caught up at a different point on the spectrum from desiring power to holding it, although the Macbeths are the ones who are unhappily carried through the whole curve of the play's action, from go to woe. Radical ambivalence in both theatrical and psychological senses rests upon the clash of different emotional worlds of human beings acting in a political context, a milieu in which the mind's construction is not necessarily registered on the face and true feelings may not be expressed in words.

Duncan

In terms of trying to discriminate between characters as morally "good" or "bad", it is not easy to be categorical about the characters in *Macbeth* as ethical beings. Duncan is the most complete victim of the plot and historical narrative, a cause more than a character, but even this depiction is ambiguous. The pro-monarchist or older orthodoxy of the play would have us believe he is, in Macduff's words, "a most sainted king" (4.3.109), and in Macbeth's description, "so meek" (1.7.17), commanding universal respect, whose undeserved fate is self-evidently appalling and a violation of his "golden blood" (2.3.110). Unfortunately, however, there is little strong evidence to support such a conclusion, although equally there is just as little evidence in the play to suggest that he is the opposite. We are simply not given enough information about Duncan in the play to make firm judgements, and he exists more in terms of his state function as king than as an individual. Ambivalence operates at the level of what the text gives us, although directors and actors do need to make choices about how to realise ("make real") the text in performance, and the position of Duncan is one area in which such decisions can be made, with implications for the effect of the play as a whole. Is he a paragon, or simply a weak cipher whose fragile hold on the state creates a power void which becomes the visible and obvious target for rebellion, invasion and usurpation? He is described by Macbeth as "meek" (1.7.17), which suggests virtuous, but this may not be the best qualification for the office of king in a warring state. Which type is chosen – meek or weak – will obviously make a great deal of difference to how we view Macbeth, and to the play as a whole.

Little is explained about what is happening to Duncan's kingdom at the start of the play. It is torn with two violent wars which are clearly aimed at Duncan himself as king. One is a civil war waged by rebellious thanes (Scottish lords or barons). We are not informed why they are rebelling, nor why their claim is significant enough to sway the original Thane of Cawdor to join their ranks. The distraction of this insurgency has secondly encouraged the traditional enemy of Scotland, Norway, to make an opportunistic strike. Alternatively (and it is not entirely clear), Norway has invaded and the thanes, rather than defend the realm, have joined forces with them to oppose Duncan jointly. "The merciless Macdonald – / Worthy to be a rebel" (1.2.9-10) has gathered a large army from the Western Isles, while the forces of Sweno, king of Norway, have invaded on the east coast at Fife, "with terrible numbers, / Assisted by that most disloyal traitor / The Thane of Cawdor" (1.2.51-2). The inbuilt perspective of the speakers here is supportive of Duncan, but their view is self-interested and partial, leaving the politics unexplained. Duncan is particularly upset by the rebelliousness of Cawdor, since he had firmly trusted him. This may be a sign of his own lack of judgement, and it is a clear irony that he confers the disgraced thane's title on Macbeth, who is also that very night to betray him. At the very least, then, there is evidence that Duncan is not popular enough to command universal obedience from his more powerful subjects, and

3 "Nothing is but what is not": Emotional Worlds of Characters in *Macbeth*

that, indeed, assailed from within Scotland and without, his closest lords are one by one turning against him. Critics such as Maynard Mack and Harry Berger have pointed out that Duncan spends a lot of time asking questions, as though he does not really know what is going on and does not have a firm hold even on his own troops. His position is being tenuously defended by a bloodthirsty military led by a professional soldier like Macbeth who thinks nothing of slicing an enemy (albeit a fellow Scottish nobleman) up the middle, chopping off his head and displaying it unceremoniously on the battlements. As Arthur Kinney sharply reminds us, "Reared in a war culture, Macbeth is its hero in warlike terms; trained to kill, his achievement is in killing large numbers and under great danger. His success is so saturated with such activity that once King, he knows no other means of rule and survival short of murder" (Kinney 2001: 199). Again, an irony is that the same ugly fate awaits Macbeth, suggesting a cyclical structure is being employed in designing the play. Such behaviour seems de rigeur for the military troops loyal to Duncan, who, although not directly linked with such bloodthirsty conduct, cannot escape the fact that the army is fighting on his behalf and under his orders. He congratulates and thanks Macbeth and Banquo for their loyal actions, and on being told that "brave Macbeth" has "unseamed" Macdonald "from the nave to th'chops, / And fixed his head upon our battlements" he says, "O valiant cousin, worthy gentleman!" (1.2.16; 22-4). Of the traitor Cawdor he abruptly and in an ominous couplet (rhyming "death" with "Macbeth") says, "Go pronounce his present death, / And with his former title greet Macbeth" (1.2.64-5). Of course Duncan has no way of anticipating that the conferral will endanger himself, but his decision makes him unwittingly and indirectly complicit in his own future fate by bringing Macbeth within expectation of a future crown. He is also fallible, if not flawed. The prototype for Duncan in Shakespeare's source emerges as an ineffectual king, unable to control rebels and his own army. For Holinshed, the two characters are opposite extremes. Macbeth, who inherited from his mother the title Thane of Glamis, is "a valiant gentleman, and one that if he had not beene somewhat cruell of nature, might have been thought most woorthie the government of a realme" (Muir 1962: 173). His cousin Duncan,

On the other part was so soft and gentle of nature, that the people wished the inclinations and maners of these two cousins to have been so tempered and interchangablie bestowed betwixt them, that where the one had too much of clemencie, and the other of crueltie, the meane virtue betwixt these two extremities might have reigned by indifferent partition in them both. (Muir 1962: 173)

The implication is that neither is fully suited to rule, but for opposite reasons, Duncan's over-merciful "inclinations" and Macbeth's "cruelty", which Holinshed regards as at least part of the job of being a king. At first Duncan's reign had been peaceful but "after it was perceived how negligent he was in punishing offenders" (Muir 1962: 173), rebellions began. Shakespeare seems to have built into his portrayal of Duncan the same amalgam of qualities in a man too "soft and gentle of nature" to perform effectively the ruthless business of ruling.

Nor do we find much in Shakespeare's play by way of disinterested, trustworthy comment unequivocally praising Duncan's stewardship of the state. Lady Macbeth gives an obsequious speech of welcome to her castle, but then, as we say now, "she would, wouldn't she?", and in fact her words are more easily understood as expressing hospitality rather than praise. Macbeth, at his moment of conscience before the murder, says of Duncan that "He hath honoured me of late" (1.7.32) and that he "Hath borne his faculties so meek, hath been / So clear in his great office" (1.7.17-18). Of these forms of praise we could say first that a king with "meek" faculties in the violent state of Scotland might not be the best candidate for such a potentially bloody job; secondly that it takes only a brief conversation with his wife to change his mind; and thirdly that Macbeth goes on, not to confirm Duncan's virtues, but to say that the memory of them will endanger him after the murder – which is a strategical and self-interested way of praising those virtues. It is of course a hypocritical rather than honest compliment for Macbeth to say to Lennox after the murder that "Renown and grace is dead" (2.3.93). As the host of the house in which the king is slain, he would have to say such things. Duncan's sons, Malcolm and Donalbain, are too fearful for their own lives to express eulogy or even tears of grief ("our tears are not yet brewed" [2.3.124]), and Malcolm curiously says he does not want to stay and pretend "an unfelt sorrow" (2.3.135): they flee, one to England

3 "Nothing is but what is not": Emotional Worlds of Characters in *Macbeth*

and the other to Ireland, laying themselves open to damaging rumours. Duncan is never heard of again in the play, not even in hindsight to contrast his reign with Macbeth's. Occasionally he is called "gracious", but this word is a formula, like calling a monarch "your Majesty". For a king whom critics have extolled, Duncan gets surprisingly little praise even from his own supporters and family. One conclusion that might be drawn is that ruling always requires violence, whether it is performed by a virtuous but weak man through his soldiers, or a regicide who becomes a tyrant – both face the same bloody outer circumstances.

Nor are Duncan's own actions any more substantial a foundation for good reputation or competence as a king. He is aware enough of dangers stemming from his political position to make sure there is a "sewer" (official taster) on hand before he eats anything in case it is poisoned at banquets given by his lords (1.7, stage direction; in Shakespeare's plays there are remarkably few original stage directions, so those that exist are of significance). But he still manages to make a series of misjudgements which amount to fatal blunders. First, looking both backwards and forwards in time, his trust has been, and will be, spectacularly misplaced: "No more that Thane of Cawdor shall deceive / Our bosom interest" (1.2.63-4). He generalises on his sense of betrayal in a manner that could equally suggest his own bad judgement:

> There's no art
> To find the mind's construction in the face.
> He was a gentleman on whom I built
> An absolute trust. (1.4.11-14)

Lisa Hopkins has traced the importance of this trope in many modern detective stories which explicitly acknowledge the quotation (Hopkins 2016, 21-7). As events turn out, by immediately trusting himself to the hospitality of Macbeth and his wife, Duncan proves the same point and his own lack of insight into people, even if he is surrounded by hypocritical subjects concealing their motives. At the battle, as J.L. Calderwood points out (1986: 80), Duncan is apart and isolated from his own troops – unlike Shakespeare's "ideal" kings such as Henry V – as if he is out of touch and subsidiary to his thanes who risk their lives on his behalf in a civil war.

Next, whether it is a misjudgement or an indiscretion, Duncan makes a clumsy and again fatal blunder when he publicly nominates his own first son, Malcolm, as Prince of Cumberland. This position, in the Scottish system, effectively makes Malcolm heir to the throne, a pivotal moment in the play carrying an implication immediately spotted by Macbeth:

> (*Aside*) The Prince of Cumberland – that is a step
> On which I must fall down or else o'erleap,
> For in my way it lies. (1.4.48-51)

Like the position of Prince of Wales in the English system, the Prince of Cumberland was that of king in waiting. We are not privy to Malcolm's thoughts at this stage and at least on the page if not the stage we cannot find the mind's construction in the face, but he must have in his mind a phrase like "And shall be king hereafter". For Macbeth, to whose thoughts we are privy, Duncan's words provoke a sudden glimpse of a future holding menace, which he already knows will not bear bringing to the daylight of consciousness. Through his rather confusing imagery he seeks to dissociate his mind from his hand:

> Stars, hide your fires,
> Let not light see my black and deep desires;
> The eye wink at the hand; yet let that be
> Which the eye fears, when it is done, to see. (1.4.50-3)

By revealing Macbeth's dread at what lies in his thoughts, Shakespeare aligns the audience with him, and we are the "light" that sees his black and deep desires, the "eye" which he hopes to blind to the "hand" of execution. Queen Elizabeth I was by contrast far more canny than Duncan in holding her cards close to her chest when she faced precisely the same decision about naming her successor. Duncan's action is both constitutionally wrong and politically risky to the point of ineptness. The Scottish system of monarchy at the time was not automatically hereditary like England's, but to some extent elective, and in Holinshed's account it is implied that Macbeth could hold a legitimate expectation that he would succeed as king, which Duncan appears to

3 "Nothing is but what is not": Emotional Worlds of Characters in *Macbeth*

encourage: "More is thy due, than more than all can pay" (1.4.21), reinforcing Ross' hint that the conferral of Thane of Cawdor on Macbeth is "an earnest of a greater honour" (1.3.104). In his letter to his wife recounting the prophetic greeting of the Witches, "King that shalt be" (1.5.9), Macbeth shows no signs of thinking he needs to kill the king, and he may assume the crown will be his as a matter of destiny. Before he is promoted by Duncan, and after meeting the Witches, he reminds himself that he may become king in the normal course of events: "If chance will have me King, why, chance may crown me / Without my stir" (1.3.142-3). Banquo might have cause to be even more resentful, since Duncan offers him no reward at all, so that in his one gesture of nominating Malcolm, Duncan potentially alienates both his powerful supporters. Until Duncan names Malcolm, it is clear that Macbeth at least, and others tacitly, do not know who will succeed Duncan, but the situation is such that Macbeth, Duncan's cousin, seems the next most senior. Malcolm's succession cannot be assumed in a system based on tanistry rather than primogeniture (see Chapter 1). What Shakespeare does not tell us is that Malcolm was a minor at the time. Where Duncan is doubly wrong, and even needlessly provocative, is in bypassing the formalities of the customary elective system, and in demonstrating overt nepotism in advancing his own son. To say the least, Duncan is unwise to provoke his few remaining loyal thanes at this moment of his greatest vulnerability, faced with both a civil war and foreign invasion. He may think the gesture will stabilise Scotland's future, but it perversely leads to the opposite outcome. However, even if Duncan's judgement and history may be open to different interpretations, he is apparently guileless and predisposed to see good rather than evil. When he approaches the Macbeths' castle, he sees only healthy and natural signs:

> This castle hath a pleasant seat. The air
> Nimbly and sweetly recommends itself
> Unto our gentle senses. (1.6.1-3)

Whether in retrospect this can be seen as a sign of Duncan's gullibility or is simply a signal that nothing bad has yet happened is open to debate, but at least Banquo confirms the general impression by noticing the "temple-haunting martlet" or house martins (swallows) nesting where "the heavens' breath / Smells wooingly here" (1.6.5-6). We shall examine Banquo's role later, but like Duncan he emerges as a figure whose destiny is shaped by his place in the plot and his motivations remain opaque. The subtle point made by Shakespeare through the imagery of birds, as perceived by individuals, seems to be that both Duncan and Banquo in their different ways demonstrate innocence and even naivety. By contrast, it is striking that Lady Macbeth, who lives in the castle, notices the birds associated with premonitions of death:

> The raven himself is hoarse
> That croaks the fatal entrance of Duncan
> Under my battlements. (1.5.37-9)

It is a rather sorry state when the only thing approaching a positive that we may say about a king whom most critics have treated as a paragon is that he is too innocent for his own good, and therefore for his office, and that he shows flawed judgement. At face value it seems that, compared with Shakespeare's other kings (certainly Bolingbroke in becoming Henry IV and his son Henry V), Duncan is strangely without obvious, positive qualities, and is presented in a kind of effacing light. For the purposes of the argument pursued in this book, there is no need to make any particular judgement either way of Duncan as some kind of rounded character, since it is his dramatic role to be the first victim in the play, and it is certainly his position as king that leads to his death, rather than some serious character flaw. Most importantly, he is not presented as a complex human being, but as no more nor less than a target in his position as king. J.L. Calderwood, while looking at the play as a whole in a different light, in this context sums up what seems to be the central point: "The impression given is that violence arises not from anything Duncan himself has done but from the mere fact of kingship itself, the royal difference" (1986: 80). It is the unlucky fate of Duncan to hold "the royal difference" at the start of the play. In the shark's bath of Shakespeare's history plays, personal motives and sentiment usually matter less than the mere existence of a piece of dented metal called a crown, which many feel entitled to and are prepared to kill for.

3 "Nothing is but what is not": Emotional Worlds of Characters in *Macbeth*

Banquo

While Duncan cannot really be said to be an ambivalent character (he does not show two opposed sides but rather stands as a possibly weak incumbent of the impersonal formality of a regal office that requires strength), Banquo, although just as briefly etched, can be seen as ambiguously presented. There is little evidence of Banquo's private attitudes, feelings or motives, but there may be some legitimate debate about whether he is expected to resist Macbeth or collude with him, since he knows about the Witches' prophecies and has an obvious vested interest in the outcome. Again, there is a tendency among critics simply to assume that Banquo is unequivocally "good", because the orthodox reading requires the isolation of Macbeth as a uniquely individual tyrant. This impression is built also on a presumption that the Witches' prophecy means that Banquo's descendants – whom the *Chronicles* claim (fictionally, as it turns out) led down to James VI of Scotland (James I of England) – will rule Scotland legitimately and wisely. These, it should be pointed out, are simply presumptions, and the text neither confirms nor denies them. The argument of this book is that the play as a whole may be seen as covertly subversive while sheltering, like Marlowe's *Doctor Faustus*, under a blander moral pattern that asserts tyrants must be punished and the good will eventually succeed. There is nothing to stop us from submitting Banquo to the same kind of close critique that we applied to Duncan, and to or from exploring his elusive role in the pattern.

When we look at the evidence, we may conclude that Shakespeare pays Banquo (and by implication King James) a double-edged but genuine compliment. He is a wary and even wily politician. The unlucky attribute Banquo shares with Duncan is that he gets in the way of Macbeth's ambitions and the play's plot. Yet unlike Duncan, the future afterlife for Banquo predicted by the Witches, and his immediate, ghostly reappearance to Macbeth at the banquet, are signs that his power is potent even after death. Banquo would make an effective poker player, never revealing what he thinks or feels, or even how much he knows of Macbeth's motives, actions and intentions, in the early part of the play. It is precisely this inscrutability which poses a threat to

Macbeth – on top of the Witches' prophecy that he will beget kings – and both lead directly to Banquo's silencing through murder.

In a political sense, Banquo certainly knows too much for his own good. As the person accompanying Macbeth when the Witches appear, he witnesses the prophecies that Macbeth will be Thane of Cawdor and afterwards king. He also hears that his own child, Fleance, will beget kings. Banquo is the more self-possessed and rational: he directly addresses the Witches, asking them questions, reproving Macbeth for his fear and questioning his "raptness". He is also more circumspect, withholding judgement about the status of the Witches, and asks questions rather than making assertions: "What, can the devil speak true?" (1.3.105):

> Were such things here as we do speak about,
> Or have we eaten on the insane root
> That takes the reason prisoner? (1.3.81-3)

He muses to himself that

> oftentimes ... to win us to our harm
> The instruments of darkness tell us truths,
> Win us with honest trifles, to betray's
> In deepest consequence ... (1.3.121-4)

By contrast, Macbeth's response is more credulous, excitable, to the point even of hysteria. Lady Macbeth, perhaps strangely, immediately believes in the Witches' powers of prophecy as soon as she receives her husband's letter.

Banquo's knowledge alone makes him somebody whom Macbeth must treat with the utmost caution, and from this point on they play a watchful game of cat and mouse, each unsure of what the other is doing. On two occasions (1.3.154-8 and 2.1.12-30) they sound each other out, but both prevaricate and neither divulges an opinion. On the second occasion Banquo goes so far as to say "All's well. I dreamt last night of the three Weird Sisters". Macbeth lies that he does not think of them, but hints that to speak more of the Weird Sisters will be to Banquo's

3 "Nothing is but what is not": Emotional Worlds of Characters in *Macbeth*

advantage: "It shall make honour for you". So hedged is Banquo's non-committal response ("I shall be counselled") that Macbeth could glean neither support nor warning from it. After the murder of Duncan, Banquo reveals in a rare soliloquy that he strongly suspects Macbeth of foul play:

> Thou hast it now: King, Cawdor, Glamis, all
> As the weird women promised; and I fear
> Thou played'st most foully for't ... (3.1.1-3)

However, at this stage he is unreadable as to his own feelings. To the audience he confides that he holds "hope" that the Witches' prophecy about him begetting kings will come true, but to Macbeth as king he shows nothing but the formalities of a loyal subject's obedience:

> Let your highness
> Command upon me, to the which my duties
> Are with a most indissoluble tie
> For ever knit. (3.1.15-18)

If only Banquo knew that Macbeth had already arranged to meet two hired assassins to plot his death, he would have spared his feats of diplomacy and fled with Malcolm and Donalbain. Macbeth cunningly persuades two poor and desperate men that Banquo was the cause of their ruin, and that they must kill him. The rest of this part of the story tells itself. The two murderers are joined by the mysterious third and in the dark night, before rain, Banquo's life is terminated in the forest while his son escapes. In a spellbinding scene (3.4), the bloodstained ghost of Banquo returns, seen by Macbeth alone as a recrimination, at the dinner party which goes horribly wrong. The play on words – Banquo and banquet – may be a kind of grisly joke on Shakespeare's part.

Fear of Banquo seems to be the only real feeling Macbeth experiences after attaining the crown:

> To be thus is nothing,
> But to be safely thus. Our fears in Banquo
> Stick deep, and in his royalty of nature
> Reigns that which would be feared. 'Tis much he dares,
> And to that dauntless temper of his mind
> He hath a wisdom that doth guide his valour
> To act in safety. There is none but he
> Whose being I do fear, and under him
> My genius is rebuked, as, it is said,
> Mark Antony's was by Caesar. He chid the Sisters
> When first they put the name of king upon me,
> And bade them speak to him. Then, prophet-like,
> They hailed him father to a line of kings.
> Upon my head they placed a fruitless crown,
> And put a barren sceptre in my grip,
> Thence to be wrenched with an unlineal hand,
> No son of mine succeeding. If't be so,
> For Banquo's issue have I filed my mind,
> For them the gracious Duncan have I murdered,
> Put rancours in the vessel of my peace
> Only for them, and mine eternal jewel
> Given to the common enemy of man
> To make them kings, the seeds of Banquo kings.
> Rather than so, come Fate into the list,
> And champion me to th'utterance ... (3.1.49-73)

The second half of this soliloquy explains something of Macbeth's resentment of Banquo, and rationalises his decision to kill him and his son Fleance. His reasoning is based on an acknowledgement of what I have called "discrepant emotional awarenesses", suggesting that such a concept is part of Shakespeare's dramatic understanding. Macbeth expresses his own feelings of fear and resentment, and suits his actions by imputing to Banquo different feelings of anticipating future triumph. Understandably, Macbeth, fearing that his own usurpation will benefit Banquo's issue, assumes that Banquo will be as ambitious as he is, despite the fact that neither Macbeth nor the audience can tell what Banquo's feelings are. The earlier part of the speech is even more

3 "Nothing is but what is not": Emotional Worlds of Characters in *Macbeth*

interesting, implying a different reason for Macbeth's fear, and one that goes to the heart of the issue of kingship itself in the play. Not only does Macbeth concede that Banquo is more "kingly" in manner than he is, and that he breathes "royalty of nature" and exhibits both a dauntless temper and "a wisdom that doth guide his valour / To act in safety" (the politician's skill); he also acknowledges that Banquo has a specific grievance that poses direct threats to Macbeth as king. The most serious of these is that, without stretching the evidence too far, Banquo could legitimately have expected to be named as a possible heir apparent in his own right. In 1.4, Duncan had named Macbeth and Banquo after the battle as equal in his estimation as his "captains" in combat (1.2.35). Banquo does not know that Duncan has received only a report of Macbeth's bravery in killing Macdonald. Therefore, when they meet King Duncan, Banquo must expect some reward for his services at least equivalent to Macbeth's elevation to Thane of Cawdor. Duncan's own words confirm this expectation, and Banquo's response shows that he hopes to "grow" as Macbeth has done:

> DUNCAN (*to Macbeth*)
> Welcome hither.
> I have begun to plant thee, and will labour
> To make thee full of growing. Noble Banquo,
> That hast no less deserved, nor must be known
> No less to have done so, let me enfold thee,
> And hold thee to my heart.
> BANQUO
> There if I grow,
> The harvest is your own. (1.4.27-33)

In a curious way, Duncan's words and their reception by Banquo reinforce the Witches' prophecies. Despite his laconic brevity, if we spare some sympathy for Banquo in terms of the role already allotted to him in the story, we can divine his feelings by summarising the chain of events. Macbeth has just been promoted for deeds in a battle in which Banquo was at least equal in status; if we take seriously Macbeth's words later we know that Banquo acts naturally like a king, and he seems in some ways superior in moral status to Macbeth, akin to the dimming of Mark Antony's light beside Octavius Caesar's, In this kind of military state the highest honours would automatically go to the most distinguished soldiers; Duncan himself raises anticipation by saying that Banquo "no less deserved, nor must be known ... to have done so"; and the only elective position apparently left in Duncan's discretion at this moment is Prince of Cumberland, the future king. The audience has been primed to expect that his descendants will be kings, so his own personal claims must have some legal validity to be argued at least in later times. Banquo in all these circumstances could be forgiven for expecting some "harvest" in his fortunes now, picking up Duncan's metaphor of planting and growing and the repeated references to "seeds". Therefore, Duncan's next statement must come to Banquo, as much as to Macbeth, as a dismaying shock, coming out of the blue and against all the expectations set up for the characters and an alert audience alike:

> Sons, kinsmen, thanes,
> And you whose places are the nearest, know
> We will establish our estate upon
> Our eldest, Malcolm, whom we name hereafter
> The Prince of Cumberland ... (1.4.35-9)

This dashes the hopes of Macbeth becoming king by legitimate means, and also signals a rebuff for Banquo, who has been very publicly passed over. His claims to advancement, which are just as compelling as Macbeth's and far more so than Malcolm's, are completely ignored. In the triangle of Duncan, Macbeth and Banquo in this scene, we have a clear and fascinating example of discrepant emotional awarenesses built up by the dramatist, of three different emotional worlds colliding, the third of which is not made explicit to the audience.

Given the withholding of clear expression of Banquo's feelings at this stage, he can be "read" in opposite ways. He can be seen as a wise, restrained and valuable counsellor (which is how Duncan and even Macbeth may view him), yet on the other hand, a further deduction by Macbeth, he is potentially a man aggrieved, politically savvy, and fully as dangerous as Macbeth himself. He knows too much for his own safety, and has cause to be at least resentful. His political discretion, as

3 "Nothing is but what is not": Emotional Worlds of Characters in *Macbeth*

well as the repetition of multiple ambivalences operating in the play, makes Banquo seem more neutral than his situation might suggest, and besides, he is soon to become a murder victim on the suspicion that he is embittered and a likely assassin of Macbeth. The question unanswered within the play is how Banquo's issue eventually gets the throne, but in the fictional scheme at least there would be a kind of poetic justice if Fleance were to kill Malcolm to avenge the insult of one father upon the other. The murder attracts audience sympathy to him, while the appearance of his gory ghost to Macbeth turns him into a spectral threat to the current king. In *Macbeth*, the real cause for evil in the world lies not in warped, individual motives like ambition, but in the very existence of the monarchy itself, which creates such motives and ambitions in men. The institution of kingship itself fuels the bloody pattern of death after death, which seems likely to be ceaseless even after the play ends.

Malcolm

Early in the play not enough is seen of Malcolm to construct a clear impression of him, though what we do see is formal rather than revealing and forceful. This character gives actors options about how to play the role, ranging from a callow, unformed youth to a future and legitimate king. He appears with his father Duncan, who nominates him Prince of Cumberland and therefore the next king of Scotland. Malcolm was saved in the battle from being taken prisoner by an unnamed captain, and he witnesses and describes the death of the disgraced Thane of Cawdor, who managed to redeem himself to some extent before dying, as Malcolm attests, by unexpectedly expressing "a deep repentance":

> Nothing in his life
> Became him like the leaving it. He died
> As one that had been studied in his death
> To throw away the dearest thing he owed
> As 'twere a careless trifle. (1.4.7-11)

After the death of Duncan, Malcolm and his brother Donalbain are too panic-stricken to mourn properly, or even to feign grief, for they see that their own lives are in danger, and they flee, Malcolm to join the king of England, which to some Scottish historians could be construed as immediate treachery:

> MALCOLM
> This murderous shaft that's shot
> Hath not yet lighted, and our safest way
> Is to avoid the aim. Therefore to horse,
> And let us not be dainty of leave-taking,
> But shift away. There's warrant in that theft
> Which steals itself when there's no mercy left.
> *Exeunt* (2.3.140-5)

Macbeth takes immediate advantage of their flight, as their defection allows him to claim that they solicited the murder of Duncan to take power themselves. While exhibiting prudence, they do not show signs of a will to resist or of future bravery, and Donalbain, having spoken very few lines, chooses to flee to Ireland and plays no further part in the play.

Six scenes then pass without trace of Malcolm, and we would be forgiven for thinking that, his claim defeated, he is like his brother, a forgotten man who will take no more part in the play. (He is not even given the role of killing Macbeth, who had murdered his father.) But in 4.1 we learn from Lennox's report that he is with the "pious" English king, Edward the Confessor, and has been joined by Macduff. This brief scene gives the background to the meeting between Malcolm and Macduff in 4.3, which is a puzzling and deeply troubling scene, stretching radical ambivalence and conflicting emotional worlds to an extreme. After his earlier cryptic and formal lines, which tell us very little about him, Malcolm's talkativeness in this scene comes as a surprise. The content is even more alarming. To a confused and increasingly alarmed Macduff, Malcolm speaks with apparent relish of the dreadful things he will do when he becomes king, or rather, as he forecasts, tyrant. He will, he says, display vices so dreadful that "black Macbeth / Will seem as pure as snow" (4.3.52-3). His "voluptuousness" or sexual depravity is so

3 "Nothing is but what is not": Emotional Worlds of Characters in *Macbeth*

insatiable that no woman will be safe from him, and he will be so avaricious as to seize wealth and land from nobles as ruthlessly as he can. Further, he says he has "no relish" of virtues but rather loves crime and division. At first Macduff indulges this inexplicable revelation, saying more or less that Malcolm as king will find enough willing women and enough wealth to keep him happy without ever approaching Macbeth's evil. But as Malcolm's monologue relentlessly continues, Macduff becomes increasingly alarmed and outspoken:

>MACDUFF
>O Scotland, Scotland.
>MALCOLM
>If such a one be fit to govern, speak:
>I am as I have spoken.
>MACDUFF
>Fit to govern?
>No, not to live. O nation miserable,
>With an untitled tyrant bloody-sceptered,
>When shalt thou see thy wholesome days again,
>Since that the truest issue of thy throne
>By his own interdiction stands accused
>And does blaspheme his breed? Thy royal father
>Was a most sainted king ... (4.3.103-10)

At this moment there comes a bewildering shift of tone. Malcolm reassures Macduff that he was in effect "just joking", testing Macduff's integrity and trustworthiness, and that in fact his life is blameless. But his explanation is very strange (4.3.114-40), and Macduff for one does not know what to think or say:

>MALCOLM
>Why are you silent?
>MACDUFF
>Such welcome and unwelcome things at once
>'Tis hard to reconcile. (4.3.138-40)

What is so "unwelcome" to Macduff is paralleled in the audience's awareness that Malcolm's somewhat gleeful nightmare vision is presented in a light very similar to Macbeth's division of mind about the Witches, reporting that Macbeth has tried to bewitch him:

> Devilish Macbeth
> By many of these trains hath sought to win me
> Into his power, and modest wisdom plucks me
> From over-credulous haste ... (4.3.118-21)

Since there are several points in the play which subtly "double" Malcolm with Macbeth even if we do not see his innermost thoughts, this may well be his "Is this a dagger I see before me?" moment, a point at which fantasy takes over from reality. It is all very well for Malcolm to say ambiguously "My first false speaking / Was this upon myself", designed to congratulate Macduff for passing the "test", but the reverie of evil has been too intense and effective to be so casually dismissed by Macduff, and by an audience attuned to assuming that those who do not speak the truth on stage may be under suspicion as liars or at least devious machiavels. Even as a test of Macduff's integrity (as most critics assume, taking Malcolm at his word) it is remarkably convoluted and barely appropriate, and the "explanation" is contradictory and unconvincing, as Macduff suspiciously protests. He has been described as a "pious fraud" in whose words "the piety does not wholly eclipse the fraudulence" (Calderwood 1986: 104).

Braunmuller writes of this scene, "Whether or not it was revised, and whether or not it was well revised, *Macbeth* Act 4, Scene 3, poses some extraordinary theatrical, dramatic, and intellectual puzzles for producers, audiences, and critics", and he speaks of "an unsettling effect" (Braunmuller 1997: 88-93, 204fn). He suggests the scene may have been "maladroitly revised" (Bruanmuller 1997: 88), perhaps by Middleton. Another explanation which has not been mooted is that perhaps Shakespeare was drawn to the episode since it is recounted at length by Holinshed, and the dramatist whose main structural unit was the scene simply could not have resisted it in its dramatic mystery. However, there are other explanations if we adopt a more subversive thematic reading. The scene would, after all, have appealed to at least

3 "Nothing is but what is not": Emotional Worlds of Characters in *Macbeth*

one witness, John Milton, whose attitude to the unreliability of monarchs and their propensity to turn into tyrants was enshrined in his published justification for the execution of Charles I. At the very least we must see Malcolm's behaviour in Act 4 Scene 3 as markedly and even dangerously ambiguous, inviting two diametrically opposed and irreconcilable readings: either he is a lily-white future king who with a kind of imaginative fancifulness tests his subject's loyalty to see how far he can go without losing support; or he is a mirror image of Macbeth, full of warring potential and self-division, torn between virtue and vice, young and as yet untested with kingship. He knows in theory that "A good and virtuous nature may recoil / In an imperial charge" (4.3.20-1) without necessarily applying the lesson to himself that he is unable to know, except through imagination, what he will be like when he does get "an imperial charge", a phrase echoing Macbeth's anticipation of "the imperial theme" (1.3.128). Malcolm's understanding of masculinity seems more like Macbeth's when he challenges Macduff for breaking under grief instead of pursuing a "great revenge" (4.3.214) against Macbeth, a callow soldier's attitude to "Dispute it like a man" (4.3.220), which is quietly reproved for lacking empathy by Macduff's feelings on being told his children have been murdered: "He has no children. All my pretty ones?" (4.3.216).

Given the scene's ambiguities and the general air in the play of duplicity, we might recall both Lady Macbeth's image of the flower with the serpent hidden under it and Duncan's worries about reading motives from the human face, and be tempted to suspect deception and self-deception at many points. The uneasy implication is that subjects in a kingdom cannot actually know in advance whether they are getting a saint or a tyrant, an Edward or a Macbeth, until it is too late, and in fact even the future incumbent will not know in advance. Which kind of king Malcolm will become on enthronement is beyond the play's brief, but the issue is certainly raised and left unresolved. The figure who becomes king at the end of the play is a revival of the earlier, bland and unknowable Malcolm, simply mouthing official language in a competent and suspiciously well-rehearsed manner, just as his father did at the beginning. As we shall see when we examine the theme of time, the uncertainty of the future is inescapable. Similarly, we might say again that the very existence of kingly power is an inducement to tyranny. Just as a question is implicitly raised about exactly how Banquo's descendants will become kings eventually (legitimately or through assassination?), even the puzzling absence of Malcolm's brother Donalbain before battle is emphasised (5.2.7-8), and he is conspicuously absent from the final scene when his brother is enthroned. Polanski, in his popular film of *Macbeth*, clearly found some possibility of an unending cycle of power-seeking, since his last, eerie and sinister scene is of Donalbain going to meet the Witches. Although he may be among the unnamed "thanes", or else more mundanely the actor who had played Donalbain is now doubled as one of the group, it is yet another open question left at the end of the play.

Once again, in the treatment of Malcolm's actions, the play's unresolved ambivalences, "smothered in surmise" (1.3.140), suggest that tyranny is not inherent in "human nature" but is an all-too-possible consequence of the simple fact of investing absolute power in any monarch. Far from being a "personality trait", it is the opposite – the potential alienation of a personal self through identification with the impersonality and inhumanity of office. This may have been one of the lessons taken by the young Milton from his experience of watching *Macbeth* on stage, given his own Puritan aversion to the trappings of authority, especially vested in the system of monarchy.

Macduff

The killing of Banquo does not solve problems for Macbeth but opens up new ones. Not only is Fleance still at large but also by definition other enemies are created by Macbeth's tyranny. He is told by the Witches to "beware Macduff, / Beware the Thane of Fife" (4.1.87-8). Enigmatically, the prediction runs that "none of woman born / Shall harm Macbeth" (4.1.96-7), and so Macbeth concludes "Then live, Macduff – what need I fear of thee?" (82). In order, however, to make "assurance double sure" he decides to kill Macduff. At this moment he learns from Lennox that Macduff has fled to England, and he authorises the sacking of Fife castle, Macduff's home, and the slaughter of "His wife, his babes, and all the unfortunate souls / That trace him in his line" (4.1.168-9). He has learned the lesson of botching the job of killing

3 "Nothing is but what is not": Emotional Worlds of Characters in *Macbeth*

Banquo's issue, and this time he is ruthless. The scene of the murder of Lady Macduff and her children (4.2) is even more horrifying because it is pointless in terms of Macbeth's aims because Macduff is absent. By this point of the play Macbeth has lost all audience sympathy and is significantly offstage for a substantial time, suggesting that the worst atrocities of a tyrant are delegated to hired functionaries.

In one sense the play presents Macduff as a hero, since he is the one who finally kills the tyrant, and he is given personal reasons alongside loyalty to Scotland for doing so. But as a moral centre he is wanting, and this play does not allow any male character to remain unscathed as unambiguously heroic. There is an uncomfortable harping on Macduff's decision to flee for England while leaving his wife and children in Scotland, first and most strongly by his wife and later by Malcolm:

> MACDUFF
> I have lost my hopes.
> MALCOLM
> Perchance even there where I did find my doubts.
> Why in that rawness left you wife, and child,
> Those precious motives, those strong knots of love,
> Without leave-taking? I pray you,
> Let not my jealousies be your dishonours,
> But mine own safeties. You may be rightly just,
> Whatever I shall think. (4.3.25-32)

Macduff is understandably offended by this untimely accusation from a young and childless man ("He has no children. All my pretty ones?" [4.3.216-17]) who goes on to lie, apparently for his own ends. He uses the occasion to lament the state of the butchered nation:

> MACDUFF
> Bleed, bleed, poor country!
> Great tyranny, lay thou thy basis sure,
> For goodness dare not check thee. Wear thou thy wrongs;

The title is affeered [confirmed]. Fare thee well lord,
I would not be the villain that thou think'st
For the whole space that's in the tyrant's grasp,
And the rich east to boot.
MALCOLM
Be not offended. (4.3.32-8)

Macduff must stoically hear of the murder of his family, blaming himself for leaving them in danger like a traitor, an accusation levelled by his own wife and child in Act 4 Scene 2. The play offers no answer, plausible or otherwise, to the question why Macduff leaves his family in so vulnerable a situation in Fife. One possibility is that he did not expect Macbeth to see his family as a threat when he himself defects to Malcolm's cause, but if so one would expect Shakespeare to make this explicit. Instead, the only explanation offered is that of Macduff's wife, "he wants the human touch", equating to a modern "he lacks common sense", by, from her point of view, putting his own safety above his family's. If Macduff's "emotional world" seems somewhat defective, the riddle that he is "not of woman born" not only means he was born by Caesarean section but also takes on a possible negative resonance through metaphor, that he lacks the qualities that are dear to the heart of the mother of his children, such as concern, care and nurturing protection of his kin. Another implication is that men in this play for the most part almost obsessively try to make themselves independent of "womanly" feelings by asserting their masculinity. Other things tarnish the image of Macduff. We can be legitimately worried about his conduct, for example, in Act 4 Scene 2, when he more or less promises to supply Malcolm with a host of willing prostitutes when he is king, and when he suggests to him how nobles' loyalty can cynically be bought. If, indeed, this is a "trial" scene, then we might suspect that Macduff also has failed some of the tests. The final battle between Macduff and Macbeth takes on the nature of a struggle between flawed men in the moral sense, and although placed among the virtuous characters and chosen to be the righteous slayer of Macbeth, Macduff faces a surprisingly double-edged treatment within the play, from his wife's condemnation to his own self-recrimination. At least his remorse

3 "Nothing is but what is not": Emotional Worlds of Characters in *Macbeth*

proves his human feelings, unlike Macbeth's hardened carapace, but his culpable misjudgement does not bring back his family.

Ambiguity of character motives and emotions marks minor characters as much as major. The Thane of Cawdor, for example, has been trusted by Duncan but turned rebel, and even more confusingly is reported then to have died a noble death, repenting and begging the king's forgiveness. Ross' actions are possibly those of a turncoat, since he is first loyal to Duncan, then to Macbeth to the extent of even apologising for Macbeth's "fit" at the banquet. He acts as messenger between Malcolm and Macduff, and finally rejoices with the others at the accession of Malcolm. His own turning point against Macbeth may be the murders of Lady Macduff and the children since it is he who warns them of danger, though it may be questionable why he does not do more to save their lives. He does not suggest any course of action, his words are enigmatically self-referential – "But cruel are the times when we are traitors / And do not know ourselves" (4.2.17-18) – and he seems to worry on his own behalf rather than solicitous of his cousin, Lady Macduff: "I am so much a fool, should I stay longer / It would be my disgrace and your discomfort. / I take my leave at once" (4.2.28-30). So suspiciously does Ross act that in some productions he is one of the murderers of the family. This may be going too far, but at the least it can be said that his early enthusiasm for Macbeth in order to gain preferment – it is after all Ross who suggests Duncan's sons have fled because they are the murderers – makes him look devious, and in the words of one critic, "By identifying himself as a Macbeth supporter, everything Ross does from this moment (2.4.27-30) onward is ambiguous (Baker 2016: 118). Lennox and Angus are more shadowy because they speak less, but they appear to follow the lead of Ross, switching allegiance midstream from Duncan to Macbeth to Malcolm in the invasion he mounts. These three may be examples of the Shakespearean characters who are used "situationally" to play differing roles required by the plot, but even so they emerge also as ambiguous figures. Few in the play are spared some taint, except some who act as subtle moral rudders at various points, such as the Old Man of seventy who discusses the unnatural weather with Ross and has a similar choric function as the Good Angel in *Faustus* in hoping unavailingly for some benign reconciliation of opposites: "God's benison go with you; and with those / That would make good of bad, and friends of foes" (2.4.41-2). There is one Doctor who reports the healing environment of Edward the Confessor in England, and another who later tends to the strange behaviour of Lady Macbeth, divining the nature of her illness as a sign of guilt amounting to a confession. Finally, there is Lady Macbeth's Gentlewoman, who notes of her mistress that "heaven knows what she has known" (5.1.47). And beyond these are the most innocent of all, children.

Children and Women

In such an apparently adult, masculine and military world as that of *Macbeth*, we find surprisingly frequent references made to children. It is instructive to look closely at some of these occurrences and ask what they add to the play. This time, we find a pattern of contrast: children are unquestionably presented as the symbols of innocence and of the future, throwing into dark relief the guilt of Macbeth's court, and in particular emphasising the apparent barrenness of Macbeth and his wife, who (despite confusing evidence) appear to be childless.

The keynote struck at the outset is the glorification of war. After the framing scene of the Witches, the first thing we see is a "bloody man" (1.2.1) who talks with relish of seeing Macbeth brandishing steel "Which smoked with bloody execution", ripping a soldier from head to toe, lopping off the head and hanging it up on the battlements. The messenger draws attention to his own "gashes", which, Duncan says, smack of "honour" as much as his words, the phrase clinching the connection between military carnage and heroic values. The Witches seem to be spirited up by the battle in a spirit of mockery or parody, one reporting that she has been "Killing swine" (1.3.2) just as the soldiers have been reported as killing each other. Pig-killing was, and to some extent still is, a distressing activity, at least to city-dwellers, since the animal must be "bled" before it finally dies, in earlier times to the sound of blood-curdling screams. In *Macbeth*, the reference is not gratuitous, but gruesomely precise in defining the nature of the raging battle as a matter of slaughter. Shakespeare does his utmost to make it an especially bloody affair. "Strange images of death" (1.3.95) receive the

3 "Nothing is but what is not": Emotional Worlds of Characters in *Macbeth*

stamp of royal approval, and become as inextricably associated with kingship and the apparent inevitability of violent death as in *Richard III*.

Pitched against this culture of adult, masculine violence are the children, and their presence, once noticed, is as symbolically and visually compelling as the "*child crowned, with a tree in his hand*" that appears to Macbeth (4.1.103, stage direction), and as unending as the descendants of Banquo, whose line stretches out "to th' crack of doom" (4.1.133). But the first references have a perversity about them which begins to make us uneasily aware of the way the world represented is an already fallen one in which the innocence of children is irrevocably and tragically lost. Macbeth equates "Children and servants" (1.4.25) as no more than images of obedience to the king. Lady Macbeth, reading her husband's letter, invokes the first of her "anti-nursing" images when she expresses her fear that Macbeth is "too full o' th' milk of human kindness" (1.5.17) to carry out a political assassination, as though he has been breastfed for too long to attain full masculinity. This adds to the destabilisation of moral values which has already been described, since intuitively we would think of "the milk of human kindness" as being wholly good rather than a fatal weakness, and it does not seem appropriate from a woman. Lady Macbeth continues this topsy-turvy morality by calling upon spirits to "unsex" her and fill her "from the crown to the toe top-full / Of direst cruelty" (1.5.41-2), and in particular she again specifies breastfeeding: "Come to my woman's breasts / And take my milk for gall, you murd'ring ministers". This perverse and sinister use of nursing imagery finds its terrible climax as Lady Macbeth galvanises her husband:

> I have given suck, and know
> How tender 'tis to love the babe that milks me.
> I would, while it was smiling in my face,
> Have plucked my nipple from his boneless gums
> And dashed the brains out, had I so sworn
> As you have done to this. (1.7.54-9)

If one thinks about this even for a brief minute, it will be seen to be truly shocking in the moral sense, and perhaps the most shocking speech Shakespeare ever wrote. Words like "tender", "love", "milks", "smiling" and even the vulnerable associations of "nipple" and "boneless gums" suddenly transpose into an image of dashing a baby's brains out. The alert reader might recall these lines of infanticide much later in the play when a Witch incants over the bubbling cauldron: "Pour in sow's blood that hath eaten / Her nine farrow; grease that's sweaten / From the murderer's gibbet" (4.1.80–2). In some productions another ironic echo is achieved when Lady Macduff is depicted as nursing a small child since she specifically has children (plural), although only one son actually speaks. Lady Macduff, as a striking contrast, is aligned with values of nurturing and parenting. Shakespeare's lines have opened up enquiries along the lines of L.C. Knights' question (parodying Bradley's general approach although Bradley himself does not ask it), "How many children had Lady Macbeth?" (Knights 1946: title), and the reference is indeed puzzling since the couple are clearly childless during the play and can have no heir. Shakespeare lost one golden opportunity to clear up this mystery and to provide motivation to both Macbeth and Lady Macbeth, since historically Macbeth had a son who was killed by Malcolm. It is often said that the text of *Macbeth* is incomplete, and this is one incident which could well have been pertinent to the theme of killing for kingship, but Shakespeare presumably omitted it because it would have put Malcolm in too bad a light early in the play when Malcolm was young (though not apparently a minor), and given unwanted sympathy to the Macbeths. As it stands, Lady Macbeth's speech illustrates the inhumanity of a society driven by lust for power, when even a woman is perversely willing to sacrifice a child for the sake of misguided honour. In this she is not necessarily alone, and she merely articulates what this kingdom is based upon: murder either in battle or for the throne. In this context, as we have noticed, Macduff who was "not of woman born" stands as prototypical.

The other disturbing point to be made about Lady Macbeth's blood-curdling speech is that Macbeth has not in fact "so sworn" to kill Duncan. From the very moment that she receives the letter, to her first words to him when he returns, it is she who fully articulates killing the king as an unavoidable act to gain power. In this instance the invocation of the child is to represent Lady Macbeth as a person whose morality has, for some reason which is not fully inscribed in the play, gone dreadfully wrong. It also focuses the underlying ambivalence

3 "Nothing is but what is not": Emotional Worlds of Characters in *Macbeth*

of the play, since Lady Macbeth, a woman, is here explicitly denying any construction of femininity which includes childrearing. She desires to be unsexed in order to perpetuate the dominant ethos of male destructiveness. In a slightly confused way, Macbeth expresses his admiration for her firm purpose by eliding the child and the male:

> Bring forth men-children only,
> For thy undaunted mettle should compose
> Nothing but males. (1.7.72-4)

He is effectively colluding in the process that links masculinity and violence as heroic values.

Early in the play the more benign use of child imagery is subdued – a subtext too quiet to drown out the darker refrain. But it is present. Duncan speaks of the martlet's nest as a "procreant cradle" (1.6.8) (curiously stirring distant echoes from nursery rhymes: "hush a bye baby, thy cradle will rock ..."). More powerfully, Macbeth uses the image of the child as a symbol of innocence which will proclaim his own guilt to future times. The train of metaphors is dense and complex, unweaving more through association than logic:

> And pity, like a naked new-born babe,
> Striding the blast, or Heaven's cherubim, horsed
> Upon the sightless couriers of the air,
> Shall blow the horrid deed in every eye
> That tears shall drown the wind ... (1.7.16-25)

A detailed close criticism of this passage as poetry can be found in Cleanth Brooks' famous essay "'The Naked Babe' and the Cloak of Manliness" in *The Well-Wrought Urn* (1947), but the significance to be drawn here is a straightforwardly moral one. This soliloquy marks the last chance Macbeth has to follow his conscience. The picture of Duncan as having a childlike meekness leads to the image of the naked newborn babe which, at least to the prelapsarian mind of Macbeth, is the most supreme symbol of original innocence (as opposed to both guilt and experience). Macbeth's use of it shows his own dawning horror at the deed he is about to do. It is the moment of moral awakening that could have saved him, but like Faustus hearing the good and evil angels, Macbeth allows himself to be steeled by his determined wife whose challenge comes soon after. Considerations of good and evil may have been swept away by this couple, and perhaps by the larger political world they inhabit, but the critical moment of Macbeth's conscience remains to haunt the mind of the reader or audience.

When he suppresses his scruples based on visualising the "naked new-born child", audience sympathy begins to ebb. The action from here on is held in a mode of hypnotic fascination with how the murder will be completed, moral bearings suspended, until one later scene reawakens all the intuitive knowledge of good and evil embodied in the image of the innocent child, allowing us to recoil in healthy shock. Until Act 4 Scene 2 we are given very little opportunity to judge Macbeth from the outside, so compellingly is his own mental state presented. Act 4 Scene 1 is the last scene in which we can say that the point of view of the play is established by Macbeth's inner processes, and it is the scene in which he visits the Witches, sees the apparitions, which include a "bloody child", and decides he must eliminate Macduff, "His wife, his babes, and all the unfortunate souls / That trace him in his line" (4.1.166-7). The next scene shows the murder of a child and a woman, and the tone switches instantly to a horror of the cold-blooded delegation of murder by Macbeth, who himself disappears from our view, hiding behind his ill-fitting robes of office, to reappear later wavering between manic bravado and desolate emptiness. We have time to breathe, collect our moral bearings, and distance ourselves. This scene is pivotal, and the deaths of the mother and children by anonymous, hired killers allow us finally to judge coolly and clearly.

Macduff has fled his castle in Fife. It may be harsh to blame him, but as we have seen, blunt questions are asked in the play itself about why he left his family so unprotected. Betrayal and equivocation are issues in this scene as in the play as a whole, since Lady Macduff feels her husband has deserted her. The scene is as much a reproach to Macduff as a badge of infamy to Macbeth, and it is disturbing that the child himself in the scene is already learning the way of such a world:

3 "Nothing is but what is not": Emotional Worlds of Characters in *Macbeth*

> SON
> Was my father a traitor, mother?
> LADY MACDUFF
> Ay, that he was.
> SON
> What is a traitor?
> LADY MACDUFF
> Why, one that swears and lies.
> SON
> And be all traitors that do so?
> LADY MACDUFF
> Everyone that does so is a traitor, and must be hanged.
> SON
> And must they all be hanged that swear and lie?
> LADY MACDUFF
> Every one.
> SON
> Who must hang them?
> LADY MACDUFF
> Why, the honest men.
> SON
> Then the liars and swearers are fools, for there are liars and swearers enough to beat the honest men and hang up them.
> LADY MACDUFF
> Now God help thee, poor monkey! But how wilt thou do for a father? (4.2.45-62)

Lady Macduff is employing a kind of bitter irony here, ostensibly saying that her husband is traitor to the king, and an "equivocator", knowing full well that Macbeth is a tyrant and deserves no loyalty. However, she has already condemned her husband on family grounds, and the accusation of treachery operates in another way:

> LADY MACDUFF
> ... His flight was madness. When our actions do not,

Our fears do make us traitors.
ROSS
You know not
Whether it was his wisdom or his fear.
LADY MACDUFF
Wisdom – To leave his wife, to leave his babes,
His mansion, and his titles, in a place
From whence himself does fly? He loves us not,
He wants the natural touch, for the poor wren,
The most diminutive of birds, will fight,
Her young ones in her nest, against the owl.
All is the fear and nothing is the love;
As little is the wisdom, where the flight
So runs against all reason. (4.2.3-14)

A law of nature is invoked here, an instinctively protective response to prolong life evident even in bird families. Ross tries to reassure Lady Macduff about her husband's nobility, wisdom and judiciousness, and says that things will improve, but the brutal action of this scene, the shocking brevity of the stabbing with the words which pick up the imagery of small birds preyed upon, "What, you egg! Young fry of treachery!" (4.2.84), prove that she is right. The scene could easily have fallen into sentimental pathos, but Shakespeare adjusts the tone so as not to focus on the boy's death in itself, which is over in the blink of an eye, but to stir outrage and judgement against tyranny itself, and secondarily upon the way in which the world of power-hungry men has betrayed the human values of a world of women and children.

The next scene shows the odd exchange between Malcolm and Macduff that was analysed previously. After Malcolm snaps out of his rhapsody in evil, news comes of the death of Macduff's wife and children. Ross breaks the news of "your wife, and babes, / Savagely slaughtered" like "murdered deer" (4.3.205-6). The dazed Macduff takes some time to comprehend, but when he does his language stirs pathos: "What, all my pretty chickens and their dam / At one fell swoop?" (4.3.219-20), and the innocent casualties signal the move. The play has shifted its centre further away from the world of male violence towards one of felt grief and human decencies, and the recantation by

3 "Nothing is but what is not": Emotional Worlds of Characters in *Macbeth*

Macduff reaches a level of moral stability which has not been attained before:

> Sinful Macduff,
> They were all struck for thee. Naught that I am,
> Not for their demerits but for mine
> Fell slaughter on their souls. Heaven rest them now. (4.3.226-9)

Malcolm seems to have missed the point when, like a "Boy's Own" hero, he utters "This tune goes manly" (4.3.235), but then he cannot afford to give way to any other mission than going to battle and maintaining the warlike ethos to ensure his father's dynasty.

In a rather unexpected way, Lady Macbeth becomes a casualty of the action which she herself has helped to precipitate. Earlier on she had embraced the idea of assassination far more readily than her husband, and her only faint sign of compunction comes after the event when the experience sinks in as real – "Had he not resembled / My father as he slept, I had done't" (2.2.12-13) – a line which psychological critics could have a field day with (although Sigmund Freud himself is very restrained, saying that the springs of her conduct are impossibly obscure) – and which carries on a long train of references to fathers throughout the play. Otherwise, she is steely and determined, carrying the plan right through to its end. As we see in the last chapter of this book, she can be portrayed by film-makers such as Polanski and Orson Welles as young, vivacious, and sexually focused, reflecting the modern cinematic taste in female villains or femmes fatales stretching from film noir, whose heyday was in the 1940s when Welles worked, up to erotic thrillers of the 1990s influenced by Polanski. However we choose to depict her, we can see Lady Macbeth as wholeheartedly committing herself to the values which the play's language links with masculinity and violence. It is she who was steadfast throughout the murder night, and who gallantly covered up for her husband's erratic behaviour at the banquet. It seems all the sadder, then, that she becomes increasingly estranged from Macbeth, unconsulted by him, particularly since at the beginning they acted so cooperatively in a deadly but genuine team, unforgettably described by the critic Barbara Everett (1989) as an almost ideally compatible couple. Lady Macbeth's increasing marginalisation comes, not necessarily because she is being treated as a woman, but because the world they both entered was one of selfish individualism, and Macbeth comes to trust, and even need, nobody. There is precious little camaraderie even between men in this cut-throat world where there is one crown and more than one competitor, and Macbeth pays the price for the system he has entered. He has no contact on stage with his wife after the banquet, although he worries enough about her health to consult doctors (5.3.37-44). He is insomniac – has indeed "banish'd" sleep – while she is defined through the image of sleepwalking. Actors make their own decisions about how to speak his words after her death, whether in sorrow (she should not have died now, but later) or weary indifference (she would have died anyway, so it doesn't much matter): "She should have died hereafter. / There would have been a time for such a word" (5.5.16-17). In the light of the play's sharp polarity between masculine violence and the helplessness of Lady Macduff, the reported moment of the death of Lady Macbeth, who has forfeited a spirit of female nurturing in a capitulation to the plan to kill the king, is a strange and haunting one:

> *A cry of women within*
> MACBETH
> What is that noise?
> SEYTON
> It is the cry of women, my good lord.
> MACBETH
> I have almost forgot the taste of fears. (5.5.8-10)

Again, Macbeth's response is enigmatic, signalling either the end of all feeling, or a regretful glimpse of feelings he has lost. The cry of women seems to be one of grief as their queen dies, and it betokens qualities of loyalty to her, perhaps even love, despite her evil actions. We can only speculate on their unexplained but vocal response. From a feminist point of view, she has been placed in a fatal dilemma, "damned if she does and damned if she doesn't" (Calderwood xiv) – another layer of radical ambivalence in the play's world. Why she entered that world in the first place is left unexplained and not answered openly, but it may in a perverse way have been a "feminist" perception that

3 "Nothing is but what is not": Emotional Worlds of Characters in *Macbeth*

the world blocks women who wish to be active, and the only way for her to achieve any power is first through her husband's agency, and secondly by being prepared to embrace the ethics of war, individualism and murder instead of peace and domesticity. The alternative is Lady Macduff's resigned and hardened perception of the impossibility of action:

> Whither should I fly?
> I have done no harm. But I remember now
> I am in this earthly world, where to do harm
> Is often laudable, to do good sometime
> Accounted dangerous folly. Why then, alas,
> Do I put up that womanly defence
> To say I have done no harm. (4.2.74-80)

The next line is the brutal stage direction "*Enter murderers*", proving her point about the ineffectuality of virtue and of women.

Arguments rage about whether Shakespeare in his works reveals himself to be or not to be a proto-feminist, and if so, of what kind (in a movement with many different styles and stances), but the question is not resolved within the terms of this play, though actors, directors and audiences may come to their own conclusions. As we have seen, the playwright certainly draws upon distinctions between concepts of masculine and feminine values, but he does so in a complex way which, as in the case of Lady Macbeth (and the Witches, for that matter), does not enforce a single or simple judgement. As at all levels in this play, ambivalence operates in its presentation of gender as of other issues. One thing we can conclude, however, is that within the play's horizon is a touchstone perception that there are children who deserve to grow up in a world safe from tyranny, cruelty, war and inhumanity – the very world which is not on offer in *Macbeth*.

The Witches

Where radical ambivalence operates at its most profound level is in making unanswerable the crucial question, "to what extent did

Macbeth freely 'choose' his course of action?" Perfectly valid arguments could be mounted to justify opposite positions. On the one hand, it could be said that the Witches in their prophecies show that, whatever Macbeth wants, his future is already mapped out, foreordained, inevitable and impervious to individual choice or agency. The other argument says that the Witches simply record the future in the way that historians record the past, that Macbeth is shown in the process of freely choosing among options, and his options then become history as the play unfolds. A kind of in-between position would be that, borrowing again from a metaphor used by Joseph Furphy in *Such Is Life*, like a person catching a train, Macbeth chooses to get on one train rather than another, and is then at the mercy of the train's route and must stay on it until it stops and he alights somewhere other than where he expected.

It is significant that in presenting the arguments above, the role of the Witches seems to be crucial but unexplained. Do they cause events or simply observe them? The questions are the same as those posed by Marlowe's *Doctor Faustus*, and by Milton in *Paradise Lost*, both within a Christian cosmology: if God knows the future of mankind, how can people meaningfully "choose" for themselves; and if they cannot choose, then is not God unjust? Does God make human history or merely observe it being made? Does omniscience include all-powerfulness? Unfortunately for those looking for easy answers, there are none, and the Witches remain inscrutable and mysterious, hovering through the fog and filthy air and apparently indifferent to human fates. The intriguing chant "Fair is foul and foul is fair" (1.1.11), throws us straight away into a moral "fog" where good and evil, fair and foul, are not opposites but somehow indistinguishable from each other and confused. The words recur: "So fair and foul a day I have not seen" (1.3.36), "Good sir, why do you start, and seem to fear / Things that do sound so fair?" (1.3.49-50). Macbeth falls "rapt" into a threshold state where "this supernatural soliciting / Cannot be ill, cannot be good" (1.3.129-30), and where "nothing is / But what is not" (1.3.140-1). The word "witches", at least in Shakespeare's time and probably generally now, would have negative associations, but there could be "white" as well as "black" witches. On the other hand, we should note that the word occurs only once in the spoken text, and that the figures are

3 "Nothing is but what is not": Emotional Worlds of Characters in *Macbeth*

nominated not witches but "weird sisters" (1.3.30). This sounds more neutral and almost certainly is a survival from the Old English word *wyrd*, which meant fate and destiny. Perhaps even in the original spelling ("weyward") there might be a touch of "wayward", namely changeable, unreliable, and it is intriguing to notice that this is the word used by Hecate to describe Macbeth himself as a "wayward son / Spiteful and wrathful" (3.5.11-12). But in fact the "sisters" are proved to be entirely correct and reliable, and their function can be strictly construed as no more than predictive and prophetic rather than causative or malicious. They are even quite friendly to everybody, in ways that others in this play are not, and indeed they are reproved by their mistress, Hecate, for revealing too much to humanity (in a scene which many doubt is by Shakespeare), as though such knowledge is dangerous, as it is to Faustus. They might be said to "put ideas in Macbeth's mind", but then again without their prophecies he may himself have built hopes of further advancement on the event of his accelerated status of Thane of Cawdor. Even without meeting the Witches he could have taken this as a signal of further success. Whichever way we look, the Witches seem to be neutral, or even to symbolise the spirit of radical ambivalence running through the play.

The actual physical status of the Witches is just as problematical as the moral space they inhabit, as Banquo reports:

> What are these,
> So withered, and so wild in their attire,
> That look not like th'inhabitants o'th'earth
> And yet are on't? – Live you, or are you aught
> That man may question? You seem to understand me,
> By each at once her choppy finger laying
> Upon her skinny lips. You should be women,
> And yet your beards forbid me to interpret
> That you are so. (1.3.37-45)

Macbeth asks not "*who* are you?" but "*what* are you?" Names like Paddock (toad) and Graymalkin (common name for a cat) place them more in the animal world than the human, while their goddess, Hecate, belongs to the spirit world of classical mythology. It is questionable even what element they are made of:

> BANQUO
> The earth hath bubbles, as the water has,
> And these are of them. Whither are they vanished?
> MACBETH
> Into the air, and what seemed corporal
> Melted as breath into the wind. (1.3.77-80)

Like water but living on land, materially visible and yet vanishing into thin air, bearded women played in the theatre by boys, the sisters defy all categories of classification and remain obdurately ambiguous in their very nature as in their relation to the past and future. Much the same can be said of the three "Apparitions" which warn Macbeth against Macduff and the rising of Birnam Wood, of the "show of eight kings" presented by the sisters, giving a glimpse into the long line of Banquo's issue holding the sceptres of office, the line stretching out to "th' crack of doom" (4.1.133) as the Day of Judgement, and even of the phantom dagger which appears temptingly to Macbeth before he kills Duncan. All these illusions would have stretched the resources of the play's original theatre – probably the Globe, an outdoor, public playhouse operating in daylight. Arguments have been mounted that it was performed indoors at the Blackfriars Playhouse or at court, but the production which Simon Forman attended in 1610-11 was at the Globe – and even today directors in presenting these "supernatural" scenes rarely escape an element of inadvertent absurdity, or at least unease in suspending audience disbelief. The repulsive ingredients tossed into the Witches' cauldron to boil in a "hell-broth" (4.1.19), and the way Birnam Wood approaches Dunsinane, are especially tricky to stage without risking laughter through either over-literalism or over-stylisation. A part of the problem is that the Witches as stage representations are on a different theatrical plane, not individuated "characters" like the others who are interacting with each other, but more like an observing chorus, especially since there are three of them. Stephen Greenblatt follows a metatheatrical approach, suggesting that the Witches stand for the dramatist in the work, and their trade of "bewitchment" is analogous

3 "Nothing is but what is not": Emotional Worlds of Characters in *Macbeth*

to the dramatist's art of intersecting fantasy and reality through a celebration of "the boundless energy and hallucinatory vividness of the imagination" (Greenblatt 1994: 31). After all (though it is a point not made by Greenblatt), they do know the plot before the play even starts, and they know where the play will end long before any of the characters themselves do.

4
"The seeds of time" and the Macbeths

Acute awareness of time was Shakespeare's nemesis, driving all his literary creations as a constant emotional pressure on human endeavours, and *Macbeth* provides one of his most urgent and sustained analyses of time's power and complexities. We might be inclined to think of time in terms of quantitative measurement of something otherwise abstract, seconds leading to minutes to hours to weeks, months, years, decades and millennia. But for Elizabethans it could mean more than clocks, hourglasses (or "sandglasses"), calendars and deadlines: more humanly apprehended events like sunrise and sunset; the sun by day and moon by night (when they were visible); recurrent and symbolically meaningful church bells tolling; birdsong (the nightingale and lark in *Romeo and Juliet*); cowbells indicating creaturely needs; tides bringing theatregoers over the Thames; guttering candles and dying embers as time for sleep – so that clocks were only one of many ways of telling time (Stern 2015). Sleep in particular is the time for watchers to protect the sleepers, and as Nancy Simpson-Younger has argued it is this fundamental ethical law of human societies which Macbeth knowingly violates in murdering the sleeping Duncan (Simpson-Younger 2016). Time could also "move" in various ways, not just as sand through an hourglass, a shadow across a sundial, or a hand circling a clock-face, but according to human, emotional rhythms, as Rosalind in *As You Like It* describes:

ROSALIND
I pray you, what is't o'clock?
ORLANDO
You should ask me what time o' day. There's no clock in the forest.
ROSALIND
Then there is no true lover in the forest, else sighing every minute and groaning every hour would detect the lazy foot of time as well as a clock.
ORLANDO
And why not the swift foot of time? Had not that been as proper?
ROSALIND
By no means, sir. Time travels in divers paces with divers persons. I'll tell you who time ambles withal, who time trots withal, who time gallops withal, and who he stands still withal.
ORLANDO
I prithee, who doth he trot withal?
ROSALIND
Marry, he trots hard with a young maid between the contract of her marriage and the day it is solemnized. If the interim be but a se'nnight, time's pace is so hard that it seems the length of seven year.
ORLANDO
Who ambles time withal?
ROSALIND
With a priest that lacks Latin, and a rich man that hath not the gout; for the one sleeps easily because he cannot study, and the other lives merrily because he feels no pain, the one lacking the burden of lean and wasteful learning, the other knowing no burden of heavy tedious penury. These time ambles withal.
ORLANDO
Who doth he gallop withal?
ROSALIND
With a thief to the gallows; for though he go as softly as foot can fall, he thinks himself too soon there.
ORLANDO
Who stays it still withal?
ROSALIND

4 "The seeds of time" and the Macbeths

With lawyers in the vacation; for they sleep between term and term, and then they perceive not how time moves. (*As You Like It* 3.2.292-325)

In the same play, the character Jaques delivers the much-anthologised passage on "the seven ages of man", reminding us of the ways in which time defines the various stages of a life, from the baby "mewling and puking in the nurse's arms", through schooldays, falling in love, working as a soldier, then as an aged justice of the peace, an elder, and finally senility without faculties (2.7.138-65). But in the Elizabethan period by no means all made it through the whole life cycle, since life expectancy was thirty-five due to infant mortality, deaths of mothers in childbirth, epidemics, and the regular bouts of plague that swept through society. Under these circumstances, a life could be abruptly terminated and was always subject to chance. This is the conditional and uncertain element in which Macbeth and his wife are located, and it comes to define their equally uncertain roles as a couple without heirs.

Time in Shakespeare is above all relative and can be measured by emotional responses rather than being a simple, objectively ascertained quantity, and it "travels in divers paces with divers persons" faced by multiple personal situations. In the sonnets in particular we appear to have a personal awareness expressed by Shakespeare about a constant dread of time, with fragility and destructiveness as its main attributes, stemming from the realisation that "Time will come and take my love away" (Sonnet 64) – but it can also be recuperative in the enduring capacity of art to overcome its tyranny, and in its ability to heal and bring about reconciliations in plays like *The Winter's Tale* and *Pericles*. The future viewed from the present is always a matter of simultaneous hope and fear: "What's to come is still unsure" as Feste the wise fool in *Twelfth Night* sings (2.3.45), where "still" can mean either "as in the past" or "always". In *Macbeth*, Shakespeare repeatedly draws attention to the peculiarity of the English language, that it has no unambiguous future tense. While in Latin the word "ambulabit" means only one thing, that at some time in the future a man "will walk", the English phrase is a present tense – he will [is willing to] walk. Feste's phrase, while referring to the future, again uses the present tense and an infinitive, "what *is* to come". No matter how we try, English cannot express the future unambiguously and must use variations on the present and past to describe events that have not yet happened: "he goes tomorrow", "he will [is willing to] go", "his departure *lies* in the future", "he will [is willing to] *have gone* by tomorrow". It is inescapable that English has only past and present tenses, and the future can be expressed only in terms of the past and present. It creates certain unique moods of existential anxiety that haunt Macbeth.

Time references pervade *Macbeth* and the word itself recurs over fifty times. It is on some occasions discussed with a "clockwork" precision:

> BANQUO
> How goes the night, boy?
> FLEANCE
> The moon is down, I have not heard the clock.
> BANQUO
> And she goes down at twelve.
> FLEANCE
> I take't, 'tis later, sir. (2.1.1-3)

However, in the topsy-turvy world of human affairs in *Macbeth*, what the "clock" says can be at odds with observations from nature: "by the clock, 'tis day, / And yet dark night strangles the travelling lamp" (2.4.7). Critics have discussed the issue of time in the play (Clark and Mason 2015: 64-82) in terms of chronology, succession, and the preoccupations of characters, but here just two larger issues can briefly be outlined since they further exemplify the aura of ambiguity that hangs over *Macbeth* as a whole. One is the role of sleep in defining day and night, and the other is a quasi-philosophical questioning of sequence between past, present and future, as a sense of reassuringly diurnal time becomes dislodged by heightened emotional states.

Macbeth defines how sleep divides time, not only between day and night but between moral equivalents, committing himself to the time of the wolf and "withered murder" while others sleep: "Now o'er the one half world, / Nature seems dead, and wicked dreams abuse / The curtained sleep" (2.1.48-53 *passim*). A bell immediately rings as if to make the shift decisive, summoning Duncan "to heaven or to hell"

4 "The seeds of time" and the Macbeths

(2.1.64). The good are all asleep, including Duncan himself and the grooms in "swinish sleep" (1.7.67). But having made himself a person of the night, Macbeth discovers that he has forfeited the capacity to sleep, plagued as he is by insomnia by night and fear of others by day. The First Witch had resolved to make a ship's pilot unable to sleep as a way of driving him mad – "Sleep shall neither night nor day / Hang upon his penthouse lid" (1.3.20) – and she could just as well be speaking of Macbeth:

> MACBETH
> Methought I heard a voice cry "Sleep no more,
> Macbeth does murder sleep" – the innocent sleep,
> Sleep that knits up the ravelled sleave of care,
> The death of each day's life, sore labour's bath,
> Balm of hurt minds, great nature's second course,
> Chief nourisher in life's feast –
> LADY MACBETH
> What do you mean?
> MACBETH
> Still it cried "Sleep no more!" to all the house,
> "Glamis hath murdered sleep, and therefore Cawdor
> Shall sleep no more, Macbeth shall sleep no more." (2.2.33-41)

His wife diagnoses the cause of his anxiety: "You lack the season of all natures, sleep" (3.4.140), and points out that one of the consequences of his insomnia is to make ambiguous other categories, since sleep becomes (in Macduff's words) "death's counterfeit" (2.3.76), and (in Lady Macbeth's) "the sleeping and the dead / Are but as pictures" (2.2.51-2). She herself comes to suffer an equally perverse but opposite state, described by the Doctor as the "slumbery agitation" (5.1.11) of sleepwalking, which he identifies as "A great perturbation in nature, to receive at once the benefit of sleep and do the effects of watching" (5.1.9-10). Both Macbeth and Lady Macbeth have "murdered sleep" with their deed done under darkness, and sleeping and waking provide another of the frequent dualities in the play.

Similarly, another pattern of three is disturbed, the apparent certainties of past, present and future. This time Macbeth is not the perpetrator but something like a victim, at the mercy of the dramatist. With great precision, Shakespeare plots the opening scenes like a filmmaker intent on creating in rapid succession a flash-forward and a flash-back, disrupting Macbeth's and the audience's sense of orderly progression. We know before he does of something which has already happened, since even before we see him, we know that he has already been promoted from Thane of Glamis to Thane of Cawdor. Only now do we see the Witches encountering Macbeth and Banquo, and they greet the former as both Thane of Glamis and Thane of Cawdor, and "king hereafter" (1.3.50). The sequence of events draws the audience into complicity with the Witches, since we have in a sense been ahead of time ("o'erleaped" or "vaulted" events) and have seen part of the future before Macbeth. When he next is told by Ross that he is already Thane of Cawdor and mutters that "the greatest is behind" (1.3.117), it is as though his own future has become his past within the present moment. Banquo interprets Macbeth's "rapt" state as understandable bewilderment, and "Like our strange garments, cleave not to their mould / But with the aid of use" (1.3.144-5). Macbeth's apparently accepting adage that "Time and the hour runs through the roughest day" (1.3.146) is little more than an uncomprehending platitude inadequate to the paradox into which he has been thrown. Immediately after, he is jettisoned further into an unlived future, when Duncan not only confirms that he is Thane of Cawdor but also nominates Malcom (Duncan's son) effectively as future king, which Macbeth instantly sees is an impediment to the Witches' third prophecy coming true. This is the moment when he begins to see the future as though it is in the present, recognising that Malcolm stands in his way to the throne:

> [*Aside*] … Stars, hide your fires;
> Let not light see my black and deep desires,
> The eye wink at the hand; yet let that be
> Which the eye fears, when it is done, to see. (1.4.50-4)

The meaning here is somewhat opaque and mirrors his confused but dawning emotional participation in future events, but the phrase "when it is done" will be repeated later ("If it were done when 'tis done …" [1.7.1]). Syntactically, Shakespeare is playing on the sense mentioned,

4 "The seeds of time" and the Macbeths

that English, like German but unlike Latin and French, has no true future tense – "when it *is* [has been] *done*" carries within itself paradoxes that the future can become the past or the present in the twinkling of an eye and, as Lady Macbeth says in the next scene, one can "feel now / The future in the instant" (1.5.57). In reading her husband's letter, she also emphasises another word which will be repeated at significant moments four times, "hereafter" (already "king hereafter" [1.3.50]; and "Malcolm, whom we name hereafter / The Duke of Cumberland" [1.4.38-9]; and most ambiguously eventually to be her own epitaph, "She should have died hereafter" [5.5.17]). Once again a word that would seem unambiguously to denote the future has become destabilised, rendering sequential time problematical in its relation to past and present. It is a conceptual knot which, try as he does, Macbeth cannot untie; even a conditional and subjunctive language based on hypotheses ("when ... then ...", "if ... may ... ") – a syntax "smother'd in surmise" (1.3.141) – comes unstuck in the temporally uncertain and paradoxical world into which Macbeth has been plunged, in which "hereafter" may already have happened. In some ways it opens up the possibility of "o'erleaping" the present (another word which is significantly repeated, recalling Macbeth's aside, "The Prince of Cumberland! – That is a step / On which I must fall down, or else o'erleap" [1.4.48-9]) but in others it prevents avoiding the consequences of actions. When he finally realises the unlikelihood of escaping these consequences, Macbeth once again sees his future in terms of the past, as though it has already happened and there is no future left (5.5.19-28). The action shows that no human agent, not even the incumbent of regal power himself, can actually know the future, but judging from the examples the prognosis is bleak. Power corrupts; but more than that, the very existence of power can lead men to forfeit their initial humanity. They are neither fully conscious agents nor helpless victims, but rather men swept up unwittingly in a historical process which can just as easily dump them later into oblivion.

Events which lie in the future exist, virtually by definition, in the realm of uncertainty that is at the heart of *Macbeth* as a play; they are "seeds of time" planted in the present which will grow in the future, whether predictably or in unforeseeable ways. Imagined events either will happen or they will not, and until the time comes they cannot be certain. Some things may be more likely than not, but they still may not happen and are dependent on a mixture of human choice and predetermined history. In *Macbeth* there are quite a lot of events in nature that overturn normal expectations: small birds attack large ones, days can be as dark as night, tame horses can turn wild. Events that are unlikely in the human world do happen: a worthy Scottish thane is projected onto the throne in a space of twenty-four hours. Both inside and outside plays, a host of factors influences whether or not an event happens or does not – some voluntary and some beyond control. We may desperately want some job, doing everything within our power to qualify and apply, but in the final analysis the decision is not entirely ours and luck may well be working against us. The situation is even more complex when you do not know what job to apply for and some influential figure says, "I can see you as an airline pilot". From then on, even if you had never thought of this, the idea of it takes hold of your mind like an obsession, and you do everything possible to open up that route (and if, heaven forbid, you are a Macbeth you may even consider killing for it). If you do not make it, failure can be attributed to possible reasons which lie in the realm of "fate", or to personal inadequacy. On the other hand, you may reach the coveted status of airline pilot and only then realise that you hate being away from home, resent the person who planted the idea in your mind, and wish you had never applied. In all these cases uncertainty operates in at least two ways: until the event occurs we do not know if it will or will not come to be; and only after the event do we know for certain what are the consequences of the decision. It is this state of existential uncertainty that Macbeth is plunged into at the beginning of the play.

Initially Shakespeare seems to do everything in his power to set a scene in which these kinds of indeterminacy and uncertainty prevail. Even the First Witch's opening words, "When shall we three meet again?", projects us beyond the present into an unknown future, and they all chant a credo of uncertainty, "Fair is foul and foul is fair, / Hover through the fog and filthy air" (1.1.10-11). Macbeth's first line is an almost exact echo: "So foul and fair a day I have not seen" (1.3.36), and the climatic ambiguity leads to a narrative uncertainty out of which come the Witches' prophecies. The Thane of Glamis will become Thane of Cawdor. We in the audience, unlike Macbeth himself, know this

4 "The seeds of time" and the Macbeths

has already happened, which puts us into a kind of alliance with the Witches, at least insofar as we know the future for Macbeth before he does, and the news is confirmed immediately after the scene with the Witches when Ross enters to bear the message, adding an enigmatic hint of "a greater honour" to follow:

> And, for an earnest of a greater honour,
> He bade me, from him, call thee Thane of Cawdor:
> In which addition, hail, most worthy thane,
> For it is thine. (1.3.101-4)

Banquo immediately sees one implication and exclaims "What can the devil speak true?" (1.3.105), while Macbeth is mystified: "The Thane of Cawdor lives. Why do you dress me / In borrowed robes?" (1.3.106-07). We know before Macbeth does that the Thane of Glamis has already become Thane of Cawdor, who is prophesied to become king, and so powerful is the logic of the three prophecies, two of which are fulfilled, that the third seems virtually inevitable whether or not the Witches "cause" it or simply foresee it. To Banquo, the prophecies are even more paradoxical and lie in the distant future of several generations: he will be "Lesser than Macbeth, and greater", "Not so happy, yet much happier", and he shall get kings though he will not be one himself (1.3.63-70 *passim*). For both men, the future takes on a strangely certain and uncertain air, at once known and unknown. At the same time the Witches themselves are of deeply ambiguous status, either fanciful or real, apparitions or substantial. "This supernatural soliciting / Cannot be ill, cannot be good ..." (1.3.129), and Banquo questions, "What, can the devil speak true?" (1.3.105), reminding those in the audience who have seen *Hamlet* of a similar question. Everything about the atmosphere and events in this early part of the play plunges us into a realm of uncertainties about the future, "horrible imaginings" which are "smother'd in surmise", while at the same time the principle of forward-moving time seems in itself a reassuring certainty: "Come what come may, / Time and the hour runs through the roughest day" (1.3.145-6).

The presentation of the future in *Macbeth* might remind those with a scientific bent of modern chaos theory in physics and mathematics, the non-linear theory accounting for seemingly random events which in fact have prior causation. From a vantage point in the future, we might say that every event was led up to with an inexorable and unavoidable logic, but to predict this beforehand (since in life, unlike in literature, we are not in league with fate and the dramatist as the Witches are) is impossible, because the future is always full of unknowable factors, choices which, when taken, open up other choices, and room for coincidences and accidents. In prospect, events are entirely uncertain, while in retrospect they are entirely certain and unchangeable. A surprise is something unpredictable, but no longer a surprise after it has happened, and can be viewed as the logical end of a complex set of interrelated events. In dramatic terms, even if the "coming on of time" (1.5.9) on the stage has been marked by extreme suspense and indeterminacy, yet a foreordained, "plotted" pattern is being played out and eventually finds an inevitable resolution. In a wider sense, the "history" on which the play is based can be assumed to have already happened in the past and is being both recreated and repeated in the "present" of the play before our eyes. "What's done cannot be undone".

In their respective attitudes to time, Macbeth and Lady Macbeth are significantly different. Lady Macbeth confidently believes that, with the help of "fate and metaphysical aid" (1.5.28), the future can be known and that all one needs to do is what one is told, or deduces (kill the king, in this case). If the future is foreknown and fixed, why worry about the passage of time intervening?

> Great Glamis, worthy Cawdor,
> Greater than both, by the all-hail hereafter,
> Thy letters have transported me beyond
> This ignorant present, and I feel now
> The future in the instant. (1.5.53-7)

For Lady Macbeth, such a suggestion acts like a reliable prophecy, liberating her from the burden of making choices and decisions, and willing to go beyond "This ignorant present" and "feel now / The future in an instant", by which she means only ruling as king and queen without any messier consequences. Macbeth, on the other hand, is less

4 "The seeds of time" and the Macbeths

confident of the prophesied future, and much more anxious about the element of human volition and choice required to achieve it. Fearful, he would want to see the future consequences before he decides to act, as the process of reaching the goal dawns on his consciousness. This is pretty well what is meant by his tangled chain of reasoning in a famous but difficult passage:

> If it were done when 'tis done, then 'twere well
> It were done quickly; If th'assassination
> Could trammel up the consequence, and catch
> With his surcease, success: that but this blow
> Might be the be-all and the end-all, here,
> But here, upon this bank and shoal of time,
> We'd jump the life to come. But in these cases
> We still have judgment here, that we but teach
> Bloody instructions, which being taught, return
> To plague th'inventor. (1.7.1-10)

If only an action could lead to its desired conclusions without having other implications. Macbeth is facing the decision made by Faustus and also by Adam and Eve in the story of the Fall. In making such a decision, knowledge gleaned from the Witches' prophecy is a dangerous distraction – "a little knowledge is a dangerous thing" in the words of another proverb. For one who used to be notorious among critics as "ambitious" by nature, Macbeth is extraordinarily dithery, fearful and indecisive, but in this case it is to his credit. His tortuously condensed soliloquy marks a strenuous attempt to resist temptation by reasoning his way through alternatives. Worried at first about the "ignorant present" and the need for making a choice to reach the promised end, he then rationally considers the moral nature of his actions and weighs his options. Duncan is visiting his house "in double trust", for Macbeth is not only his subject and "kinsman" but also his guest. Lady Macbeth enters upon his meditations, and immediately scorns his qualms, questioning his love for her, and going so far as accusing him of being a coward. A crucial ambiguity in the word "man" turns the conversation around:

MACBETH
Prithee peace.
I dare do all that may become a man;
Who dares do more is none.
LADY MACBETH
What beast was't then
That made you break this enterprise to me?
When you durst do it, then you were a man;
And to be more than what you were, you would
Be so much more the man. (1.7.45-51)

Macbeth uses the word "man" to mean a moral agent, a human being as distinct from one who, like Faustus, tries to usurp God's position. Lady Macbeth, either wilfully or unconsciously, sees "man" as separate from "beast", and says that if Macbeth is being a man now, then he must have been an animal when he broke the enterprise to her. As she goes on, vowing that as a mother she would have dashed her baby's brains out rather than break her word if she had sworn as she asserts Macbeth had done, she throws out another implicit challenge to his honour and his masculinity (with the sense that his scruples now make him more effeminate than a suckling mother). By a mixture of sexual taunting and spirited persuasion, Lady Macbeth manages to "screw [his] courage to the sticking-place" (1.7.61). Curiously, if the actual discussion had not been over murder, the mutual supportiveness of this married couple would be quite touching, as Barbara Everett (1989) has argued. If only the decision had been whether or not to apply for a particular job, to acquire a dog, or whether to holiday by the beach or in a city, the partnership of the Macbeths might be seen as collaborative and frank in a positive way. As it is, they spur each other on towards a course of action which, as Macbeth instinctively knows, is criminal in deed and potentially disastrous in consequence. Onwards from the point when Macbeth decides, they act more or less as trapped, unable either to change their choice or to avoid the destined future. In the words of Joseph Furphy's *Such Is Life*, they have at first a completely unfettered choice, but having chosen they must then live through rigorously unfolding consequences which they cannot avoid. After his moment of wavering in Act 1 Scene 7 – his moment of resisting temptation and of questioning the apparently fatalistic chain of events leading him to kill the king – Macbeth takes his place within a kind of historical process of rise and fall. Far from being a "man" in any of the senses canvassed above, he gradually forfeits human feelings altogether, becoming more an automaton, a programmed machine going through the motions of life, hiring others to do his killing to protect his ill-gained position. The most shocking of these actions are the murders of Banquo, and of Lady Macduff and her children, from both of which Macbeth is absent.

A turning point seems to come at Macbeth's rueful line after the murder: "To know my deed, 'twere best not know myself" (2.2.72), and so he chooses not to know his deed. The editor of the Oxford Shakespeare edition of the play glosses the sentence as "'if I must acknowledge my crime I must forget the man I have been, and am' – he is condemned to self division" (Brooke 1990: 130). At this moment of self-reflection, the deed separates from the person, but by committing to regicide Macbeth's self becomes identified with the deed, and his actions alone are the things by which he is to be judged. They determine what is left of his life. Then comes a knocking at the door, as the world is awakening and outside influences in the person of Macduff are coming to stir this castle of claustrophobia and death. Macbeth mutters, "Wake Duncan with thy knocking: I would thou couldst" (2.2.73). This day is the first of the rest of his life, but carrying the opposite tone from this common anonymous saying, which is invariably used optimistically.

Whatever his past feelings and thoughts may be (so far as we can judge them from the text), his immediate present is tied to a "deed". He is now, in a very real way, defined by his crime. The play could be renamed to anticipate Dostoyevsky's title *Crime and Punishment*, and as crime begets more crime, punishment inevitably looms. The only "inner self" left to Macbeth is the tortured conscience, and even this becomes cauterised to the point of insensibility in his increasingly beleaguered position; as a scholar of conscience concludes, "thereafter only imperfectly accessible to his reason, as the light of his conscience thickens, darkens, and becomes finally extinct" (Wilks 1990: 143). On the one hand, the reckless bravado of the condemned criminal drives Macbeth from now on, and conscience is externalised in the figure of the bloody ghost of Banquo, which acts as a form of vengeance rather than a moral compass. By the end of the play, Macbeth's consciousness of good and evil has been "used up", exhausted and effaced by the relentless and alienating processes of getting and keeping power, with literally nothing else left to live for. It is the report of his wife's death that stirs this speech, but the sentiment expresses more generally the fate of one who has had life squeezed from him by the very office he had so eagerly and apprehensively sought:

> To-morrow, and to-morrow, and to-morrow,
> Creeps in this petty pace from day to day,
> To the last syllable of recorded time;
> And all our yesterdays have lighted fools
> The way to dusty death. Out, out, brief candle.
> Life's but a walking shadow, a poor player
> That struts and frets his hour upon the stage,
> And then is heard no more. It is a tale
> Told by an idiot, full of sound and fury,
> Signifying nothing. (5.5.18-27)

We should remember that this passage was written by a working dramatist who also acted in his plays, and there is both an audacity and scepticism about his profession of using poor players as "walking shadows". In his fondness for metatheatrical statements (drawing attention to the theatre itself as context), Shakespeare here links time as an emotional and psychological quality with the experience of an actor who is speaking lines already written for him by somebody else which cannot be varied, nearing the end of his time on the stage for this particular performance. In recognition of a kind of tragic farce, the actor will repeat his actions and lines on the next night, and the following, and the following – "To-morrow and to-morrow and to-morrow" – until the script has all been spoken to "the last syllable" of its "recorded time", and after which there is "nothing". To some extent then, Shakespeare is reflecting on and reproving his own professional practice of telling tales to be enacted over and over again with feigned emotionalism, "full of sound and fury", by actors upon a stage. But just as important as the metatheatrical reference is the substance of what it expresses of the mood of the character in context: Macbeth has

4 "The seeds of time" and the Macbeths

come to the ultimate end of the process he had begun, and he now understands that he has been merely an insignificant agent in a play drawn from historical sources recording events which lie in the past, his words written by another as a script rather than expressing his own thoughts, and that now there is no more need for his existence.

> I have lived long enough. My way of life
> Is fall'n into the sere, the yellow leaf,
> And that which should accompany old age,
> As honour, love, obedience, troops of friends,
> I must not look to have ... (5.3.23-7)

Macbeth's tragic awareness at this moment that the play is over lies in the consciousness of having lived at least the second half of his life on the wrong values, excluding the decent, safe and warm stabilities of community, family and self-respect. The assassination has not trammelled up the consequence, but instead has created a purgatorial state of living through those very consequences. We are returned to our initial question – victim or hero? – and the answer seems to be, both.

5
"Palter with us in a double sense": Leading Ideas – Temptation, Equivocation, Evil

Recent research in the emerging field of the history of emotions has established that emotions and ideas, or passion and reason, are rarely separate categories, least of all for Elizabethans. Scholarly ways of analysing emotions suggest a symbiosis between feelings and physiological processes, as if both body and feelings have their own, interrelated basis, as in the doctrine of humours mentioned elsewhere as one explanation of the "choleric" nature of Macbeth. This is not to deny that they could also go "beyond the humours" and recognise that passions are explained in terms of the non-corporeal soul (Meek and Sullivan 2015). Concomitantly, the world iew of Shakespeare's contemporaries included a fundamental concept of "right reason" in which rational understanding of moral issues, such as right and wrong, could be held so innately and strongly as matters of belief as well as reason that the two were inextricable as categories. One could have a passion for reason, and reason for passion. The most comprehensive explanations and exemplifications of this integrated and inclusive theory of "the little world of man" (Bambrough 1952, his title quoting from *King Lear*) were Thomas Wright's *Passions of the Soul* and Robert Burton's *Anatomy of Melancholy* (Sullivan 2016). "The Elizabethan malady" (Babb 1951) shows that melancholy could be an affliction involving both the body and the soul, and could explain diverse behaviours encompassing ecstasy, religious frenzy, scholarly despondence and despair as manifestations of creative to debilitating feeling. The relevance to this chapter is that the schema enables us to explore ideas as motivated ("moved") by feelings underpinned by concepts and beliefs, in the dynamic interplay of characters placed in extreme dramatic situations.

In an earlier chapter we glanced at Sidney's argument that imaginative literature can effectively amalgamate and surpass the disciplinary work of history and philosophy by "proving" their factual and didactic lessons on the emotional pulses, in tales and plays that move our feelings to new understandings of morality and human, emotional complexity. Shakespeare's history plays, for example, are based on historical, chronicle sources and show us "what happened", albeit in ways that are slanted towards confirming a Tudor myth, but they do far more than tell the "bare was" of facts (Sidney's phrase) by showing characters making history by following their passions. Now we turn to philosophy. Ideas about good and evil can be presented aridly, or at least abstractly, in logical arguments or, as Shakespeare shows, in affectively based demonstrations which invite us to share the dilemmas of plausible characters who face life-and-death decisions. These plays can make us understand, through changing sympathies and exercise of empathy, how ideas are more than abstractions. In *Macbeth*, this is especially important, because this play in particular invites us to understand how otherwise exemplary people can be driven through strength of feelings in certain situations to commit evil acts; how they are tempted and fall, even against their instincts and reason. The play is a moral test for readers and audiences as much as for the characters we observe and whose actions we trace through circumstances. It also constitutes a meditation on the power of time, apprehended subjectively through the feelings it inspires as well as an objective imperative, guiding and haunting the actions of human agents, as we saw in the previous chapter.

Temptation

One would think that Christianity is unlikely to figure prominently in a play set in eleventh-century Scotland dominated by an atmosphere suggesting Celtic paganism, but in fact the religion of Shakespeare's day pervades *Macbeth*. For example, there are some references to the day of

5 Leading Ideas - Temptation, Equivocation, Evil

judgement, twenty to heaven and eleven to hell, sometimes coming in tandem: "Hear it not, Duncan; for it is a knell / That summons thee to heaven or to hell" (2.1.63-4). The Porter, at the door of a castle inside which a murder has been committed though unknown to him, likens himself to the porter of hell-gate, concluding facetiously, "But this place is too cold for hell. I'll devil-porter it no further: I had thought to have let in some of all professions that go the primrose way to the everlasting bonfire" (2.3.18-21). Even the ethic of patience preached in the Gospels is mentioned specifically by Macbeth himself, albeit with some sarcasm and with an ulterior motive to solicit the assassination of Banquo:

> Do you find
> Your patience so predominant in your nature
> That you can let this go? Are you so gospell'd
> To pray for this good man and for his issue,
> Whose heavy hand hath bow'd you to the grave? (3.1.93-8)

Macbeth suggests that "Turn the other cheek" is not a feeling likely to be held by hardened men, persuaded that Banquo has made their life a misery. Some Christian references are casual sayings ("God's benison", "God above" [4.3.139-40]) but others are strong in their context, in particular those aligning Macbeth with Christian hell: "O hell-kite" (5.1.218), "Turn, hell-hound" (5.10.5), and others:

> Come, thick night,
> And pall thee in the dunnest smoke of hell,
> That my keen knife see not the wound it makes,
> Nor heaven peep through the blanket of the dark,
> To cry "Hold, hold!" (1.5.49-53)

"Hell is murky" (5.1.35) intones the sleepwalking Lady Macbeth, distantly recalling Marlowe's Mephostophiles in *Doctor Faustus* – "I am damned, and am now in hell" (Ormerod and Wortham 1985: l. 584) – suggesting that Lady Macbeth now has the status of a devil and also that the version of living hell she faces is the guilty conscience she reveals through her compulsive hand-washing. Although references to heaven outnumber references to hell in *Macbeth*, the latter carry more weight in informing the play's atmosphere, linking the Second Witch's chant, "For a charm of powerful trouble, / Like a hell-broth boil and bubble" (4.1.18-19), with Malcolm's personal vision of evil, "Nay, had I power, I should / Pour the sweet milk of concord into hell" (4.3.99). Macbeth's name is defined by Young Siward as worse than Lucifer's – "thou call'st thyself a hotter name / Than any is in hell" (5.7.23) – and the tyrant's theological status is suggested by Macduff: "Not in the legions / Of horrid hell can come a devil more damn'd / In evils to top Macbeth" (4.3.58). The repeated verbal association of Macbeth and hell is one of many examples of the unfairness of Shakespeare and Holinshed to the historical King Macbeth, who, although known to Scottish historians as the last of the Celtic kings, was also sympathetic to Christianity and even helped establish it in Scotland. But Shakespeare did not let this get in the way of a morality tale, and he did not need to, since his audience and his own king had no vested interest in giving credit to an ancient enemy of the Stuart line. The historical moment when two religious schemes were in play is turned against the very man who helped establish Christianity in Scotland. More thematically functional than these references, however, are two guiding Christian concepts that were of special significance in King James' Protestant Britain in 1606, temptation and equivocation, and both invite closer analysis in understanding the play. Both reach back to the Reformation, Henry VIII's break from the Catholic empire, and the resulting tensions between Protestantism and Catholicism, which were very much live issues in Shakespeare's time as two schools in conflict with each other within a single religion.

From the morality plays in the late fifteenth and early sixteenth centuries, through Marlowe's *Doctor Faustus* to Milton's *Paradise Lost*, one of the major Protestant theological debates centred on temptation, a theme which features prominently in other plays by Shakespeare, such as *Hamlet* and *Measure for Measure*. It is even more ubiquitous in the period than revenge, which was a pre-Christian ethic derived in drama from Seneca. Temptation is absolutely central to *Macbeth* and indeed defines the moral design of the play, as the protagonist clearly and sequentially understands how wrong murder would be, wrestles with his conscience, but finally in conversation with his wife succumbs to the temptation of seizing power and kingship by violent regicide. It is

5 Leading Ideas - Temptation, Equivocation, Evil

his temptation and fall that provide the central fulcrum of the play's psychological dimension, and in broader terms temptation underpins the questions raised by the Witches' prophecies concerning whether the future is predetermined or changed by human choices acting with free will. The likenesses to Marlowe's *Doctor Faustus*, a story of a man who railed against Christian orthodoxy and sold his soul to the devil to gain knowledge, and one of the most influential plays in the whole Elizabethan and Jacobean period, has been mentioned already several times as a recurrent reference point for *Macbeth*. The function of the Old Man in *Macbeth* is a direct structural parallel with *Faustus*, as he dispenses pious advice to Ross and Macduff: "God's benison go with you; and with those / That would make good of bad, and friends of foes" (2.4.40-1). Edmund Spenser in *The Faerie Queene*, another major source for Shakespeare in some of his plays, shows his knights perfecting their virtue by confronting and overcoming temptations to evil. Half a century later, John Milton was heavily influenced by Shakespeare and even contemplated writing a work (either poem or play) adapting *Macbeth* (Braunmuller 1997: 60-1). This was because to Milton temptation was the foremost issue facing Protestants, and the longer poems he wrote are based on this theme. In his masque *Comus*, a virtuous lady is tempted by the cavalier royalist credo "seize the day" (*carpe diem*) but she resists and although her body is immobilised her mind cannot be changed; in the epic *Paradise Lost* the story comes from Genesis as Adam and Eve are tempted by Satan and fall to gain knowledge; in *Paradise Regained* Christ resists the multiple temptations of the devil to despair and to forfeit his faith in God; in *Samson Agonistes* the struggle between temptation and resistance is replayed in another Biblical myth as Samson, taunted and tempted, literally brings the house down on his enemies. Central to Milton's Puritan thinking was the belief expressed in his prose work *Areopagitica*, "I cannot praise a fugitive and cloister'd vertue, unexercis'd & unbreath'd, that never sallies out and sees her adversary ... that which purifies us is triall, and triall is by what is contrary" (Milton 1974: 213), and he returned again and again to stories which showed in action the process of purification through temptation. It was a major theme of Protestant Christianity for over a century, and *Macbeth* is Shakespeare's contribution. Anticipating the scheme of *Paradise Lost*, Malcolm's statement and Macbeth's fate go to the heart of the major issue of the rebellion of Satan against God: "Angels are bright still, though the brightest fell" (4.3.28). Such phrases are ultimately from the Bible (for example, Luke 10.18, Isaiah 14.12, 2 Peter 2.4). Significantly, the Witches' advice, "Seek to know no more" (4.1), is echoed twice by Milton in *Paradise Lost*: "To know no more / Is woman's happiest knowledge" (4.635), and "Oh yet happiest, if ye seek / No happier state, and know to know no more" (4.773). I have not seen the idea advanced by a critic, but what happens to, and between, Macbeth and Lady Macbeth bears further striking resemblances to the Biblical Adam and Eve story, or at least to Milton's retelling in *Paradise Lost*. The dynamics between the couple, their emotional closeness, and the way that the Eve figure is the first to fall to temptation and then uses appeals to her love to draw her husband into the decision, all occur between Adam and Eve before the Fall, and in their case the Fall is equivalent to the Macbeths' murder of Duncan, which brings them both knowledge of evil and power. After Milton came John Bunyan's quintessentially Protestant allegory, *The Pilgrim's Progress* (1678), in which Pilgrim is destined to carry his pack of sins on his back and face temptations at every turn, until he is declared one of the elect and welcomed into heaven. A corollary to temptation central to all these mainly Protestant writers, and to *Macbeth* and *Doctor Faustus*, is the nagging and supreme question raised by the Christian cosmology: if God foresees all – which must include whether an individual will resist or succumb to temptation – can there be any true exercise of free will, or do we exist within a predetermined and deterministic context? The apparent neutrality of the Witches, whose prophecies seem aligned with the things they foretell, directly raises such questions, though in an ethos that smacks of demonology rather than scripture. If they foresee the future, do they cause it? If not, can they cause events to come about simply by stating that they will, activating a kind of auto-suggestiveness in the listener? A.P. Rossiter for one is confident:

> They are not the Fates: for they have "masters", and the Fates do not need the chemistry of corruption to call forth their powers. They are not the real or supposed human witches that James tortured to the greater glory of God: for they predict the future and predict it truly.

5 Leading Ideas - Temptation, Equivocation, Evil

They are not the Devil (and therefore not in control of Macbeth) ...
(Rossiter 1961: 220)

But the questions remain around the haunting, riddling figures.

The Renaissance can be seen as a bridge between medieval and modern, old and new worldviews. In science, for example, we see the emergence from reliance on ancient authorities and occultism into the observational science of Francis Bacon, Thomas Browne and Galileo. In religion we see in the sixteenth century, not surprisingly given the successive changes in the state of Britain, a fluctuation between the "old religion" of Catholicism with its explanation of good and evil as external to humans (as in the fifteenth-century play *Everyman*), a divine plan working itself through punishment, and the "new religion" of Protestantism after the Reformation, in which writers like John Milton and George Herbert emphasised each person's individual choice between good and evil and their emphasis on election of the virtuous rather than salvation for sinners. They portray man as a constantly tempted being who must vigilantly exercise conscience to choose good, or else face the consequences with full severity. Catholic confession and remission of sins are impossible in this view. Marlowe's *Doctor Faustus* draws on both religious perspectives, reflecting their equal cultural availability in England at the time. The protagonist's desire to pursue knowledge beyond the limits allowed by God is the moralistic framework, providing a judgemental, external perception from "old religion" which begins and ends the play. The Chorus judges Faustus under "old religion": "regard his hellish fall, / Whose fiendful fortune may exhort the wise ... To practise more than heavenly power permits" (Ormerod and Wortham 1985:1533, 1536). But "inside" Marlowe's play is a more internalised psychomachia, a battle in, and for, the soul, of individual conscience tempted by what seems a legitimate human aspiration for knowledge and as constantly advised by a Good Angel and an Evil Angel. Faustus falls, and suffers the consequence of damnation. But enacted in the theatre there is something heroic in his struggle, and Marlowe at least strongly implies a subversive sense of injustice in a god who gives inquisitiveness to humanity but forecloses on knowledge and insists on obedience and maintaining a state of ignorance.

At many thematic levels of *Macbeth* we see in operation the Witches' thesis and antithesis, "fair is foul, and foul is fair". Macbeth is a victim of the moral relativity, thrown into a situation that seems to require a choice between expediency, which will have a benign and safe outcome for him, or an immoral action that will lead to power but also damnation. The question posed by Shakespeare revolves around whether Macbeth's destiny is as inescapable and fore-written as the Witches seem to imply, or whether he positively chose his fate – was he pushed or did he jump? If there is a possibility of predestination, as the Witches seem to suggest, does Macbeth really have a free choice? And if the Witches had not put ideas into his head would he have had a more or less free choice, in the sense that killing the king may not even have occurred to him? There is evidence for both views. On the side of predestination ("he was pushed") are the prophecies imposing a general sense of inevitability, and Lady Macbeth's persuasion reinforces this by not contemplating options. On the side of personal choice ("he jumped") is his own recognition in soliloquy that he faces a crisis of conscience which will entail living with the consequences of his actions.

> He's here in double trust:
> First, as I am his kinsman and his subject,
> Strong both against the deed; then, as his host,
> Who should against his murderer shut the door,
> Not bear the knife myself. Besides, this Duncan
> Hath borne his faculties so meek, hath been
> So clear in his great office, that his virtues
> Will plead like angels, trumpet-tongued, against
> The deep damnation of his taking-off,
> And pity, like a naked new-born babe,
> Striding the blast, or heaven's cherubin, horsed
> Upon the sightless couriers of the air,
> Shall blow the horrid deed in every eye,
> That tears shall drown the wind. I have no spur
> To prick the sides of my intent, but only
> Vaulting ambition, which o'erleaps itself
> And falls on the other. (1.7.12-28)

5 Leading Ideas - Temptation, Equivocation, Evil

Here Macbeth struggles with his conscience and is clearly fully aware of the risk he runs, the foreseen punishment being intuitive and imagined through imagery rather than the product of rational thought. He first decides not to do anything – "If chance will have me King, why, chance may crown me / Without my stir" (1.3.143-4) – but then succumbs to his wife's argument in favour of action. Both suffer consequences which are worse as mental torture than physical suffering, as Macbeth acknowledges:

> better be with the dead,
> Whom we, to gain our peace, have sent to peace,
> Than on the torture of the mind to lie
> In restless ecstasy. (3.3.21-4)

"Ecstasy" here has its semantic meaning of "placed outside oneself" or "beside oneself" with anxiety, and "restless" literally means without rest. Such "torture of the mind" is evidenced in his "horrible imaginings", as in the banquet scene; in Macbeth's anxious and paranoid insomnia; in Lady Macbeth's somnambulistic, agitated replaying of the murder; in the taunting vision of future kings stretching out "to th', crack of doom"; and in Macbeth's changed perception of himself: "To know my deed 'twere best not know myself" (2.2.73). His determination to wield complete control over what becomes a police state is obsessional and he thinks of everything (and so does Shakespeare) in covering all possible risks: "There's not one of them but in this house / I keep a servant fee'd" [bribed] (3.4.130-1). His final state of mind is not exactly repentance or acceptance, but a hollow despair which can be ended only by death when all "to-morrows" are used up.

Other characters face their own versions of temptation. Both Malcolm and Banquo give signs that they have been tempted and forced to exercise their consciences, but they choose good – or at least inaction – over evil. Macduff's is the most tragic and subtle, since the temptation he faces is to save his own life without foreseeing a likelihood that his own actions will lead to the deaths of his wife and children. It is an unfair test perhaps, but nonetheless he chooses wrongly. Lady Macbeth does not initially realise the nature of temptation – her conscience is metaphorically dormant or "asleep" in the early stages, and she does not acknowledge personal responsibility in making the decision. Her moment of personal recognition and incrimination comes just seconds too late to do anything about it – "Had he not resembled / My father as he slept, I had done't" (2.2.12-13). Much later she suffers revenge from her conscience, now ironically awakened in her state of sleep, revealing not just guilt but remorse, which drives her illness, eventually leading to death.

Equivocation

Nowadays, the word "equivocation" means sitting on the fence, unable to make a decision when faced with choices, or, changing the metaphor, hedging one's bets. However, when *Macbeth* was written it had more specific and technical senses relating to taking religious oaths (Huntley 1964). Both the old and the new meanings depend on an underlying attitude of evasiveness, whether culpable or congenital. When Macbeth at the end of the play begins "To doubt the equivocation of the fiend, / That lies like truth" (5.5.49-50), he joins the specific meaning of lying while appearing to tell the truth with the wider sense of riddling doubt aroused by the equivocator, creating a question over where truth exists. By this stage the Witches' final prophecies have come true – Birnam Wood has come to Dunsinane and Macduff has revealed that he was not of woman born – and Macbeth feels betrayed by "these juggling fiends no more believed, / that palter with us in a double sense" (5.8.19-20), but it is in fact Macbeth's faulty interpretive faculties which have "lied" to him, not the Witches. However, the modern definition is just as appropriate in describing a play which is based on ambivalence at several levels, and where fair can be foul depending on how one sees events.

It is the Porter, rousing his hungover self to answer the knocking on the door, who is preoccupied with equivocation in its topical, Jacobean sense. Earlier critics held up this scene (2.3) as a classic example of "comic relief", breaking the tension of the grim murder scene with some lowlife comedy and bawdy jokes. There are some problems with this. There is no evidence that Elizabethans necessarily found people

5 Leading Ideas - Temptation, Equivocation, Evil

funny simply because they were of a serving class, and also the jokes on drunkenness and male lechery hardly seem lighthearted. Nonetheless, the scene is crucial to the design of the play, and tells us much about its nature. It is placed pivotally. After the murder of Duncan comes a knock on the door, which provokes Macbeth to quip "Wake Duncan with thy knocking: I would thou could'st" (2.2.73), and which rouses the Porter to action. We discover the person knocking is Macduff, who will eventually kill Macbeth, but more symbolically the knock that wakes the Porter is equally a knocking from outside the narrow confines of the chamber – at this moment the stage itself – which has the effect of awakening the audience from the "rapt", spellbound state that dominates the preceding scenes between Macbeth and Lady Macbeth. Moral bearings are being reinstated in the world of the play, and this moment carries Macbeth across from crime to consequences, from kingship to tyranny, from the first murder to the bloodbath that will follow. The world has changed irrevocably for Macbeth, and the knock on the door which signals this cannot go unanswered. A common reading hinges on the reference, "if a man were porter of Hell gate" (2.3.2), as though the Macbeths' castle is hell and is about to be opened up for inspection. The Porter harps on "equivocation":

> Knock, knock. Who's there in th'other devil's name? Faith, here's an equivocator, that could swear in both the scales against either scale, who committed treason enough for God's sake, yet could not equivocate to Heaven: O come in, equivocator. (2.3.7-10)

Later he puns on the subject of alcohol and its ambiguous results:

> Therefore much drink may be said to be an equivocator with lechery: it makes him, and it mars him; it sets him on, and it takes him off; it persuades him, and disheartens him; makes him stand to, and not stand to – in conclusion, equivocates him in a sleep, and giving him the lie, leaves him. (2.3.28-33)

It is generally agreed that the whole speech, the import of which is largely lost today, refers specifically to the Jesuit, Father Henry Garnet, who, on being prosecuted for aiding and abetting the Gunpowder Plot in 1606, swore evidence while holding mental reservation that his evidence was not the whole truth (Thomas 2014: 141-60). Garnet had written a book, *A Treatise Against Lying and Fraudulent Dissimulation*, advancing a theological justification for the practice of quibbling on words so that one tells "the truth, but not the whole truth" or does not exactly lie but also does not exactly tell the truth. It rested on the assumption that God would understand and forgive the duplicity, as part of his higher plan. The ruse did not work in a worldly way, since Garnet was executed. He had been living in hiding for twenty years, using aliases including Farmer, apparently alluded to in the Porter's "Here's a farmer, that hang'd himself on th'expectation of plenty". This chimes with the words of Lady Macduff and her son in the grim scene leading to their deaths, as she defines a traitor as "one that swears, and lies" (4.2.50). These, and many other points of relevance surrounding the executions of the Gunpowder plotters to *Macbeth*, are advanced by Henry N. Paul in *The Royal Play of Macbeth* (1950).

Taking all the definitions together, the argument in the first four chapters of this book has led to the point of claiming that every significant character in the play is an "equivocator". The Thane of Cawdor's death is represented as at odds with the way he lived his life. Duncan may be "mild", but his regal office is the source of extreme violence and civil war. Malcolm, his son, is inscrutably contradictory in claiming and then denying that he will be a far worse tyrant than Macbeth, to which Macduff replies, "Such welcome and unwelcome things at once / 'Tis hard to reconcile" (4.3.139-40). (One point behind this puzzling scene may be that all men are subject to temptation – and Malcolm is also in a sense tempting Macduff in his "false-speaking" [4.3.131] – but equally that resistance to evil is also available to all.) Banquo never reveals his true ambitions but it is clear that he is colluding with Macbeth's crime when he knows that Macbeth "hath play'dst most foully for [the crown]" (3.1.3) and yet remains silent – and we know also that he has a grim fascination in the prophecy that his issue will be kings. Macduff spends much of his time in the play in the modern state of equivocation, wavering between alternative actions. Even characters like Ross and Lennox are, in less significant and less blameworthy ways, inadvertent equivocators, for they first serve and then betray Macbeth as king. Macbeth himself equivocates in

5 Leading Ideas - Temptation, Equivocation, Evil

several senses, ranging from treachery to indecisiveness and a kind of impenitent remorse. Lady Macbeth at the very least acts hypocritically towards Duncan and the banqueters, maintaining an image of the perfect hostess while concealing her guilt. The Witches "hover" with "double" meanings, neither one thing nor its opposite, morally and physically ambiguous, equivocating between the present and the future.

All this is underpinned by a strain of imagery throughout *Macbeth* focused on the face as an unreliable signifier of truth and of emotional states. The play gives us Shakespeare's most systematic account or even theory of the significance of facial gestures; recurrently he implies that motivations behind expressions are unknowable and that at best the face is an unreliable signifier – it may be a mask, a surface, a "dial", or a disguise. What is significant is the way the viewer interprets or constructs meaning out of semblance, due to his or her own emotional state ("this is the very painting of your fear"). The extreme is when the viewer "sees" a face that is not there at all but is wholly a projection of (in this case) a guilty conscience – the apparition of Banquo's hideous face that only Macbeth sees – a highly meaningful signifier but visible to one person only. The implication, as in other aspects of the play's design, is that the visible is neutral and becomes meaningful only in the interpretive viewer's imagination.

The first to notice that equivocation can be facial is Duncan, who is bewildered by the treachery and later apparent sincerity of repentance in the Thane of Cawdor: "There's no art / To find the mind's construction in the face" (1.4.11-12). The second comes as a kind of echo to Duncan's words, as advice from Lady Macbeth to her husband:

> Your face, my thane, is as a book where men
> May read strange matters. To beguile the time,
> Look like the time; bear welcome in your eye,
> Your hand, your tongue; look like the innocent flower,
> But be the serpent under't. (1.5.61-5)

Her lesson is reinforced later by Macbeth himself: "Away, and mock the time with fairest show: / False face must hide what the false heart doth know" (1.7.82-3), and in his resolution to "make our faces vizards to our hearts, / Disguising what they are" (3.2.33-4). However, he is unable consistently to dissemble, and is reproved by Lady Macbeth for his inability to "make such faces" (3.4.66) on seeing the ghost of Banquo. There are other references to faces in *Macbeth* which invite further exploration, but these ones provide more evidence of the tight fit between imagery and concept that marks Shakespeare's poetic drama.

If, as seems inevitable, almost all characters in *Macbeth* are inescapably compromised in equivocation of one sort or another, and if the play is built upon a riddling and inconclusive ambivalence, then we can at least isolate the true source of conflict. The existence of the throne – the impersonal and depersonalising symbol of ultimate power in the state – has literally caused regicide, tyranny and murder. Like alcohol in the Porter's jokes, it provokes service but also takes it away by inviting treachery; it rewards ambition by promoting those who prove themselves in bloody battle, and yet its occupant has much to fear from ruthless people. The ultimate, inscrutably double equivocator, and the cause of equivocation in others, is the crown, and always, in the words of another play, "uneasy lies the head that wears the crown" (*2 Henry IV*, 3.1.31). We can conclude, then, by upturning the conventional reading of the play as a parable showing the evils of disobedience and the dangers of personal ambition, by saying that the play is at the very least radically ambivalent and equivocating, and that it can be read just as convincingly as a parable showing the evils of power vested in one person, and the dangers it poses for social life and communities by its mere existence.

Evil

Many treatises on evil have been written in branches of philosophy, religion and other fields. Murder with intent and genocide are usually assumed to be the ultimate examples of evil as actions demanding the strongest possible moral condemnation and legal sanctions. *Macbeth* is generally regarded as a major, imaginative exploration of evil – among the most profound treatments in literature. But it also suggests some ambivalence inherent in the subject of evil, just as much else in the play is ambivalent. There is, for example, an initial question which

5 Leading Ideas - Temptation, Equivocation, Evil

brings some problems into focus. The play begins with a very clear example of murder when Macbeth and Banquo kill in battle, and far from these actions being condemned as evil, they are regarded as cause for congratulations and promotion. Likewise, at the end there is an equally brutal murder, albeit offstage, when Macbeth is killed and decapitated, but once again this is hailed as cause for jubilation rather than opprobrium. It is, however, what happens in the middle of the play, the murders of Duncan, Banquo, and Macduff's family, which are held to be truly evil, by characters and audiences alike. In at least this sense, whether or not the very same action is evil seems at the very least to be not such an absolute as would first appear, but relative to other considerations. G. Wilson Knight calls his chapter on the play "*Macbeth* and the Metaphysic of Evil", and says "this evil, being absolute …" (Knight 1949). But is it? A.C. Bradley suggests that even among Shakespearean characters, evil need not be the same thing: "Evil, again, though it shows in *Macbeth* a prodigious energy, is not the icy or stony inhumanity of Iago or Goneril; and as in *Hamlet* it is pursued by remorse" (Bradley 1904: 331). Coleridge, musing about Iago, also casts doubt on whether it is necessary even to have a particular intention, motive or state of mind (the law calls it *mens rea*) to do evil, and coined the resonant phrase "the motive-hunting of a motiveless malignity" (Bate 1992: 485) to describe the various treatments of Iago's actions, suggesting he saw evil as neither absolute nor unambiguous.

A related question is whether only individual human beings can do evil, or if nature and its agents ("weyward sisters" who appear and disappear like bubbles of the earth), or man-made institutions (such as monarchy) can be inherently evil insofar as they incite evil deeds, even if in themselves they lack apparent motivation for wrongdoing. Even more abstractly, can a concept or ideology be inherently evil, since fascism and Nazism led to the holocaust, and racial hatred and supremacism have led to murder, genocide and "ethnic cleansing"? This brief discussion can only scratch the surface of such profound issues, in a necessarily selective way, but at least it should cast some doubt on any easy conclusions about the nature of evil in a play where we have a criminal as hero.

To what extent can Macbeth be described as evil, and what is Shakespeare's vision of evil in the play? The terribly sad fact of

Macbeth's mercurial and blighted "career" is that he was so completely unfitted to play the role that history (fate, *wyrd*, the Weyward Sisters) prophesied for him. Everything we hear and see of him initially is favourable, in terms of his profession as soldier and as one deserving respect. He displays courage in battle, loyalty to his leader, the heightened imagination of a poet, and a conscience capable of resisting temptation. He seems initially to have little or no personal ambition and knows his place as a retainer of the king. In his profession as soldier he is licensed to kill without remorse, but otherwise he appears to be temperamentally indecisive and not prone to self-advancement. Although earlier critics imputed to him overweening ambition, if we accept Alison Hobgood's excellent account (2013), Macbeth is afflicted with something like its opposite: fear, which Hobgood shows was accepted as both a physical and mental ailment in Shakespeare's time, its modern equivalent perhaps being chronic and crippling anxiety. Working from contemporary medical models based on Galen, Hobgood concludes that he suffers from "fear-sickness", and that it is a state which is contagious and can spread to others, both within the play and through the at-risk audience. (The argument concerning audience "contagion" may need more buttressing, since some of the evidence Hobgood presents comes from "anti-theatrical" critics who were predisposed to believe that drama would incite rebellion; by contrast, Forman's eyewitness account of *Macbeth* on stage gives no hint of fear in the audience.) The word "fear" runs through the play at a breathless rate. Right at the beginning Banquo questions Macbeth as to why he would "seem to fear / Things that do sound so fair?' (1.3.49); Macbeth himself finds his heart knocking at his ribs as "Present fears / Are less than horrible imaginings" (1.3.136-7). His wife points out, "… that which rather thou dost fear to do / Than wishes to be undone" (1.5.23-4), accuses him of fearing "a painted devil" (2.2.53), and in her sleep-talking recalls, "Fie, my lord, fie, a soldier and afeard?" (5.1.35). Macbeth gives voice to his "fear" of Banquo alive, and of his ghost when dead. It is not until very late in the play (5.3) that he claims to relinquish fear in new-found bravado, but on quite the wrong grounds, assuming that Birnam Wood will never come to Dunsinane and that no man exists who was not born of woman. The question raises itself, then,

5 Leading Ideas - Temptation, Equivocation, Evil

how can such an emphatically fearful man be described as evil, or be induced to carry out evil acts?

A conservative, moralistic reading of the play might argue that there are always bad men who will opportunistically kill good kings for personal gain, and that bearing guilt they will themselves rule as tyrants and eventually face their fate. But where are the premonitions in the play that Macbeth is a bad man? Shakespeare seems to have gone out of his way to avoid showing him as an evil person although he does evil acts, unlike, for example, Richard III and Iago, who arguably are evil men. The factors that catapult Macbeth into power are an amalgam of luck, coincidence, temptation, precipitate speed that gives little time for reflection, and whatever is represented by the misguided supportiveness or pressure of his wife and the suggestibility of the Witches. The terrible revelation of this play is that a perfectly ordinary man, who is in some ways weak and uncorrupted, is capable of killing to attain power, and then of vicariously killing again and again to retain power. When we ask "why does such a man as Macbeth do evil actions to get and hold power?", one answer might be, "because power exists", because there is a throne and a crown which incite men to kill for it. The logic is a little like that of Edmund Hillary who, when asked why he climbed Mount Everest, is said to have answered "because it was there"; axiomatically, if it had not been there he would not have been drawn to climb it. The question is constantly raised in Shakespeare's history plays: why do men routinely kill for the throne? The answer seems to be, because it is there. It provides a sometimes irresistible challenge and incitement to those who seek power, an aspiration which in itself is not necessarily an evil impulse (if it were, very few politicians would wish to be a president or prime minister, and the exceptions would be the very people considered unsuitable for such offices). Men may become alienated from their own humanity, their "better selves", and do things which are "out of character" when faced with the possibility of gaining worldly power. In this consideration, Macbeth's initial readiness to elide his human qualities with the professional necessities of a trained soldier, to subsume even human fear in the trappings of his occupation, are worrying forecasts. The radical ambivalence of the play as a whole lies in the fact that it can equally plausibly be enacted as monarchist propaganda against regicide and tyranny, or as its opposite, subversion of the notion of absolute monarchy as an inherently destabilising and alienating institution that invites challenges from those who feel for one reason or another entitled to the office. By recognising the latter possibility we see in the play a more deeply moral experience, which, like the movies of Alfred Hitchcock, takes us into the mind of a wrongdoer and forces us to travel his journey into territory of undoubted evil.

There are, of course, deeper questions to be asked about apparently "good" people who do evil deeds, and both religious and secular thinkers have perennially wrestled with these. So, it appears, did Shakespeare. We may extend consideration to a range of characters such as the Duke of Cornwall in *King Lear*, Goneril and Regan and Edmund in the same play, and Claudius in *Hamlet*, but for the sake of analysis we may concentrate on three figures in particular, who represent prototypes. The first need not detain us since he exists in a comedy where events are safely rescued from his malevolence. Don John in *Much Ado About Nothing* is a character type recognisable from comic traditions as the "malcontent", or in his own phrase, "a plain-dealing villain" who, if he were not "muzzled" by social conventions would happily wreak havoc on others in incorrigible fashion: "If I had my mouth I would bite. If I had my liberty I would do my liking. In the mean time, let me be that I am, and seek not to alter me" (1.3.33-4). Since he works surreptitiously through slander, Don John's character type led on to Iago in *Othello*, who has provoked as many discussions of evil as Macbeth. Coleridge's phrase "motiveless malignity" suggests that, like Don John but more dangerously concealed from view, Iago is "naturally" or "essentially" evil, not tempted as Macbeth is, but determined from the outset to cause harm. There are some problems with this approach, since Iago does in fact express a range of "motives", in fact too many to be able to dismiss him as simply "a plain-dealing villain": hatred for Othello, who has passed over Iago for Cassio as his lieutenant; hatred for Cassio for the same reason; an apparently unfounded jealousy of Othello, thinking he has slept with Iago's wife; envy of Othello for his marriage to Desdemona; and his promise to help Roderigo in pursuing Desdemona. If he is fuelled by one emotion over others, it is jealousy, which he skilfully transfers to Othello in an example of emotional contagion. The targets and tactics of his evil

5 Leading Ideas - Temptation, Equivocation, Evil

seem to be chosen more by chance and opportunity than by forward planning or controlled plotting. The third of Shakespeare's prototypes is the Duke of Gloucester, who systematically murders his way with malicious delight to the throne in *3 Henry VI* and *Richard III*. It is he who most clearly represents the kind of evil perpetrated by a man who, unlike Macbeth, is without moral scruples and needs no temptation in seeking power because he sees it as his legitimate right. Given the unending violence in the world he inhabits, all of which stems from power struggles over political succession, Richard simply accepts, clarifies and exploits the potential for evil already invited by the institution of monarchy. In this rogue's gallery of evil prototypes Macbeth does not seem to belong, given his conscience, congenital fear, and resistance to temptation. And what of Lady Macbeth, who seems no "plain-dealing villain" nor one driven by "motiveless malignity", but instead one whose devotion and support for her husband resembles his own unquestioning professional assumption that his office as soldier overrides scruples of killing? She too is no doubt led on by the existence of the role of queen, but just as strongly by her role as loyal wife.

The capacity in both protagonists to alienate humane feelings in pursuing an impersonal office suggests another approach to illuminate the kind of evil at work in *Macbeth*. In coining the phrase "the banality of evil", Hannah Arendt (1963) referred to deeds carried out by men who accepted unquestioningly the authoritarian structures on which their political existence was based and predicated. Arendt constructed her theory by studying the behaviour of Adolf Eichmann in his prosecution for genocide of the Jews in Germany, and his apparent lack of remorse or even understanding since he was "just obeying orders". All the Nazi officers in the Nuremberg trials depended on such a defence, but it was Eichmann who showed the most consistent lack of empathy for the victims. Interestingly, Arendt even draws on Shakespeare for her analysis, though asserting contrast rather than similarity:

> When I speak of the banality of evil, I do so only on the strictly factual level, pointing to a phenomenon which stared one in the face at the trial. Eichmann was not Iago and not Macbeth, and nothing would have been farther from his mind than to determine with

Richard III "to prove a villain." He merely, to put the matter colloquially, never realized what he was doing. (Arendt 1963: 287; quoted in Curthoys 2014: 26)

Arendt distances the Shakespearean villains no doubt because each of these characters did have a desire to cause evil of some kind, whereas the argument runs that Eichmann did not. Macbeth could also be said to have, at least initially, a conscience telling him the difference between right and wrong, which again Eichmann seems not to have had. However, there are some parallels to be drawn in that both Macbeth and to a greater extent Lady Macbeth persuade themselves to regard the Witches' prophecies as something akin to a command which must be obeyed, and that given the existence of a power structure they are legitimised in seeking it by violent means. Macbeth as a soldier also accepts his wife's persuasions with the immediacy of following a military command presented as a test of his masculinity: "When you durst do it, then you were a man; / And, to be more than what you were, you would / Be so much more the man" (1.7.49-51). Later, and further down the chain of command, Macbeth uses the same strategy in issuing orders for the murder of Banquo to the two hired assassins:

> Now, if you have a station in the file,
> Not i' th' worst rank of manhood, say 't;
> And I will put that business in your bosoms
> Whose execution takes your enemy off. (3.1.103-06)

The choice of language demonstrated in "station in the file", "rank", "business", and "enemy" inadvertently reveals Macbeth's continuing reliance on a military model in his thinking, where orders are issued and obeyed.

All-important in this didactic scheme is Shakespeare's presentation of innocent victims who suffer most in the world we have been observing, a world in which men may be led to violate natural law to such an extent that they cease to be men. This is explicitly raised in *Macbeth*, first by Macbeth in conversation with his wife when he decides against murdering the king:

5 Leading Ideas - Temptation, Equivocation, Evil

> Prithee, peace:
> I dare do all that may become a man;
> Who dares do more is none. (1.7.45-7)

The sense of "a man" he uses here is clearly "humanity" or "mankind", and turns on the central concept of natural law (*lex naturale*), derived mainly from classical texts and Aquinas. Eternal law is an unwritten but universal and innate moral construct which was said to outweigh man-made or "positive" law, to the extent that if the latter contravenes the former then it is no law at all, as both Augustine and Sir William Blackstone clarified. At its heart was a belief that the primary drive through "right reason" for every species is survival of its own, and this impels people to follow virtue and shun vice, to follow what "ought to be" rather than "what is", asserting "the underlying integrity of all nature inclining to the Natural Law which prescribes to each thing its purpose and fulfilment" (Wilks 1990: 125). Theologians in the Renaissance linked it with conscience, while it can also be used as a justification for "poetic justice" in literature, where the good are rewarded and the bad punished (White 1996). Murder is self-evidently against the natural law of preservation of life, and this is the initial conclusion Macbeth had reached in the soliloquy in which he thinks of himself as Duncan's kinsman, subject, host, and even protector (1.7.12-16). Lady Macbeth, however, picks up a different sense of Macbeth's words, that what "may become a man" is what distinguishes humans from animals:

> What beast was't, then,
> That made you break this enterprise to me?
> When you durst do it, then you were a man;
> And, to be more than what you were, you would
> Be so much more the man. Nor time nor place
> Did then adhere, and yet you would make both.
> They have made themselves, and that their fitness now
> Does unmake you. (1.7.47-54)

She is demonstrably wrong, however, in changing her husband's logic at this point and arguing from a positive law basis that he should do what he has "sworn" to do (a proposition which is doubtful in itself since it is not clear that Macbeth has "so sworn" to do anything), and follows up with the infamous statement that every Renaissance audience would proclaim as against natural law:

> I have given suck, and know
> How tender 'tis to love the babe that milks me.
> I would, while it was smiling in my face,
> Have plucked my nipple from his boneless gums
> And dash'd the brains out, had I so sworn
> As you have done to this. (1.7.54-9)

She also introduces a gender consideration, that "being a man" and behaving like one is a specifically masculine quality, and if he flinches from the plan to murder then he is effeminate. It is the realisation of her earlier fear about her husband, "Yet do I fear thy nature. / It is too full o'th' milk of human kindness / To catch the nearest way" (1.5.15-17). But her words are juxtaposed in the play with Lady Macduff's later assertion of a principle of femininity which is consistent with dictates of natural law – that the primary obligation of human beings, most acutely known by mothers, is to preserve and protect their children. However, Macbeth allows himself to be persuaded by his wife's forceful rhetoric, sidetracked from his initial natural law premise by the taunt that he is "cowardly". It is the moment when he clearly denies conscience and reason, and the consequences of his decision for both are profound and disastrous.

Further evidence of the corruption in Macbeth's thinking comes after "the Fall" when he tries to shore up his power by the murder of Banquo and Fleance. In commissioning the murderers, he draws not on natural law but on a different model of "law of nature", anticipating both Hobbes and Darwin in suggesting that each species is involved in intra-species conflict where it may be necessary to kill or be killed:

5 Leading Ideas - Temptation, Equivocation, Evil

FIRST MURDERER
We are men, my liege.
MACBETH
Ay, in the catalogue ye go for men,
As hounds and greyhounds, mongrels, spaniels, curs,
Shoughs, water-rugs and demi-wolves are clept
All by the name of dogs. The valued file
Distinguishes the swift, the slow, the subtle,
The housekeeper, the hunter, every one
According to the gift which bounteous nature
Hath in him closed; whereby he does receive
Particular addition, from the bill
That writes them all alike. And so of men.
Now, if you have a station in the file,
Not i' th' worst rank of manhood, say 't,
And I will put that business in your bosoms
Whose execution takes your enemy off,
Grapples you to the heart and love of us,
Who wear our health but sickly in his life,
Which in his death were perfect.
SECOND MURDERER
I am one, my liege,
Whom the vile blows and buffets of the world
Have so incensed that I am reckless what
I do to spite the world.
FIRST MURDERER
And I another
So weary with disasters, tugged with fortune,
That I would set my lie on any chance,
To mend it or be rid on't. (3.1.90-114)

Macbeth's reasoning allows him to exploit an impulse to revenge, using the grievance the desperate men have against Banquo (or more likely have been persuaded by Macbeth to hold against him) to overcome any scruples they may have about being members of the human race. At the same time Shakespeare, with his unerring dialectical mode of thinking, envisages the possibility that these men are not innately evil but shaped by unjust adversities which have embittered them.

The general issue of violence in art is relevant to the discussion of portraying and witnessing evil in a play. It is often said that violence in films or books should be banned. If this were to become universal policy, *Macbeth* would be one of the first scripts to go. However, depicting evil is not the same thing as endorsing it, especially in a work of art and the imagination where there is a general context that may provide a guiding moral control. In *Macbeth*, Shakespeare in an audaciously paradoxical move makes empathy the central issue for both characters and audiences. He takes us first inside the murderers' consciousnesses, to empathise with their feelings and reasoning as they contemplate committing a violent crime. In order to do so, the dramatist unmoors us from ways of too easily and too adversely judging what is fair and what is foul about their conduct. He then shows the central character exercising his own capacity for empathy by visualising the horror of the act of murder and realising that the victim is owed hospitality and obligations of kinship. It is partly the lack of such empathy in Lady Macbeth's functional approach that allows Macbeth to distance his actions, and partly also the historical determinism implicit in the Witches' prophecy. The murder takes place offstage, since Shakespeare wants the audience not to invest their sympathy in the dying victim but to keep us for the time being focused on the criminals' dawning emotional state after the event, which continues until after the banquet scene. However, the dramatist then decisively detaches us from the murderers by allowing several scenes to pass without our seeing the Macbeths at all while their regime proceeds towards impersonal tyranny. With devastating power, the scene of the killing of Macduff's family enables us to find our moral perspectives and begin to condemn the villains, even with a prior understanding of their value systems. The switch is rather like that of a novelist beginning with first person narration then abruptly changing to third person. In short, if ever we have "sympathy" for Macbeth and Lady Macbeth, the play does not allow us to stay on this level, but forces us to stand back, judge and condemn, while humbly acknowledging that we too have for a time inhabited murderers' minds, and as in Dostoyevsky's *Crime and Punishment*, we know what it feels like from the inside. Violence is morally contained and finally condemned, but no complacency about its roots in human behaviour is allowed. Furthermore, the radical ambivalence of the play at every level suggests that power itself has an intimate and sinister link with violence: "the golden round" of the crown leads men and women to murder; while hardly absolving them, it can plausibly explain their actions. Shakespeare subtly presents a critique of power and authority as potentially open to abuse and tyranny, and allows us not to be seduced into simple moral judgements or condemnation. *Macbeth* allows us to see violence and the aspiration to power as linked, in complex and sometimes dangerous ways. Shakespeare's treatment of violence is morally contained and educative, a condemnation of, not an incitement to, evil.

6
"This is the very painting of your fear": Imagery and the Emotional World of *Macbeth*

The study of imagery was once a central area of analysis in literature in general and Shakespeare in particular. However, with the rise since the 1980s of theory-driven concentration on themes like politics, gender, and cultural identities, this aspect of the local texture of works of literature has been neglected. For example, in the entire 2758 pages of the apparently exhaustive *Norton Anthology of Theory and Criticism* published in 2010, the word "imagery" occurs only once, in an essay, and not at all in the commentary. It may also be symptomatic that in Emma Smith's edited volume on tragedy in the Blackwells Guides to Criticism series (Smith 2004), there are sections on genre, character, language, gender and sexuality, and history and politics, but none on imagery, and nor does the word figure at all in the index. However, the study of imagery deserves resurrection, since it is central to the power of Shakespearean drama, complementing and enriching the design and effects and establishing emotional content in sometimes unconscious or barely conscious ways. Contemplation of just two lines which open *Richard III* reveals that the meaning is expressed metaphorically and advanced through images rather than logic: "Now is the winter of our discontent / Made glorious summer by this son of York" (1.1.1-2). The meaning proceeds by contrasting winter and summer, discontent and glory, and by a pun on "sun" and "son". Without at least unconsciously assimilating this we lose the all-important, politically manipulative tone of the rhetoric, as used by a persuasive politician pretending he rejoices in the coronation of a new king even as he plots himself to take the crown. There are as many figurative passages and underlying visual patterns in *Richard III* as in *Macbeth*, and in the latter they contribute to its singularly powerful atmosphere of palpable, all-encompassing fear. More than this, close inspection reveals an extraordinarily dense and rich tapestry of imagery which is capable of subliminally guiding our emotional responses moment by moment, as well as suggesting broader frames of reference against which we interpret the action, placing the play in broader contexts. Macbeth himself, some critics have observed, is perhaps Shakespeare's greatest poet among his characters, an impression derived from the compelling vividness of his imagination and the way in which he characteristically "thinks" and expresses himself through metaphors rather than logical speech. In an especially acute sense, *Macbeth* is a play built upon imagery, real and imagined, in its enhanced atmosphere and emotional expressiveness.

Nowadays we may underestimate how visual were Elizabethans' imaginations, apparently attuned to expressing themselves through what Sir Philip Sidney in *The Defence of Poetry* called "speaking pictures". Emblem books in which pictures represented and reinforced moral lessons were common. In churches, stories from the Bible were illustrated with minimal text in vernacular English on the walls in *biblia pauperum* or "bibles of the poor". Moreover, using imagery to convey feelings was considered a crucial skill for the orator and, by association, the writer. Quintilian, a Roman rhetorician whose *Institutes of Oratory* (*Institutio Oratoria*) were revived in the Renaissance and well known to writers such as Petrarch, Erasmus and Ben Jonson, deals with imagery. To some extent he was drawing on works by Cicero, who was even better known. In Book 6, Chapter 2 of the *Institutes*, Quintilian extols the use of "*visions*, whereby things absent are presented to our imagination with such extreme vividness that they seem actually to be before our eyes" as the most powerful appeal to the emotions possible (Quintilian 1920-22: 433), relevant in every part of a speech, and particularly in the peroration, where it is crucial to affect the feelings: "Whoever shall best conceive such images will have the greatest power over the emotions" (433). He gives the example of reporting a murder in such a way that the judge will have a "'mental view' of the event":

6 Imagery and the Emotional World of *Macbeth*

> From such impressions arises that *enargaia* which Cicero calls *illumination* and *actuality*, which makes us seem not so much to narrate as to exhibit the actual scene, while our emotions will be no less actively stirred than if we were present at the actual occurrence. (435)

This must have been music to the ears of the poet Shakespeare, whose plays stir emotional effects through their poetic deployment of imagery.

In addition, however, there is an important, theatre-centred reason for the imagery-rich poetry of Shakespeare's plays, and it is apt to be overlooked today since movies can visually show landscape, for example, in naturalistic forms, without the need for description. On the bare boards of the Elizabethan stage, open to the elements, there would literally be no way for the audience to know a play's setting without the benefit of Shakespeare's descriptive language, his "speaking pictures". Within a few lines we have crucial, verbal evidence for us to know that *The Tempest* begins with a shipwreck, *Othello* in the darkness of night outside Brabantio's house, *Hamlet* again at night, this time on the battlements of a castle, and *Macbeth* in stormy weather which limits visibility, on a heath near a place where a battle has been raging. When his plays are turned into movies which can give us immediate "ocular proof" without the need for explanation, Shakespeare's poetic descriptions can seem redundant and are shortened or dropped. If we can be *shown* sights and sounds with our eyes, we do not need so graphically to be *told* what to see and hear in what Hamlet calls the "mind's eye". In some ways this might downplay the evocative, poetic descriptions by Shakespeare, such as the sunset described with some incongruity by the hardened First and Third Murderers:

> FIRST MURDERER
> The west yet glimmers with some streaks of day.
> Now spurs the lated traveller apace
> To gain the timely inn, and near approaches
> The subject of our watch.
> THIRD MURDERER
> Hark! I hear horses. (3.4.5-9)

Otherwise inconsequential characters are sometimes given these kinds of descriptions which establish time and atmosphere, for example the Old Man in *Macbeth* who marks an unusually bleak and ominous daybreak after a "sore night": "By the clock 'tis day, / And yet dark night strangles the travelling lamp" (2.4.6-7); although obviously major characters also contribute, as in Lady Macbeth's "I heard the owl scream and the crickets cry" (2.2.15). Such local colour may sometimes be conspicuously superfluous to the plot and action, but it is part of Shakespeare's signature in capturing rich effects in the intimacy of the moment.

To Shakespeare, and more broadly to his contemporaries, the word-painting was fundamental to the illusions created by drama itself, and necessary to the stage business, since without it the narrative would be little more than functional and denuded of ambience and atmosphere. One extremely strange example from *King Lear* shows that Shakespeare was well aware of the sheer power of his imagery and could even daringly draw attention to a logic of emotion and imagination that overrides rational thought. Through words alone, Edgar convinces his father, and initially at least the audience, that he stands on the very edge of Dover Cliff looking down to the beach far below. He then switches perspective to describe the same scene from the beach, pretending to look up at the cliff-top from which Gloucester believes he has fallen. We gradually become aware, however, that Edgar is playing a trick on his father and that they are not on the cliff edge nor are they on the beach. In fact in this case we do not know where they are except a flat place outside, and throughout the dislocating sequence all the Elizabethan audience would actually see is a flat, bare, wooden stage. It is interesting to see modern directors wrestling with what to do with this strange set of verbally induced illusions, given the technological possibilities available now and audience expectations that we should be able to "see" what the play is "saying". Another odd moment comes in *Macbeth* when the protagonist asks "Is this a dagger which I see before me, The handle toward my hand?" He concludes it is a "fatal vision / Sensible to feeling as to thought" and "A Dagger of the mind, a false creation" (2.1.33-8), which must leave the audience perplexed, making the effect deeply ambiguous – is there something there, or is it just a creation of words? The uncertainty hangs over each play as a whole, full as they are of "shadows" created by a poet with words alone. In another

6 Imagery and the Emotional World of *Macbeth*

play, *As You Like It*, the main action takes place in a forest, and again the original audience would not know this without the play telling us. Rosalind, speaking for the playwright in an epilogue, boasts "my way is to conjure you" (Epilogue, 9), and in all cases it is the dramatist whose word magic has been conjuring the audience and reader, persuading us through language alone that we can "see" certain landscapes, belying the evidence of the eyes. In *Henry V*, the Prologue, again speaking for the playwright, apologises to the audience for the paucity of visual stimuli "Within this wooden O", and promises "On your imaginary forces [to] work" so long as the audience will reciprocate: "Piece out our imperfections with your thoughts" (Prologue, 13, 18, 23). Descriptive poetry, and imagery in general, is fundamental to Shakespeare's art in ways that are not self-evident today, and its significance extends beyond the visual to the creation of atmosphere, manipulation of the audience through illusion, to consolidate thematic and emotional issues.

The critical school most alert to imagery in literature prevailed in the mid-twentieth century as New Criticism, consisting significantly of critics who were also poets – Mark van Doren (who taught John Berryman, Allen Ginsburg and Jack Kerouac), William Empson, Allen Tate, Robert Penn Warren, I.A. Richards, John Crowe Ransom – and academic critics who moved in poetic circles (Cleanth Brooks, Reuben Brower, W.K. Wimsatt, Ronald Crane, Wayne C. Booth). Because of their close links with the world of practising poets, they tended to follow assumptions of predecessors like A.C. Bradley and G. Wilson Knight who focused on imagery, and L.C. Knights who asserted that "a Shakespeare play is a dramatic poem" (Knights 1946: 16) rather than primarily an evocation of character. It is also symptomatic that most of these critics gave just as much attention to Shakespeare's sonnets as to his plays, recognising that both are essentially poetic constructions. These critics' main preoccupation was identifying unity in literary works, extending this to incorporate the contribution which metaphors, symbols and images make to the effect of the whole, and asserting that particularity, even if it is based on ambiguity, rather than abstract theories, is the starting point for reading with emotional understanding. Their great predecessor was Samuel Taylor Coleridge, another poet, who was among the first to probe into Shakespeare's imagery as a clue to emotional effects and unity of vision in the works.

A backlash may have followed among critics who considered internal contradictions and *lacunae* to be more critically interesting than assumptions of unity, and found historical and cultural contexts to be more revealing of meaning than rhetorical surfaces. But it is not necessary to think in terms of exclusive critical binaries, but instead to accept that each critical school has something to offer in interpreting texts. In this case I hope the analysis complements that in Chapter 5, revealing both congruities and incongruities in the texture of *Macbeth*, adding up to a unity which incorporates functional discordances.

Macbeth in particular has an aura that transcends the sum of its parts. The very mention of the play's title evokes an ambience and mood constituent of and incorporating its imagery, character types, themes, language, ideas and world views, the unique "*Macbeth* universe" with a pervading atmosphere which is like no other. Like much of the play's design, the distinctiveness of this impression, on closer inspection, is seen to be created from internal clashes and disruptions which also define the whole. For all its dramatic unity, it contains fractures which contribute to the whole, even as mirroring ruptures between nature and humanity are enacted. A.C. Bradley spoke of the importance of the play's "general effect" and "atmosphere", pointing out that whereas the other tragedies open with conversations, "here the action bursts into wild life amidst the sounds of thunderstorm and the echoes of a distant battle ... Darkness, we may even say blackness, broods over this tragedy" (Bradley 1904: 332-3). G. Wilson Knight speaks of Shakespeare's plays as "spatial metaphors", advocating that "we should regard each play as a visionary whole, close-knit in personification, atmospheric suggestion, and direct poetic-symbolism" (Knight 1930: 11). However, in *Macbeth* we find that "the whole" – its unity – contains disunities, which contribute to its special and disturbing effect.

It may be no coincidence that the generation of image critics focused in particular on *Macbeth*, as a tacit acknowledgement that it is the most "poetic" of all Shakespeare's plays except – in some ways paradoxically – *Romeo and Juliet*. One by one, each critic identified a particular kind of recurring imagery or cluster of images. Caroline Spurgeon, a pioneer of imagery study in the twentieth century, noticed the ill-fitting clothes of Macbeth: "why do you dress me / In borrow'd robes?" (1.3.106-7), followed by Banquo drawing attention to "strange garments" which have not yet been worn in to fit the shape of the body, and several other references through to the end of the play. Angus verbalises: "Now does he feel his title / Hang loose about him, like a giant's robe / Upon a dwarfish thief" (5.2.20-2), clearly imagining a man promoted well beyond his ability. Ian McKellan played the role in conspicuously over-sized clothes. Spurgeon's work now seems dated because of her primary objective to find clues about Shakespeare's biography rather than seeing images within their dramatic context, but in this case her perception provides an insight into the play. In a more modern fashion, Wolfgang Clemen explored how images relate to other parts of a play and can illuminate the work as a whole, as if it is an organism with all parts interconnected. L.C. Knights followed another of Spurgeon's suggestions by exploring the frequent references to disease and sickness that afflict the body politic as well as characters. There are two doctors on hand in the play though the one is unable to cure Lady Macbeth's illness and the second merely reports the distant king of England's ability to cure "the evil" by touch. Cleanth Brooks fastens on "Pity, like a naked babe" as providing "the most powerful symbol in the tragedy" (Brooks 1947: 37), one that is simultaneously natural and supernatural, an image of helplessness and power, as a paradoxical evocation of the operation of conscience on the guilty mind. Once again, Brooks finds many substantiating and enriching references to children in the play (some noted elsewhere in this book), a perception perhaps too literally and single-mindedly visualised in the recent movie of the play by Justin Kurzel. More generally still, William Empson finds in *Macbeth* a host of lines – perhaps more than in other plays – exemplifying his suggestive notion, advanced in the brilliant *Seven Types of Ambiguity*, that the most complex poetry works by producing functional ambiguity of language which generates multiple meanings. This chimes with the theme of the present book – that ambiguity operates at all levels of the play. Empson teases out a remarkable range of ambiguities in passages of poetry in *Macbeth*, especially in those which often baffle critics since they seem almost incomprehensible, such as the one beginning "If it were done, when 'tis done / 'Twere well it were done quickly" (1.7.1-2), where Macbeth struggles to materialise the immaterial and understand the non-visual subject of time in visual terms.

Interestingly, these critics' preoccupation with imagery in *Macbeth* has found a different, more technical justification recently, as the work in which Shakespeare most extensively uses a rare rhetorical figure of speech drawn from his classical learning, *metalepsis*. Brian Cummings uses several speeches from this play to explain how the "extreme figurative complexity" works by piling up figures or images which have an emotional rather than rational or logical connectedness. The speeches are memorable but often virtually impossible to paraphrase because they set up "metaphors in chain with one another" as though each image gives birth to the next without causal sequence. One effect is that "The speaker shares with us a powerful sense of living on the edge, of life and reason under threat of collapse". It is this process which Cummings describes as *metalepsis*, a figure of speech available from ancient times in Quintilian but rarely used by Elizabethan writers – "a process of transition, doubling or ellipsis in figuration, of replacing a figure with another figure ..." (Cummings 2007: 219). The Elizabethan theorist Puttenham describes *metalepsis* as "strangely entangled" and resting on "farfet" (far-fetched) associations. The passages used for analysis by Cummings are the famous ones where we *feel* we understand but cannot explain the meaning in a logical sequence: "Tomorrow, and to-morrow, and to-morrow ..." (5.5.17ff); Lady Macbeth's "was the hope drunk / Wherein you dress'd yourself?" (1.7.35-6ff); "Present fears are less than horrible imaginings ... And nothing is but what is not" (1.3.137ff); "If it were done, when 'tis done ... We'd jump the life to come" (1.7.1ff). Significantly, it appears to have been Romantic poets in particular who, without necessarily using or even knowing the word *metalepsis*, seemed to understand the guiding idea. Coleridge comments in *Biographia Literaria* how imagery in Shakespeare's sonnets is linked not by logical thought but by emotional progression; and more vividly John Keats, describing Shakespeare as "the Whim King" and again focusing on the sonnets and the "whimsical" way the images spill out of each other describes the effect:

> I neer found so many beauties in the sonnets – they seem to be full of fine things said unintentionally – in the intensity of working out conceits – Is this to be borne? Hark ye!

6 Imagery and the Emotional World of *Macbeth*

> When lofty trees I see barren of leaves
> Which erst from heat did canopy the herd,
> And Summer's green all girded up in sheaves,
> Borne on the bier with white and bristly beard.
> (Keats 1958: 1. 188-9).

As in the passages from *Macbeth*, it is difficult to trace a logical order of thought here, but instead we find association of images, one leading to the next, which takes us from winter trees, to sheltering cattle, to harvested corn, and finally death through a pun on "bier" as both the plank on which the corn is carried and also a coffin. *Metalepsis* may be the technical word but the peculiarity of these Shakespearean usages is that we somehow understand them imaginatively and emotionally without actually understanding them rationally. Here is another from *Macbeth*, though it is not mentioned by Cummings. In its density of imagery it has more or less baffled editors attempting to explain the meaning:

> Now o'er the one half world
> Nature seems dead, and wicked dreams abuse
> The curtained sleep. Witchcraft celebrates
> Pale Hecate's offerings, and withered murder,
> Alarumed by his sentinel, the wolf,
> Whose howl's his watch, thus with his stealthy pace,
> With Tarquin's ravishing strides, towards his design
> Moves like a ghost. (2.1.49-56)

In the Oxford edition of the play, Nicholas Brooke takes thirty-eight lines of notes explaining individual words, but an overall paraphrase is elusive, while in the New Cambridge edition, A.R. Braunmuller takes thirty-seven lines, again without offering a satisfactory explanation of the overall meaning. Specific words are comprehensible or can be glossed in their local meanings, but the general sense is at most an impression, built up through images and metaphors that link tangentially, becoming images within images: darkness > dreams > sleep > witchcraft > Hecate (not necessarily the figure in the play) > murder > the wolf as murder's sentinel > wolf's howl > Tarquin the rapist of Lucrece > striding > goal > ghost. The condensed phrase "Tarquin's ravishing stride" imports an ominous memory of the context of Shakespeare's earlier poem *The Rape of Lucrece*. In teasing out the associative connections it is probably easiest to work backwards, treating the sentence as one of Milton's epic similes, asking "*what* moves like a ghost?" But even so, there is a truly impossible set of ambiguities which editors cannot explain and on which they disagree, the connection between the wolf, murder and Tarquin, yet it remains one of the greatest poetic passages in Shakespeare's works. It seems to attempt to describe an experience through a set of questions that hinge on "what is it *like*?" rather than "what does it *mean*?" or "what does each image *look like*?"; and as in the figure of *metalepsis* some of the links between metaphors are missed out as the sense "o'erleaps" itself. This happens in other tangled, obscure, but memorable passages by Macbeth, and it gives the impression of a mind racing beyond its capacity to process thoughts in any logical way. It is what happens verbally, for example, in the "When 'tis done" passage, as Macbeth wishes that the deed could be done without consequences and he could find himself on "the other side" of the event – "We'd jump the life to come" (1.7.7), as if a sentence could be begun and ended without a middle. More specifically, the "wolf" passage is prefaced and perhaps created by Macbeth "seeing" the illusory dagger and consciously debating whether it is "sensible to feeling as to sight" or alternatively a "fatal vision ... A dagger of the mind, a false creation / Proceeding from the heat-oppressed brain?" (2.1.34-50). He is aware of being in a visionary state, and no matter how much he resists, the power of "false creations" of the mind overrides consecutive thoughts. In other words, Macbeth exhibits throughout the state of mind and mode of expression of a poet, and a Romantic poet at that, like the Coleridge of "Kubla Khan" or Keats of "Ode to a Nightingale" (both of which show signs of indebtedness to *Macbeth*), and in the latter we recall specifically the key transition, "Was it a vision or a awaking dream?" All the rhetoricians had made it clear that *metalepsis* is an exclusively and even quintessentially poetic figure of speech, and it has no place in prose or advocacy, whose burden is carried by discursive argument. There is no other character in Shakespeare who speaks so consistently like a poet (except to a lesser extent Richard II), and it is somehow a daring choice of the dramatist to turn a poet into a murderer, a murderer into a poet, through the concentration on imagery as the dominant mode of thought.

Drunkenness

A curiously lateral link explaining the prevalence of *metalepsis* in this play might be the insistently recurrent imagery of drunkenness. The rhetorical figure can produce effects that resemble those of alcohol on the brain, as if a drunken but emotional person is trying hard to express some thought which will not quite come into focus through words constructed in a logical order. Liberated from control by conscious reasoning and logical thought processes, the imagination or unconscious mind comes to the fore, with a series of intensely realised but tumbling, barely connected pictures revealing feelings without syntactical connectives. This is not such a whimsical suggestion as it seems when we consider the prominence of drinking in the play. The imagery of banqueting begins innocently enough when Duncan praises Macbeth as a "peerless kinsman" in whose commendations, he says, "I am fed; / It is a banquet to me" (1.4.55). It becomes a little more specific and sinister when Lady Macbeth berates her husband for his indecisiveness: "Was the hope drunk / Wherein you dressed yourself? hath it slept since?" (1.7.35). Her reference may even give her the idea for fomenting her plan, which is literally saturated in intoxicating liquor, and depends on its predictable effects:

> We fail!
> But screw your courage to the sticking-place
> And we'll not fail. When Duncan is asleep –
> Whereto the rather shall his day's hard journey
> Soundly invite him – his two chamberlains
> Will I with wine and wassail so convince
> That memory, the warder of the brain,
> Shall be a fume, and the receipt of reason
> A limbeck only. When in swinish sleep
> Their drenched natures lie as in a death,

> What cannot you and I perform upon
> The unguarded Duncan? What not put upon
> His spongy officers, who shall bear the guilt
> Of our great quell? (1.7.61-72)

The plan works well, since Banquo reports to Macbeth that the king has retired to bed "in unusual pleasure" and has even given Lady Macbeth a valuable diamond in thanks for her hospitality (2.1.11-16), and we hear that the hapless chamberlains are dead drunk. Meanwhile, Lady Macbeth has not deprived herself: "That which hath made them drunk hath made me bold. / What hath quenched them hath given me fire" (2.2.1-2), and Macbeth proposes drinking on, ordering the servant, "Go bid thy mistress, when my drink is ready, / She strike upon the bell" (2.1.31-2). Everything suggests that this night's events, in the modern phrase, are alcohol-fuelled.

This brings us to the famous but problematical inset scene of the Porter's "morning after" rambling. Why is it there and what does it do to the emotional design of the play? After addressing a jaundiced soliloquy to the audience on traitors, equivocators and "all professions, that go the primrose way to th' everlasting bonfire" (2.3.20-1), the "porter of hell-gate" opens the gate to Macduff. The conversation turns explicitly to the party of the previous night and the effects of alcohol, before and after inebriation:

> MACDUFF
> Was it so late, friend, ere you went to bed,
> That you do lie so late?
> PORTER
> Faith sir, we were carousing till the second cock: and drink, sir, is a great provoker of three things.
> MACDUFF
> What three things does drink especially provoke?
> PORTER
> Marry, sir, nose-painting, sleep, and urine. Lechery, sir, it provokes, and unprovokes; it provokes the desire, but it takes away the

6 Imagery and the Emotional World of *Macbeth*

performance: therefore, much drink may be said to be an equivocator with lechery: it makes him, and it mars him; it sets him on, and it takes him off; it persuades him, and disheartens him; makes him stand to, and not stand to; in conclusion, equivocates him in a sleep, and, giving him the lie, leaves him.
MACDUFF
I believe drink gave thee the lie last night.
PORTER
That it did, sir, i' the very throat on me: but I requited him for his lie; and, I think, being too strong for him, though he took up my legs sometime, yet I made a shift to cast him. (2.3.21-40)

Usually explained as "comic relief", this cameo speech is somehow too seedy and emotionally mixed to be genuinely funny, and it is also more disturbingly apt to the situation in the play than a merely comic distraction from the serious business. A part of the effect was identified by Thomas de Quincey in his famous essay "On the Knocking on the Gate in *Macbeth*", which was written in the Romantic age but is still regarded as illuminating. He begins his account by exhorting readers "never to pay attention to his understanding, when it stands in opposition to any other faculty of his mind", an example being "intuitive knowledge". He says he regards the "knocking at the gate" scene as providing "a fresh proof that I was right in relying on my own feeling, in opposition to my understanding", finding a fuller, more imaginative awareness. He describes the "knocking on the gate" as marking the moment when a transitory suspension of time during which the murder is committed is now over and a healthy "reaction" has begun. It is "that moment when the suspension ceases, and the goings-on of human life are suddenly resumed ... the murderers are taken out of the region of human things, human purposes, human desires. They are transfigured" (Bate 1992: 433). The human heart returns after the "fiendish heart" has dominated. However, de Quincey's account addresses only the knocking sound marking the refreshing entrance from an outside world in the figure of Macduff, without explaining also the disquieting effect of the Porter's soliloquy, which makes the moment more ambiguous. It asks us to wonder whether the "goings-on of human life" are in reality all that honourable and admirable, if they amount only to a reminder of men treading "the primrose path" of corruption and the sleaziness of "nose-painting, sleep, and urine" along with the ups and downs of male "lechery". His groggy and inconsequential rambling does several things to the rhythm and perspective of the play which qualify de Quincey's positive response. After the hectic violence of the explosive night-time events, it slows the pace down to a point of near inertia; it conveys the amoral lassitude of a hangover on waking from drunken somnolence, with no more than a vague memory of what happened the night before; and the words "I pray you, remember the porter", addressed directly to the audience, lure us into recognising our own covert and uneasy alliance with the characters who committed murder and return with bloody hands. It turns on us a vestigial sense of recrimination that we have unquestioningly shared in the most shocking events imaginable, apparently transfixed and mesmerised by their theatrical contagion. By emphasising the effects of alcohol in suspending moral judgement and in providing the thrills and disappointments of unfulfilled sexual excitement, Shakespeare turns on us a shaming gaze, implying that in our fascinated suspension of judgement we have been impotent voyeurs to a truly shocking event, and that if anything we have responded to the perpetrators who are so much more intelligent and alive than the gross, unbuckled degenerate we now witness. If we laugh at the Porter's words, then it is we who are being judged and uneasily found morally wanting, in our recent intoxication with violence. At this point in the play we are placed alongside a man awaking from a sleep induced by drunkenness which "in conclusion, equivocates him in a sleep, and, giving him the lie, leaves him". Any relaxation after the taut tension is tinged with the shame which Ewan Fernie (2002) and Buckner Trawick (1978) have argued accompanies references to alcohol in Shakespeare's plays.

Light and Dark, the Natural World

Contrasts of darkness and light, night and day, provide an overarching and dominant image pattern in the play, as most commentators agree. The play begins with a stage direction, "Thunder and lightning", and the First Witch emphasises the visual impression: "When shall we three meet again, / In thunder, lightning, or in rain?" (1.1.1-2). On Shakespeare's stage there would have been at least a "thunder machine" for rolling a cannon ball down a wooden chute, but the lightning must have existed more in the words than in ocular evidence, the first of many examples of illusionary word-painting in the play. Elizabethan audiences were trained to trust the words as guides to what they were "seeing". Whether the performance was in broad daylight on a sunny afternoon or under a lowering grey sky in drizzling rain, to the auditors' imagination for a split second everything is either plunged into darkness or brilliantly lit in a static tableau through the evocative power of words; then clarity is gone and once again we are plunged into darkness. By the end of the short scene, the sudden juxtapositioning of light and darkness is elevated to a moral quality which problematises good and evil. Moral perception is confused and switches with terrifying speed from mode to mode, from good to evil and foul to fair, so quickly that we cannot tell the difference between them. Everything is "Double, double, toil and trouble" (4.1.10).

Imagery connecting and disconnecting the natural world and the human persists through the play. There is initially some logic to the hierarchy in nature: we are told that battle no more dismays Macbeth and Banquo than "sparrows eagles, or the hare the lion!" (1.1.35), but steadily the "thunder and lightning" announced in the first stage direction becomes a sign of persistently perverse events in nature:

> LENNOX
> The night has been unruly. Where we lay
> Our chimneys were blown down, and, as they say,
> Lamentings heard i'th' air; strange screams of death,
> And prophesying with accents terrible
> Of dire combustion and confused events
> New-hatched to th' woeful time. The obscure bird [owl]
> Clamoured the livelong night. Some say the earth
> Was feverous and did shake.
> MACBETH
> 'Twas a rough night. (2.3.53-60)

Others notice the way nature seems increasingly troubled by events in the human world:

OLD MAN
Threescore and ten I can remember well,
Within the volume of which time I have seen
Hours dreadful and things strange, but this sore night
Hath trifled former knowings.
ROSS
Ha, good father,
Thou seest, the heavens, as troubled with man's act,
Threaten his bloody stage. By th' clock, 'tis day,
And yet dark night strangles the travelling lamp.
Is't night's predominance or the day's shame
That darkness does the face of earth entomb
When living light should kiss it?
OLD MAN
'Tis unnatural,
Even like the deed that's done. On Tuesday last
A falcon, tow'ring in her pride of place,
Was by a mousing owl hawk'd at and killed.
ROSS
And Duncan's horses – a thing most strange and certain –
Beauteous and swift, the minions of their race,
Turned wild in nature, broke their stalls, flung out,
Contending 'gainst obedience, as they would
Make war with mankind. (2.4.1-20)

If the earth can be "feverous" like an organism and respond to human events, so can it spawn beings which appear to be human, as Banquo describes the Weird Sisters: "The earth hath bubbles as the water has, And these are of them" (1.3.77). Banquo asks the question which occurs to many in the play concerning the experience they are undergoing, "have we eaten on the insane root / That takes the reason prisoner?" (1.3.84-5), an unnerving and primal doubt which comes to infect the audience too, as we watch unfolding events in an increasingly "rapt" state. The Witches in particular seem especially associated with the animal world, mentioning (and using in their unpalatable recipes [de Sousa 2014]) animals, reptiles and rodents, and they are accompanied at one stage by a "spirit of a cat".

6 Imagery and the Emotional World of *Macbeth*

Imagery of birds in the passage above is sustained throughout the play, leading Alexander Leggatt to speak of "Shakespeare's own ornithological obsession in *Macbeth*" (quoted Leggatt 2006: 112; see also Spurgeon 1936: 73, 187-90), so insistent that it evokes Hitchcock's disturbing movie, *The Birds*, which seems to dwell on fear of alienated winged creatures attacking humanity. Some of the allusions indicate a topsy-turvy world where nature has been perverted, as when the mousing owl attacks the majestic falcon. There are five references to owls, including Lady Macbeth's "It was the owl that shrieked, the fatal bellman / Which gives the stern'st good night" (2.2.3-4), and her repeated, "I heard the owl and the crickets cry" (2.2.15-16). Lennox's descriptions of the "confused events" with his image of their being "new hatched" suggest imaginatively to him the owl which cannot easily be seen at night: "the obscure bird / Clamoured the live-long night" (2.3.59-60).

Alternatively, birds can stand for safety and nurturing in contrast to the treachery which is rife among humans. Duncan notices "the temple-haunting martlet" nesting around the Macbeths' castle, referring to the sight as a reassuring "procreant cradle" (1.6.8) of young life, and reflecting his own optimistic view. Lady Macbeth, by contrast, is predisposed to spot a more ominous bird associated with graveyards:

> The raven himself is hoarse
> That croaks the final entrance of Duncan
> Under my battlements. (1.5.37-9)

Her husband thinks also of funereal birds as evening approaches: "Light thickens, and the crow / Makes wing to the rooky wood" (3.3.51) and nocturnal, predatory creatures, "night's black agents to their preys do rouse" (3.3.54). Lady Macduff, we recall, speaks of the natural law that requires protection of the young for the survival of species when berating her husband:

> He wants the natural touch, for the poor wren,
> The most diminutive of birds, will fight,
> Her young ones in her nest, against the owl. (4.2.9-11)

To her frenzied question to her son in the belief that he is dead, "How will you live?", the innocent boy replies "as birds do, mother", to which she drily replies, "What, with worms and flies?" (4.2.31-3). The underlying train of thought in this case and in some others is that the world of creatures lives more in accordance with nature than men, or at least their responses are a recrimination to mankind. The murderer of the children sadistically displays the inhumanity by driving the imagery strand to its source in the beginning of life in the act of killing: "What, you egg? / Young fry of treachery!" (4.2.84-5).

If there is an emphasis upon unnatural reversals in the physical world, they also affect the human. Restful sleep, the harbinger of night-time, becomes a problem for Macbeth. Much to his wife's alarm and derision, he expresses his anxiety when he finds he cannot say the word "amen", which he links with prayers before bed:

> MACBETH
> One cried "God bless us" and "Amen" the other,
> As they had seen me with these hangman's hands.
> List'ning their fear I could not say "Amen"
> When they did say "God bless us!"
> LADY MACBETH
> Consider it not so deeply.
> MACBETH
> But wherefore could not I pronounce "Amen"?
> I had most need of blessing, and "Amen"
> Stuck in my throat.
> LADY MACBETH
> These deeds must not be thought
> After these ways. So, it will make us mad.
> MACBETH
> Methought I heard a voice cry "Sleep no more,
> Macbeth does murder sleep" – the innocent sleep,
> Sleep that knits up the ravelled sleave of care,
> The death of each day's life, sore labour's bath,
> Balm of hurt minds, great nature's second course,
> Chief nourisher in life's feast –

6 Imagery and the Emotional World of *Macbeth*

> LADY MACBETH
> What do you mean?
> MACBETH
> Still it cried "Sleep no more" to all the house,
> "Glamis hath murdered sleep, and therefore Cawdor
> Shall sleep no more; Macbeth shall sleep no more." (2.2.26-41)

It is difficult not to invest some sympathy in Macbeth at this point, so eloquent and terrified is his emotional state, expressing an almost childlike helplessness and yearning repetition of the word "sleep" seven times in less than ten lines. Lady Macbeth diagnoses him as being "brain-sickly" (2.2.43) and advises him to wash his hands of the blood while she goes to "gild" the grooms.

> LADY MACBETH
> You lack the season of all natures, sleep.
> MACBETH
> Come, we'll to sleep. My strange and self-abuse
> Is the initiate fear that wants hard use:
> We are yet but young in deed.

Insomnia continues to plague him for the rest of the play, and even when he can sleep he is wracked by "terrible dreams / That shake us nightly" (3.2.20), knowing that Duncan "sleeps well" (3.2.25). The final irony is that his wife sleeps only too well, revealing her guilt in that state. While not exactly an image in the visual sense, in *Macbeth* sleep and its deprivation as psychic states exert a continuing and palpable presence. There may be a further, authorial layer to Macbeth's heartfelt pleas for the balm of "tired nature's sweet reviver" in sleep, since some of Shakespeare's sonnets, for example 27 and 28, indicate that he suffered from the same affliction of sleeplessness, though the cause in those poems is not a guilty conscience but absence from his lover.

"Blood will have blood"

The leading image sustained through a play which defines major themes and their complexities in visual references is blood, the word itself recurring more frequently in *Macbeth* than in any other play by Shakespeare. Its significance can, like much else in the play, be ambiguous, "equivocating", "fair and foul", and lead in different directions, to the extent that it is astonishing how many different meanings and significations it is given in the play. This plenitude of meanings may be especially surprising in the light of how little was known in Shakespeare's time about the physiology of blood as we understand it scientifically today. William Harvey's discovery of circulation of blood lay in the future. The Elizabethans knew of course that blood "flows" freely, but it was Harvey in 1618 in *De Motis Cordi* who postulated that it circulates through the heart and around the body, reported later in his observation:

> that when he took notice the Valves in the Veins of so many several parts of the body, were so plac'd that they gave free passage to the Blood Towards the Heart, but oppos'd the passage of the Venal blood the Contrary way: He was invited to imagine that so Provident a Cause as Nature had not so Plac'd so many Valves without Design: and no Design seem'd more probable, than That, since the Blood could not well, because of the interposing Valves, be Sent by the Veins to the Limbs; it should be Sent through the Arteries and Return though the Veins, whose Valves did not oppose its course that way. (Boyle 1688: 157-8)

Oddly enough, there are links between Harvey and the circumstances of the writing of *Macbeth*, since he was physician to King James I (and later Charles I) and he was also involved in interrogations concerning witchcraft. For 4000 years before Harvey, Galen's teaching prevailed, that blood was one of the four "humours" governing the body and temperament (along with phlegm, yellow bile and black bile), that it governed the "sanguine" type of person (optimistic and cheerful), and that its primary function was to distribute vitality through the body to its extremities. In a healthy body, then, blood is life, reflected in the metaphorical description of Duncan's death to his sons as "The spring, the head, the fountain of your blood / Is stopped, the very source of it is stopped" (2.3.97-8). Hereditary ties of bloodlines hold families together, signifying survival into the future, and this is clearly an issue in Shakespeare's plays on the theme of succession. This significance is multiply important in *Macbeth* because the tyrant is childless, he orders the murder of Macduff's children, and realises that Fleance, whose line has been nominated by the Witches as future monarchs, still lives. In his moment of pricking conscience, Macbeth also realises he is violating the "double trust" of Duncan, who is not only his king but also his kinsman, a blood relation. The connotations could be positive, and even "bleeding" was considered a health-giving remedy for those who had an imbalance of too much blood (which could cause choler or anger), so the death and beheading of Macbeth could be seen as a kind of ritual bloodletting for the nation, returning Scotland to health.

However, right from the beginning of the play, blood is also associated with destructive violence, especially in war. Duncan's first line is "What bloody man is that?" (1.2.1), and battle is described in terms of blood: "with his brandished steel / Which smoked with bloody execution" (17-18). Macbeth is introduced in terms of the honour bestowed by shedding the blood of rebels. He is a "man of blood" in the humoral sense, not so much indicating a sanguine and cheerful spirit but, with the body out of balance, the choler and anger of the professional soldier. In *Macbeth* as a play, the indiscriminate and bloody violence of military death is built into the fabric of its imagery. Glorification of war as "honour" in Duncan's word, paying lip service to the connection between military carnage and heroic values, is immediately and rapidly juxtaposed with the first of many bloody images. The Witches seem to be spirited up as scavengers after battle, and one reports that she has been "Killing swine" (1.3.2) just as the soldiers have been reported as killing each other. As we noticed in Chapter 3, the reference to pigkilling is not gratuitous but placed with a gruesome precision, defining the horrifying nature of the raging battle and undercutting appeals to honour. A later Witch's recipe includes "baboon's blood" and "sow's blood that hath eaten her nine farrow" (4.1.37-8, 81), the latter providing a subliminal link with Lady Macbeth's apparently physiological reference to infanticide, when she calls on spirits to "make thick" her blood in order to "Stop up th'access and passage to remorse" (1.5.42-3). It heralds the appearance before Macbeth of the second apparition, which is a bloody child.

Whereas in war, violence is legitimised, the most reprehensible act of all is murder as violation of the sanctity of human life. Macbeth has a premonition of the bloody nature of what is to come when he follows the dagger, whether real or imaginary:

> I see thee still,
> And on thy blade and dudgeon gouts of blood,
> Which was not so before. There's no such thing.
> It is the bloody business which informs
> Thus to mine eyes. (2.1. 45-9)

This murder, unlike later ones such as Banquo's and Macduff's family, occurs offstage, and the need to verbalise in reporting gives the opportunity for emphasising even more intensely the sheer amount of blood and the way it has been transferred from Duncan's body to Macbeth's hands: "This is a sorry sight" (2.2.20), a sentiment which Lady Macbeth reproves even though later she will share it: "A foolish thought to say a sorry sight" (21). She urges him, "Go get some water,/ And wash this filthy witness from your hands" (45-6). First, however, the daggers must be planted and since Macbeth refuses to re-enter the bedchamber, his wife must "smear / The sleepy grooms with blood" (48-9). This gesture implicates her, and the incriminating blood is now transferred also to her hands but not yet to her mind:

> MACBETH
> What hands are here! Ha, they pluck out mine eyes.
> Will all great Neptune's ocean wash this blood
> Clean from my hand! No, this my hand will rather
> The multitudinous seas incarnadine,
> Making the green one red.
> [Enter LADY MACBETH]
> LADY MACBETH

6 Imagery and the Emotional World of *Macbeth*

> My hands are of your colour, but I shame
> To wear a heart so white.
> ...
> A little water clears us of this deed. (2.2.57-63)

It sinks in much later for her in her sleepwalking as she tries to wash out the spots of blood from her hands: "Yet who would have thought the old man to have had so much blood in him?" (5.1.37ff). She goes on, "Here's the smell of the blood still. / All the perfumes of Arabia will not sweeten this little hand. O, O, O!" The common phrase, "blood on one's hands", is here literalised, and blood is now the visible badge of guilt. So it become for the First Murderer of Banquo:

> MACBETH
> There's blood upon thy face.
> FIRST MURDERER [*aside to Macbeth*]
> 'Tis Banquo's, then.
> MACBETH
> 'Tis better thee without than he within.
> Is he dispatched?
> FIRST MURDERER
> My lord, his throat is cut. That I did for him. (3.4.11-15)

The words of the two reveal another complicity through black, private humour here in Macbeth's "'Tis better thee without than he within" and the Murderer's "That I did for him". When the image of Banquo's head appears to Macbeth, it is the blood, caked dry and cold, which marks it out and provokes Macbeth's incoherent rant beginning "Blood hath been shed ere now, i' the olden time".

Cryptic, repeated phrases act as constant reminders, making it impossible to avoid the image of blood: "this most bloody piece of work" (2.3.127); "this bloody stage" (2.4.6); "this more than bloody deed" (2.4.22); "our bloody cousins" (3.1.31); "such bloody distance" (3.1.117); "thy bloody and invisible hand" (3.2.49); "The secret'st man of blood" (3.2.125); "untitled tyrant bloody-sceptered" (4.3.105); "Those clamorous harbingers of blood and death" (5.6.10). These phrases hold both literal and metaphorical significances, and Macbeth adds to these the self-propagating contagion of guilt which invites revenge: "It will have blood, they say. Blood will have blood" (3.2.121). Eventually the impossibility of washing away guilt becomes as wide as the sea itself in Macbeth's extraordinary, anguished vision, juxtaposing for intensification simple Anglo-Saxon and orotund Latin-based language: "The multitudinous seas incarnadine, / Making the green one red" (2.2.61-2). The inevitable revenge in Macbeth's case comes not from Duncan's issue nor Banquo's but from Macduff, a man more directly wronged than others in the play after the slaughter of his wife and children. Revenge, or blood-law, is a constant theme throughout Shakespeare's canon, even in the comedies (Anderson 1987), but it is usually problematised in some way in other plays, as an ethically questionable form of justice (Keyishian 1995), especially in *Hamlet*, but Macduff's slaughter of Macbeth comes in open battle as a righteous response to personal aggrievement and as a final closure of the bloody sequence of Scottish history presented in the play. In this case forgiveness, the antidote to spiralling revenge, is not presented as an option for one so steeped in blood as Macbeth.

Imagery in a play like *Macbeth*, then, functions as a major determination of aspects beyond the merely narrative sequence of events. It can establish atmosphere, colour our judgement of the action in ways that go beyond rational analysis, and suggest states of mind and feelings not confined to the expression of thought or attitudes alone. It is the underlying and ubiquitous secret to the play as an emotional world, containing within itself a multitude of particular emotional worlds interplaying in the imagination as the experience of the total work which individual audience members take away with them after the hurly-burly of action is done.

7
Macbeth on Stage and Screen

Literary interpretation and performance on stage are different disciplines but they are complementary and can be mutually enhancing. Critics working from the language of the written play can identify theoretical options and possibilities which may even be in contradiction with each other, and as long as they can be justified from the evidence of the text they may be held in suspension in the mind, opening up a plurality of emotional worlds. However, directors and actors must make decisions about everything they propose to do in the theatre or on film, from their large conception of the play's meaning, setting, character traits, general ambience and specific emotional effects, down to the minutiae of how lines are to be spoken. While it is possible for them to maintain an ambiguous stance, for example on issues of good and evil, leaving it up to audiences to close the circle in sometimes unpredictable ways, they nonetheless do need to make such decisions in the interests of a unified production. Literary approaches can suggest ideas to work with that may appeal to performers, and the latter can show unexpected possibilities that may not occur to us when simply reading the text. The one deals in potential, the other in realisation.

Very detailed information about the history of *Macbeth* in performance can be found in two excellent earlier books: Dennis Bartholomeusz's *Macbeth and the Players* (1969) and Marvin

Rosenberg's huge book *The Masks of Macbeth* (1978). However, it is probably true that up to the 1990s performance was confined to theatre spaces and neglected as an object of academic study in books. Then there was something of a revolution, and recent years have helped to rectify the imbalance with theatre history, performance and audience studies, and analyses of Shakespeare in popular culture including cinema becoming mainstream. In an age which may become known for "information overload" and one in which virtually everything is recorded, written traces are keeping pace with the stage. As a consequence, the last twenty years have seen a plethora of books and articles, and the sprouting of multiple digital databases devoted to the subject. Prompt – books from the past have been published by Adam Matthew Digital in collaboration with the Folger Library, which owns an enviable number of them, while the Internet Shakespeare Editions website has a huge cache of theatre documents and information. Here one can search for productions of *Macbeth* using various criteria – title, person, character, company, artifact – and the results are overwhelming, if also intimidating by their unsifted bountifulness. In print, the series "Shakespeare in Performance", published by Manchester University Press, includes a volume on *Macbeth* edited by Bernice W. Kliman and Jim Bullman (2004), while the New Cambridge editions of the plays concentrate on performance issues and history (the *Macbeth* edition is edited by A.R. Braunmuller), as do the skimpier "RSC Shakespeare" editions of each play, in which *Macbeth* is edited by Eric Rasmussen.

Movie versions are comprehensively covered in books like Kenneth S. Rothwell's pioneering *A History of Shakespeare on Screen* (1999) and Richard Burt's more recent, voluminous *Shakespeares after Shakespeare* (2007). Another set of approaches involving multimedia and focused on issues of race in America is Scott Newstok's edited volume *Weyward Macbeth: Intersections of Race and Performance* (2010). It is full of extremely stimulating and original essays, and is especially illuminating in recovering historical American material regarding *Macbeth*'s place in race relations and cultural diversity. They range from issues like violence and slavery in American history, through Orson Welles' famous so-called "voodoo" *Macbeth*, some movie versions, to Duke Ellington's jazz adaptations of Shakespeare.

7 *Macbeth* on Stage and Screen

These can be supplemented by more recent editions of the play, which customarily have a section on film. In line with the scope and thematic concentration of this book, here is an all too brief chapter which sketches a few lines of development, and mentions some versions on film and some of the more recent spectacular and original performances. Ambivalence marks the performance history because of the open questions concerning Macbeth's motivation and culpability, and the uniquely problematical role of Lady Macbeth. Whether they are villains, victims or heroes is a question that must be raised in performances. More generally, *Macbeth* is like an open space, full of potential, to be made whole, realised by readers' imaginations and actors' voices and bodies; and the outcomes may be extremely diverse, and even non-committal or contradictory in representing a morally problematical figure, "the murderer as victim" (Honigmann 1976: chapter title) or "the criminal as tragic hero" (Heilman 1967: title). The play itself becomes "fair and foul", paradoxical and radically ambivalent. On stage and screen, we find so many and varied versions that the point is effectively proved in practice. As Ruby Cohn (1976) demonstrated, adaptations of *Macbeth* alone provide a virtual history of stage conventions and approaches in different historical periods and inevitably many more are to come, like the endless line of future children seen by Macbeth.

The playing of Macbeth himself requires choosing options from sets of conflicting possibilities. Is he to be played as an anguished and misguided hero, or as an unequivocal villain like Richard III, or something in between (if that is possible)? Is he ambitious and acting decisively on his own inner drives and compulsions, or is he a weak man driven by forces outside his control and persuaded by his wife? Or an exemplary and conscientious man who spectacularly falls by succumbing to temptation? In brief, did he fall, or was he pushed – and if so, by whom, or what? Or if we take the line that he is himself a dramatically divided character, almost schizophrenic or manic-depressive in swinging from nobility to crime to tyranny, elation to despondency and despair, we then raise similar questions about his emotional drives. Is the division within his own psyche the result of a pre-existing temperamental flaw (and if so, what is it?), or is he later divided by the external existence of power and kingship which alienates him from his human feelings? This latter interpretation has been proposed here, because it is less often put, but the other options are by no means discredited or in any way "wrong" since they can all be justified by reference to parts of the text. The main point is that actors and directors need to make bold decisions about their interpretation of the play as a whole, in order to clarify how individual roles are to be played. This is especially so in plays like *Macbeth* and *Richard III* where a protagonist is cast in a criminal role. And how is one to convey this mixed emotion swinging in a single line between anguish and love for his wife: "O, full of scorpions is my mind, dear wife!" (3.3.37). A particular problem has been identified by performers over the centuries as to how the ending should be played, since most star actors are reluctant to accept that the major character, who has been by turns courageous, warrior-like, conscientious, ruthless and altogether larger than life, should be dismissed in what could be played as facing a humiliating end – possibly (though not necessarily in some performances) killed offstage and represented only as a severed head. Stars being stars, few might be satisfied with a directorial instruction to end one of the most demanding roles of their careers, drawing on emotional extremes of bravery, vulnerability and terror, not with a bang but a whimper. The same goes for actors playing Lady Macbeth, the role which, apart from Cleopatra, is the most memorable, powerful and demanding female part in Shakespearean drama. In contrast to Cleopatra, who orchestrates her own death with magnificent awareness of her historical importance, Lady Macbeth suffers an offstage death which is not fully explained, lamented by an ambiguous "cry of women". Clearly, on the decisions about playing the Macbeths hang others which are equally open. Do the Witches simply observe, or do they determine the action? Is Lady Macbeth a victim of Macbeth's evil impulses or a cause of them? Are Malcolm and Macduff flawed parallels to Macbeth or polar opposites as paragons of virtue? – and so on, the questions multiply.

Another political option has been suggested by the argument in this book. It is quite possible to step back and regard the play not as actors playing "real people" who have unique characters and feeling-states, but as the representation of an externalised struggle of political forces being enacted in a historical process, which can be called regicide

7 Macbeth on Stage and Screen

or assassination, raising questions of authority and tyranny in a monarchical state. People cease to be individuals but are rather agents standing for conflicting attitudes to power, which can be activated by "supernatural solicitings" (1.3.129). Bertolt Brecht consistently espoused a kind of theatre which invites detached analysis of issues rather than empathy with characters, and he claimed to find this theory of "epic theatre" in Shakespeare. His play *The Resistible Rise of Arturo Ui*, a parable of the rise of Hitler set among Chicago gangsters, bears comparison with *Macbeth* in many ways, and has pointed to new stagings of Shakespeare's play. Given that all we know about the original performances overseen by Shakespeare is that most were presented on a bare, open stage, in daylight, and without scenery or artificial lighting, either the Elizabethan audiences were capable of great feats of imaginative projection, or Brecht was right that we are dealing with a kind of theatre which was very different from the stage of illusion and character prevailing from the eighteenth century through the nineteenth and twentieth, and into the medium of film.

Richard Burbage must have been a powerful and charismatic actor, since Shakespeare wrote his great tragic roles specifically with him in mind. However, we know little for sure about whether he played Macbeth let alone his style of doing so, and less about the boy actor who played Lady Macbeth. John Rice has been proposed (Bartholomeusz 1969: 11) though without a lot of firm evidence. The actor may have been an older youth rather than the figure conjured up by the word "boy", since Shakespeare had always written remarkable parts for mature women from Queen Margaret in the early history plays and Constance in *King John*, to Lady Macbeth, Cleopatra and Volumnia in the Jacobean plays. No doubt pitch of voice was important in playing young women in comedy of courtship, but for older women clothes may have been enough to signify gender. It is likely that *Macbeth* was first performed outdoors at the Globe Theatre to a cross-section of London's population, and later revived in a more exclusive, indoor theatre, Blackfriars, where more atmospheric touches could be achieved through darkness, candles and torches. A gap in drama history occurred between 1642 and 1660 when public theatres were closed by the Puritan Commonwealth because of religious suspicions about representation, and the reopening in 1660 was marked by such profound changes – women playing women, generally aristocratic audiences in specially designed indoor theatres rather than a social cross-section on outdoor stages, and wholly revised and rewritten scripts – that we can never hope to retrieve fully the flavour of Shakespeare's own theatres. In fact, the text of *Macbeth* which monopolised the stage from the 1660s until 1744 was not Shakespeare's but William Davenant's rewritten or "alter'd" version, which was spectacular and "operatic" in including a set of singing and dancing Witches (Kliman 2004: 16–20). Davenant regarded himself as "Shakespeare's son" with such a licence to "correct" where the text did not accord with neo-classical norms of composition. The most famous Macbeth of this era was Thomas Betterton, known for depicting terror rather than tenderness, described by John Wilders as having "an ungainly figure with a large head, a thick neck, fat arms, which he seldom raised higher than his stomach, a corpulent body, and large face" (Wilders 2004: 11). His Lady Macbeth was Mrs Betterton.

After Burbage, the next most influential Shakespearian actor and theatre entrepreneur was David Garrick. He performed a service in restoring at least some of the excised, Shakespearian text though he retained some of Davenant's changes and made excisions of his own from Shakespeare's text. For better or worse, he also initiated the cult of bardolatry – uncritical admiration of Shakespeare to the point of making him a god – and as his career developed he seemed egotistically to invite an equation between Shakespeare, his characters, and himself in the role of the bard reincarnated. Garrick's approach to Macbeth, inevitably, was the most sympathetic one possible. He played the character as a "reluctant, sensitive murderer" (Bartholomeusz 1969: 44), marked by remorse while his wife remained steely. His style was naturalistic as he tried to emulate the language of an ordinary man rising to a "tragic dignity". A contemporary painting is quite revealing, since it shows Garrick as being very short and somewhat childlike beside Mrs Pritchard's large and decisive Lady Macbeth, an image reflecting their roles in this production. Garrick established a tradition of playing Macbeth as a vulnerable "henpecked husband", as this style has somehow been called (with some disrespect for his strong-willed wife).

7 *Macbeth* on Stage and Screen

The next great Macbeth, at the end of the eighteenth century into the early nineteenth, was John Philip Kemble, who played alongside his own sister, Sarah Siddons, as Lady Macbeth, who was the more emotionally striking character. Kemble's presence seems to have been unmistakably aristocratic, stately and rather solemn, and we imagine a stiff-upper-lip grandee, burdened by opening knowledge of the awesome consequences of his ambition. Siddons, on the contrary, was a much less formal, more intuitive and passionate actress. Her role as Lady Macbeth, which she recorded in written memoirs and which has been analysed by Glenn McGillivray (forthcoming), was ferociously ambitious, demonically possessed and impulsive. Her contemptuous taunting of her husband, her "fiend-like" beauty, and an intensity which terrified the audience and acted as a spell cast upon Kemble's Macbeth, dominated the performances. He in turn seems, like Garrick, to have achieved the effect of a man led and distracted, though in Kemble's case he was no naive victim, but rather an honourable (English) aristocrat trying to do the "proper" thing after making a fatal mistake. Almost certainly in reaction against Kemble, the "radical" and populist Edmund Kean sought to shock his audiences from 1814 onwards. He was an actor made for the Romantic period. Contemporary accounts contrast the declamatory style of Kemble against the fitful Kean. Imagery of lightning flashes and electrifying moments dominate the descriptions of an essentially energy-driven, naturalistic style. In such an approach there was little room for a strong Lady Macbeth, and Kean played Macbeth as a ruthless, self-centred man who changes into a fearful, moral coward.

After Kean came William Macready in the 1820s and 1830s. He restored heroic grandeur and fatal impressionability to the role of Macbeth, but since Kean was an inescapable theatrical presence Macready had to build into his acting some volatile and paradoxical elements, "the animal ferocity and the sensitiveness, the courage and cowardice, the primitive impulsiveness and dignity of his Macbeth" (Bartholomeusz 1969: 169). He had various Lady Macbeths, most notably Fanny Kemble and Charlotte Cushman, the latter being an American actress who had "a forbidding physical massiveness" (Rosenberg 168), towering over her Macbeth. Macready seems to have been the actor who realised most effectively the ambivalences of

Macbeth, leaving it up to the audience to form its own moral judgements. Kemble, Kean and Macready, their careers overlapping in quick succession, displayed not only vividly contrasting Macbeths, but also in total the most fertile period of male Shakespearian acting in England since Burbage. In the mid-nineteenth century, one of the most remarkable international actors was Ira Aldridge, a black African from Senegal who toured across the whole of Europe, Britain and Russia. Curiosity drew audiences to his Othello, but Macbeth was as much his signature role, admired by among others George Eliot, whom Aldridge met (Lindfors 2015: 15-16). He acted with impressive passion and energy and came to command high fees in the many countries he visited. Towards the end of the nineteenth century the Shakespearian stage was dominated by Henry Irving and Ellen Terry. Irving played Macbeth as "gloomy, and mischievous, far from an amiable tool in the hands of a fiendish woman" (E.R. Russell in 1875, quoted in Bartholomeusz 1969: 198). Irving played the role realistically, sceptically, and with a pervading sense of cold, disillusioned cynicism, as if ruthlessly playing a game of power politics. Meanwhile, Ellen Terry subdued her playing of Lady Macbeth into a house-proud, sugary and cajoling figure.

Twentieth-century male Shakespearian acting in Britain has been dominated by two inescapable and opposite influences: John Gielgud and Laurence Olivier. The mellifluous Gielgud restored poetry to acting, and his advice to Olivier, "You must sing the lines, Larry, my dear boy", although not heeded, revealed his own approach to the language of Shakespeare. Gielgud's entrancement is with voice and rhythmic language, and as a result his Macbeth becomes "a prisoner of his own fantasy" (Bartholomeusz 1969: 233), a poetic spellbinder convinced by his own eloquent rhetoric. This approach influenced a generation of critics who saw Macbeth as the greatest poet among Shakespeare's tragic heroes. Olivier, in stark contrast, was ever aware of the power of the body, using his physical presence in a charged, "tigerish" way to present a Macbeth which sent critics scurrying for comparisons back to the records of Kean's dynamic acting.

Olivier's natural successor is Ian McKellen, who in 1976 played beside Judi Dench's chunky and practical-minded Lady Macbeth. It was a brilliant production which, luckily for posterity, was filmed at the time. McKellen as Macbeth gradually retreated into himself, clutching dolls, imagery identified with Orson Welles' famous production in New York in 1936, and trembling in paranoia. His clothes become ever larger and more ill-fitting to reflect the references in the text which suggest a man promoted beyond his ability and lacking in natural command. I was privileged to attend a performance of this production, in a small, Gulbenkian theatre-in-the-round in Newcastle upon Tyne, which seemed especially suited to this play. The audience's proximity to the actors in the cramped, dark space made palpable a sense of the domestic intimacy between husband and wife in their home, along with a menace outside beating on the door to get in, and Macbeth's own state of mental entrapment, "cabin'd, cribb'd, confined, bound in / To saucy doubts and fears" (3.4.23-4). Without props and with constant entrances and exits, the taut economy and breathless pace of the action was accentuated. My own seating positioning led to an especially riveting and unnerving moment. The banquet scene was played with chairs in a circle around the perimeter, very close to the audience. On each chair sat a thane – except on the one in front of mine, which was left empty. Of course, this was where Macbeth sees the head of Banquo. I shrank from the ferocious hostility and dread which was directed at me personally by one of the greatest actors of his time in full flight. My first, flinching instinct itself was flight, and I desperately wanted to run out of the theatre but at the same time felt paralysed. Nor did it reassure me to have an irritable Judi Dench pointing at me and in a tone of ridicule declaring to McKellen "Shame itself! / Why do you make such faces? When's all's done, / You look but on a stool" (3.4.66-7). The moment of my shock can be recaptured on the filmed version since the camera is placed at this exact spot, but somehow the frisson and sense of terrified involvement evoked by the event in the theatre itself does not really come over on screen.

If Macbeth can be played in such a variety of incompatible ways, so can his wife. Marvin Rosenberg presents the variety of different potential styles. I summarise these here in my own words but under Rosenberg's headings (in which I change his "lady" to "woman" in conformity with contemporary practice):

(1) The Terrible Woman: a fierce Lady Macbeth who keeps recurring through stage history (for instance, Sarah Siddons and

Charlotte Cushman), leading Macbeth rather than being led. A woman worthy of the line, "Infirm of purpose! / Give me the daggers" (2.2.50-1).

(2) The Loving Wife: "whose ambition is all for the husband to whom she is entirely devoted" (Rosenberg 1978: 174), an image which was particularly popular in nineteenth-century Germany, and one which Edmund Kean encouraged in his leading ladies (for example, Helen Faucit), to complement his fiery individuality. The greatest of all was Ellen Terry, who played alongside Irving, and interpreted the role by anticipating Lady Macbeth's madness as that of a gentle woman, devoted to her husband, not seeing through him until the banquet, and through loyalty, finding herself in very deep waters.

(3) The Maternal Woman: mature, strong and protective (Flora Robson in 1934).

(4) The Child Woman: a mixture of innocent vulnerability and open terror (Francesca Annis in Polanski's film [1971] begins very young and seems to age during the action, as if undergoing a rapid and dismaying rite of passage into adulthood).

(5) The Sensual Woman: a passionate, physical and sexually dynamic woman, full of erotic allure and dangerous vitality, a style especially associated with French actresses. Even the English actor Sarah Bernhardt, popular in France, "shocked some Victorian English tastes" (Rosenberg 1978: 198) by playing Lady Macbeth as a voluptuous seductress. Orson Welles in his film emphasised the vamplike role in his casting and direction, and it has been a popular interpretation in the twentieth century. Many critics, such as Calderwood (1986), find and trace this potential in the language of the play.

(6) The Upwardly Mobile Woman: one who skilfully plots the course of her husband's business career, is a phenomenon of the twentieth-century stage, demonstrated, for example, by Sybil Thorndike, and in some of the recent creative adaptations which set the play in commercial venues like restaurants. Interestingly, we have seen on reality television shows like *My Restaurant Rules* the apparently unavoidable and fierce competitiveness this context brings out in participants and audiences.

(7) The Woman Possessed: where a demonic connection between Lady Macbeth and the Witches is implied through symptoms of

possession and later madness. This approach plays up the supernatural elements in the play.

(8) The Woman as Barbarian: full of primitive cruelty and with only a veneer of civility.

(9) The Nerve-Driven Woman: full of nervous excitement hiding behind a fragile, cool exterior. Diana Rigg played Lady Macbeth in 1973 as brittle and insecure.

(10) To these we might add "The Broken Woman" as apparently played by Faucit, after the banquet scene becoming "broken, exhausted, melancholy" (Wilders 2004: 33).

Taken as a whole, these groups seem to exhaust the gamut of constructions of femininity over the centuries, though it remains to be seen if more styles will emerge. It would be interesting to explore these, and to locate in the text lines which may have stimulated each image, and to speculate on other possible approaches to the role. One other which comes to mind would be a more psychological interpretation, since both characters can be said to be obsessional types: once they get ideas into their heads, they are compelled to enact them, and they exhibit various unusual mental states. This reading would be in stark contrast, for example, to some of the film versions mentioned below, where sometimes extroverted action and absence of inwardness propels the action forward, as though the characters are victims of fate rather than free agents. There is a great spectrum available, and it may be true to say that Macbeth and Lady Macbeth are the most "open" roles in all Shakespeare's plays. On Lady Macbeth in particular, Bradley wrote, "The reader is at liberty to imagine Lady Macbeth's person in the way that pleases him best, or to leave it, as Shakespeare very likely did, unimagined" (Bradley 1904: 379fn). Despite Bradley's attribution to "the reader" and an odd hypothetical attitude of Shakespeare, the same general point goes for actors and audiences. There are few, if any, who have been played with such fundamental differences.

One group which is not often considered, but whose influential contribution to the world of theatre is important, are reviewers. In a recent book, *Reviewing Shakespeare: Journalism and Performance from the Eighteenth Century to the Present*, Paul Prescott entertainingly traces critics from the past, using *Macbeth* as a running comparison. Usually male, they remain like ghosts, their prickly egos as large as actors', and they continue to roam the theatre world like unquiet souls eager still to settle old scores with enemies. Their implacable enemies have always been the famous actors from Garrick to Kean and Olivier, whose profession required them, if they were playing a tragic protagonist, to die every night and rise the next night to die yet again, making even their final demise seem provisional. The words of reviewers can live on disconcertingly. Between the two groups, reviewers and actors, war often rages, as we see in the cult movie *Theater of Blood* (1973), starring Vincent Price, which depicts a malmsey-soaked series of macabre murders where the corpses are theatre reviewers, the perpetrators vindictive ghosts of actors whose reputations have been tarnished and even ruined by the critics. Prescott's erudite and entertaining book traces the sometimes hazardous profession of theatre reviewing in Britain from the 1740s through to the present day. Iago, the villain in *Othello*, had ominously proclaimed that he is "nothing if not critical" (2.1.122), thus immediately placing professional critics in sinister company, the intensifying "nothing" adding an alternative threat of potential, insignificant oblivion for some whose words are forgotten and forgiven. They process in all their waspish pomp across the pages of Prescott's book, "elegantly regurgitating their erudition" (Shaw's scathing words on music critics), not in full glare across the lighted stage but patrolling the shadowy perimeters as a "night-watch constabulary" (quoted Prescott 2013: 1). Nowadays, in London's "Shakespeare's Globe", for example, reviewers often comment in superior fashion on the unavoidably visible behaviour of the audience, as much as on the acting.

In foregrounding critics, the example of *Macbeth* is an interesting choice, since actors are often uneasy with the lead role in this play, not just because of the "curse" but because of some inbuilt ambiguities. Although clearly requiring the services of a star performer, history has shown that the role can polarise critics into seeing the actor playing Macbeth as either an impotent weakling or a blustering megalomaniac, neither of which is particularly appealing to any self-respecting actor, to whom even an outright villain like Iago or Richard III holds more appeal. Garrick, responding to his age's valuing of sensibility, attempted to portray the character as courageous and dignified, but as many actors have found, something in the play resists such efforts. Among other factors, Macbeth is the only major tragic protagonist who cannot redeem himself with a dignified or spectacular death scene (unlike, for example, Othello, whose final speech allows him to repent before committing suicide). Macbeth is violently dispatched offstage, and only his bloody head returns on a pole – not a fate that many self-respecting star actors who love a death scene would relish. Many have fought against Shakespeare's ignominious send-off: Garrick, for example, wrote a dying speech recalling Marlowe's *Doctor Faustus*, and some later actors borrowed this.

> 'Tis done! The scene of life will quickly close,
> Ambition's vain, delusive dreams are fled,
> And now I wake to darkness, guilt and horror.
> I cannot bear it! Let me shake it off. –
> 'Twa' not be; my soul is clogged with blood.
> I cannot rise! I dare not ask for mercy.
> It is too late, hell drags me down. I sink.
> I sink – Oh! – my soul is lost forever!
> Oh! (*Dies*). (Holland 2010: 24)

Others eliminated the very final scene so the play could end with Macbeth's death. Edmund Kean at the end eschewed dignity for dangerous vehemence and agitation, but his efforts to assert a different kind of manhood were at times undermined by his diminutive stature. His more famous roles were the less warrior-like Iago and Richard III. Kean was lucky, however, in having as his chronicler the greatest critic of them all, William Hazlitt, who wrote of one speech when Macbeth is represented at his most vulnerable and shocked at his own actions:

> as a lesson of common humanity, it was heart-rending. The hesitation, the bewildered look, the coming to himself when he sees his hands bloody: the manner in which his voice clung to his throat, and choaked his utterance: his agony and tears, the force of nature overcome by passion – beggared description. It was a scene, which no one who saw it can ever efface from his recollection. (Hazlitt 1994: 213–14)

Kean is a rare example of an actor whose posthumous fame was clinched by the equally moving prose of the critic, Hazlitt, who has the capacity to bring the past to life and give some permanence to the otherwise ephemeral experience of performance. He could equally diminish Kean's rival, Kemble, who had both the size and dignity of a "noble" Macbeth, but paradoxically used these assets in the service of a wooden delivery skewered by Hazlitt for its emotional deficiencies. To overcome all the inbuilt difficulties in the role, and to be exalted and remembered as a "great Macbeth", the actor has always needed to persuade one layer of arbitration above all, the serried ranks of critics in the press.

It used to be in some ways easier when the convention held that theatre reviews would be published anonymously and the grandee could opine safely from behind a nom de plume. 1867 was the year that marked the inception of the removal of the mask, and the practice of anonymous reviewing gave way to attribution of authorship. With such public accountability came, however, not humility but aggrandisement, and the rise of the celebrity reviewer was complete by the end of the century. Enter Bernard Shaw, by turns cantankerous, self-contradictory, provocative, and always quirkily individual. While claiming incorruptibility, he was not above interviewing himself about his own plays, and leaking the third-person transcription to the press. Shaw was essentially a whimsical iconoclast, but he consistently tested performances by their relevance to the modern world and the respect they paid to the "music" of poetic language. His successors were equally distinctive in their own idiosyncratic ways: Beerbohm the dandy, minimally informed but entertaining; James Agate fulminating against what he saw as the pernicious rise of directorial "interpretation" over the power of acting; Kenneth Tynan as *enfant terrible* driven by his libido and admiration for the Oliviers, and later by his discovery of Brecht. Michael Billington, not yet a ghost, is more temperate than his predecessors, but unlike them he faces impertinent rebellion from readers of the online *Guardian*, who are licensed to comment publicly and frequently acidly on his reviews. On any hint of derision for "ignorant groundlings" who stand at Shakespeare's Globe (usually assumed to be foreign), Billington and his contemporaries provoke a swift and sure backlash as "the groundlings write back", reversing stereotypes of unruly ignorance by quoting Barthes and indignantly bridling at snobbishness, racism, misplaced pseudo-sophistication or dismissive archness. Although each audience member will have personal preferences, Ian McKellen seems to have passed the test. He may have been lucky in being born too late to face the magisterially opinionated and often scathing reviewers of yesteryear like Hazlitt, Shaw and Max Beerbohm, since generally speaking they are a more tolerant and benign lot these days.

Including in this book a brief critical review of reviewers, thereby possibly in turn attracting indignant readers' comments amounting to another tier of hecklers, seems to be taking meta-reviewing to new heights. Hounded by ghosts fulminating from the past, and peppered with pot-shots or "tweets" from the living, anybody brave enough to become a reviewer will need to be aware of Prescott's repeated point that "theatre criticism, no less than the art it captures, is haunted by nostalgia. A diachronic awareness of past achievement and contemporary inadequacy pervades the game" (Prescott 2013: 138). Most playgoers have a fond memory of some particular actors (like mine of McKellen and Dench) – for those old enough it may be Lawrence Olivier and Vivien Leigh (RSC 1955), more recently Antony Sher and Harriet Walter (RSC 1999), for spring chickens Kenneth Branagh trudging along a muddy trench in a deconsecrated church in Manchester (National Theatre 2013, transmitted around the world as "live" filmed performance). As the present becomes the past, the whirligig of time will bring in more of its revenges, and no doubt many more Macbeths.

Music and Opera

Another version transposed into a different artistic medium altogether is the magnificent opera scored by Giuseppe Verdi, first performed in 1847 and again in revised form in 1865. Although Verdi follows reasonably faithfully the sequence of events in Shakespeare, the whole nature of opera is to achieve emotional effects by building up in crescendos of music towards a scenic conclusion that can leave both performers and audiences physically and emotionally drained. The words are less significant than the voices and orchestra, and many were dropped or changed from Shakespeare's text by the librettist Francesco Maria Piave. Duncan's role is reduced to a non-speaking, ceremonial one. No doubt Verdi, as a staunch republican, had a hand in diminishing still further any potential audience sympathy for the king, while retaining only his essential, institutional power which causes others to be ambitious. It is quite possible to argue that Verdi's music can give us just as intense an awareness of the potential in Shakespeare's text as any spoken version, at least in its strong concentration on Macbeth's own psychology. Indeed, the medium of opera is not so far from Shakespeare's theatre as we might imagine. The introduction to the New Oxford edition gives prominent discussion to the ways in which music has been central to *Macbeth* ever since it was first staged, while Graham Bradshaw (2004) has analysed the opera itself more thoroughly. Verdi's opera shows that the play can emerge triumphantly in a medium which does not depend upon the spoken language of the text – what most people would assume is the most essential element of any Shakespearean play.

Film

With the invention of new technologies, there have been dramatically different approaches to *Macbeth* which prove that the linear story, the body and the image, even without words, can directly create the play. The neatest examples of this are the silent films made in the very early years of the twentieth century. They are hard to get hold of, but their very existence shows that Shakespeare can be played without words and still be Shakespeare. Silent films of *Macbeth* were made in 1908 (USA), 1909 (Italy), 1910 (France), 1911 (Great Britain), 1913 (Germany), 1916 (France and another in USA) and 1922 (Germany). They were limited by the length of the film rolls available at the time, and were usually eight or twelve minutes long. After these short extracts, it seems to have taken a surprisingly long time for feature films to appear. Indeed, compared with some other plays like *Hamlet* and even *The Tempest*, such an irresistibly cinematic play has attracted relatively few adaptations. Of those, and because of possibilities inherent in the medium and the existence of film genres known to audiences (horror movies, murder mystery, gangster films, action movies and so on), movie-makers tend to prioritise atmosphere, even over character. Welles uses effects identified with film noir of the 1940s, Kurosawa emphasises the strangeness of the play, Polanski turns it into an erotic thriller, a popular genre in the 1990s, and Kurzel wants to make evil something felt by the senses rather than merely a thematic or metaphysical abstraction. Equally, since filming can be carried out anywhere and allows for endless visual tricks, the film-maker can go to town with settings and magic, especially in adapting this particular play.

Orson Welles' innovative film version of *Macbeth* was made in 1948 in the wake of the Second World War, under severe financial constraints. In 1936, Welles at the age of twenty had created on stage in New York a sensational, all-black-American performance of the play, which caused riots. It became known as the "voodoo" *Macbeth* since the medieval witches were replaced with a culture based on nineteenth-century Haitian supernatural practices. The famous version (part of whose spectacular conclusion can be seen on YouTube) has influenced many subsequent performances, in particular Ian McKellen's, and more comprehensively black, African-American productions (Newstok 2010: 91-100). Welles claimed in interviews that he deliberately did not instruct the black actors in how to speak Shakespeare's lines, but encouraged them to develop their own music and traditions of speech. Welles' film, however, was conceived as a wholly different work located in a more historically defined period in Scotland, though it is made in such a stylised and non-realistic way that it is a kind of Druidic dreamland. Ironically, the Scottish accents, including Welles' own and Jeanette Nolan's as his wife, seem false in contrast with the impression gained from reports of the African-American style on stage earlier. The film-maker was beset by problems, particularly in the soundtrack, which had to be entirely re-recorded and is still today very flawed. The sets are minimal, cave-like, and monolithic, partly the result of the lack of funding but also of an artistic decision by the *auteur* film-maker whose preference was for the low-budget film noir genre. They are in stark contrast to the spectacular open-air cinematography in his *Othello* (1951), filmed mainly in the glaring sunlight of Morocco. Welles uses the medium of black and white to make a thematic point about the clash of evil and good, and also to attune the pagan atmosphere to suggest a murky and menacing society full of paranoia and claustrophobia, giving images to Macbeth's state of mind as "cabin'd, cribb'd, confined, bound in / To saucy doubts and fears". The scene in which Macbeth sees the ghost of Banquo at the feast is extraordinarily powerful, as close-ups of Welles' face show graphically the character's encroaching terror. Welles uses at the end rather than the beginning the Witches' chant (given to Hecate this time), "Peace, the charm's wound up" (1.3.37). This in itself provides an inscrutable ambiguity, since the phrase could mean equally "completed" or "ready to begin" like a clock, as if Macbeth's fate represents a cycle which will repeat itself over and over again, with different protagonists. Beginning at the end (as in Welles' filmed *Othello*) and ending at the beginning is an effect commonly used in the film noir genre on which Welles is drawing. Also a sign of the times is that the movie can be interpreted partly as a warning against dictatorship, totalitarianism and tyranny, a common theme in the postwar era, reflected also in Joseph Mankiewicz's *Julius Caesar* (1953).

In contrast, Roman Polanski's version (1971) is full of colour and youthfulness set against an ugly underworld of demonism and black magic. As the director of *Rosemary's Baby* and vampire films, Polanski may have been predisposed to emphasise these aspects in his vision of the play. He cast two actors who were unusually young (Jon Finch at twenty-nine and Francesca Annis at twenty-six). Polanski seems to have taken rather literally Macbeth's words "We are yet but young in deed" (3.4.143), though the main meaning suggests "we have more to do". The casting makes Lady Macbeth in particular seem to appear as an inexperienced woman out of her depth, undergoing a rite of passage and enhanced acceleration from reckless innocence to precocious knowledge of evil and despair. Made under the Playboy franchise, this production had no scruples about showing Lady Macbeth and the more obese Witches nude. Polanski also uses the story as a vehicle for questioning monarchy and power, showing that monarchy itself is a temptation to evil and that the acquisition of power is by no means secure, physically or emotionally. In his version, the turncoat Ross is the one who hands the crown to the equivocator Malcolm, and Donalbain ominously slinks off to consult the Witches at the end of the movie, suggesting the whole sequence of usurpation will repeat itself (as it did in the historical record). The movie emerges as reflecting the permissive and anti-authoritarian 1960s and 1970s, an era when youth culture and a "generation gap" between elder power figures and their rebellious teenagers dominated Western society.

Creative adaptations or "offshoots" of *Macbeth* abound. The most well known is the remarkable Japanese film made by Akira Kurosawa, *Throne of Blood* (1957; also titled *Cobweb Castle*). While not completely doing away with the Shakespearian text, this movie certainly minimises its language and Scottish setting, placing it among samurai warriors, and turning the Witches into one old person of dubious gender who sits endlessly spinning yarn and speaking in a mesmeric chant about the futility of ambition. The production generally prefers abrupt explosions of action before words, evoking a culture that runs on warlike violence. So powerful is the effect of this film that it is possible to say it is more authentically "Shakespearian" than a version which might have all the words spoken beautifully but has no emotional or visual impact. Or, to put it another way, the example may show us how impossible it is to talk of "authenticity" when dealing with a play by Shakespeare written and first performed over 400 years ago adapted into different times and media.

Adaptation is also international, as the example of Kurosawa shows. Another is *Siberian Lady Macbeth* (1962), also known as *Fury Is a Woman*, directed by Poland's most internationally prominent director, Andrzej Wajda, although he made it in Yugoslavia using Serbian language. It is based not directly on the play but a Russian short story, Nikolai Leskov's *Lady Macbeth of the Mtsensk District*, and its music is (according to its acknowledgements) "based on the motives of the opera" by Dmitri Shostakovich (1934), which itself was turned into a movie directed by Petr Weigl in 1992 as *Lady Macbeth of Mtsensk*. As the title implies, Wajda's film is a localised version of the story. Katarina, a Madame Bovary character, is an ambitious, spirited and manipulative woman who feels frustrated and trapped in a stultifying (and rat-infested) Siberian social and political system, "imprisoned like a bird in a cage" yearning to conceive a child but in a loveless marriage. The opening makes its relationship to *Macbeth* clear by using a quotation from Lady Macbeth, transcribed thus, the sexual connotations and unsentimental emotions given priority:

> Come, you spirits that tend on mortal thoughts,
> Unsex me here ...
> And fill me, from the crown to the toe,
> Top-full of direst cruelty! ...
> Come to my woman's breasts
> And take my milk for gall ...
> *Act I Scene V – 'Macbeth'*
> *By William Shakespeare*

While her husband is away, Katrina impulsively makes love with an itinerant labourer, and to avoid punishment on her husband's return, she murders her vindictive father-in-law with rat poison. She and the serf, Sergei, then murder the husband, resulting in plenty of blood, which Katrina compulsively washes not from her hands but from the stairs. They later begin to smother in his bed a child who stands between inheritance of the farm by them and their unborn child, upon which they are besieged by the furious mob of villagers and exiled as prisoners. Katrina herself drowns trying to kill the young woman who has now become her rival in love. The whole story has spiralled from apparently innocuous beginnings in a moment of Katrina's understandable boredom and sexual recklessness, and proceeds through her frustrated sexuality and thwarted ambition. Although we are not invited to invest much sympathy in Katrina, the events unfold with a certain tragic inevitability from love, but also from the bleak environment from which she cannot escape. In this, a more sympathetic connection with Shakespeare's character might be drawn, and although in the play the murderous liaison exists between husband and wife, there is an imputed agency to the woman in her role as a femme fatale. The film has been remade as *Lady Macbeth*, transposed into a rural setting in Victorian England (2017). In this version Katherine is presented as an extremely young and inexperienced woman who has been married as part of a deal for her husband's family to acquire land. She is immensely bored, with an apparently impotent and absent husband, and constantly berated for not bearing an heir.

The real villain is the sadistic father-in-law, who in one scene forces a servant to walk on all fours, saying "behave like an animal and you will be treated like one". As Katherine is increasingly driven by her instincts into amoral adultery and hardened into horrific murders of her tormentors, the statement could be reversed to apply to her: "treat me like an animal and I will behave like one". The film, like the story on which it is based, presents the heroine as a deeply ambiguous figure, and it is difficult to judge whether she is more sinned against than sinning.

At least two Hollywood movies transplant *Macbeth* into mafia culture, where the succession of godfathers seems commonly to proceed by assassination. The first was an Anglo-American collaboration film noir, *Joe Macbeth* (1955), where the mafia link is not directly drawn but strongly implied. Certainly the *Macbeth* reference is proclaimed at the beginning with a text-over: "Not in the Legions of Horrid Hell, / Can come a Devil more damn'd / In evils to top Macbeth. / Act 4 scene 3 MACBETH / WILLIAM SHAKESPEARE", followed by an external view of Tommy's Bar followed by two gunshots after which a "closed" sign is hung on the door. A fortune teller called Rosie quotes and acts as the Witches, prophesying three things for Macbeth, beginning with "the house on Lakeview Drive" which happens to be Tommy's, and ending with "king of darkness, king of the city". Lady Macbeth is Lily, who is initially furious at being kept waiting two hours to marry Joe. He suffers from delusions and nightmares, and after accidentally killing Lily, suffers a violent end himself. The writers had clearly done their homework, because just as Shakespeare includes a "sewer" to ensure Duncan's food is not poisoned, so it is in this version: "being a taster, that's dangerous, I could get killed". "Duke" (Duncan) is undoubtedly up to his eyeballs in corruption as a cold-blooded gang leader and even flirts with Lily Macbeth, while Joe is a malleable and obedient softy ("I'm as far as I want to go right now ... the Duke's the boss") whom Lily relentlessly badgers and provokes ("It's got to be done, Joe, it's just got to be done ... We only have to go through it once ... The knife knows where to go, just follow it step by step"). She makes quite sure Duke is thoroughly dead, stabbed in his own swimming lake, to the raucous sound of birds ("boids") which punctuates the movie. The rest unravels in surprisingly close fashion to the events in

Macbeth. In fact, the screenwriters' fidelity to the source is ironically Joe and Lily's undoing, since if they had been allowed to be more alert and opportunistic, and not so wedded to death by stabbing, the death of Duke could have been plausibly explained by drowning, and they would not have been suspected. As it is, their fates are sealed. The only significant change is that the role of Macduff is elided with Fleance's as Lenny, who loses his wife and children but is Joe's nemesis, and a butler called Angus does service for Shakespeare's Porter and the enigmatic Rosse, as an economy of action to facilitate the plot.

The second mafia adaptation is *Men of Respect* (1990), which follows Shakespeare's story quite closely and signals the influence in some of the names. The sound of Mike Battaglia is not far from Macbeth and his resentment is sparked when he is passed over as lieutenant in the mafia hierarchy; his wife is named Ruthie, which was an open choice since Shakespeare does not name her; D'Amico is not quite Duncan but shares consonants and highlights the fact that this doomed godfather is a "friend". Others are more recognisable: Bankie Como is close enough to Banquo (his son Philly, on the way to Fleance), D'Amico's son is Mal, Donalbain is Don and Seyton Sal, while the rival to the new tyrant Mike is Matt Duffy, whose wife and children are "rubbed out" because the hired killers cannot find Duffy. The latter murders Mike, and Mal inherits as the new godfather, but one suspects his own days are numbered.

A third mafia example, not from Hollywood, is an Australian version of *Macbeth* (2006) with local Sam Worthington starring. For such a peaceful city, Melbourne is still plagued by gangland killings with close ties to Sicily, the latest of which was in 2016 when a lawyer who had defended prominent underworld criminals, but ended his association, was gunned down outside his gelato cafe. This adaptation retains Shakespeare's language though delivered in "Strine" accents. It seems to be the only one that has sought to make sense of Lady Macbeth's "I have given suck" speech, by showing her in a graveyard mourning the death of a child. It also suggests the main motivation for Macbeth's actions is his overwhelming love for his wife.

A recent, important movie version of *Macbeth* offers the opportunity of seeing the play in a culturally different light, and also to look in more detail into the process of adaptation into the different medium. The Indian *Maqbool* (2003), directed by Vishal Bhardwaj, is a compelling and highly atmospheric movie in its own right, and due to its recognisable basis in the Hollywood genre of "godfather" crime drama, it is accessible to audiences in all cultures without further explanations. The fact that it is also an adaptation of Shakespeare's *Macbeth*, announced in the opening credits, is not something we need to know in order to understand it, though the reference does enrich the experience and show how the film approaches the major issues in the play and takes a stance on the central character. On the whole, Maqbool seems to be at the less active end of the spectrum of available Macbeths, in the sense that he tends to let things happen to him, at least initially. This is an odd thing to say about a man who ends up shooting several others and is actively involved in the violent gangland affairs – mainly gold smuggling, contract killings, and mafia-like operations controlling the Bollywood film industry – which are shown as ruling Mumbai life. He is more fatalistic than active, mainly because ambition is not to the fore among Maqbool's motivations, and he is, instead, gradually sucked in. His slaughter of the "godfather", Abbaji (literally "revered father"), takes longer to effect than in *Macbeth*, and in the meantime Maqbool's loyalty and fealty are touchingly shown in a kind of strong, father-son relationship. Like Duncan, Abbaji's stated intention is to secure his lineage by nominating as successor his own son-in-law, Guddu, who will be married to Sameera, thus promising an heir and future successor. This stirs Maqbool to realise the impossibility of any thoughts he might harbour to take over peacefully from Abbaji some day, but still his loyalty holds him back. Abbaji is certainly no "saintly" figure, but a hardened criminal who is far less sympathetic than Maqbool. Most centrally, it is the seduction by Nimmi, a discarded mistress of Abbaji who is now filled with the desire for revenge, who implicates Maqbool by working on his own latent desire for power. For the Witches, the film substitutes two corrupt policemen who owe more to Shakespeare's Dogberry in *Much Ado About Nothing* than the "weird sisters" in *Macbeth*. In a sense they do see the future by using the horoscope or *kundal* chart, a repeated image in the movie, but they are presented as corrupt and superstitious rather than spookily supernatural. India is a country where religion rubs shoulders with superstition and the latter in turn is ridiculed and undermined by the energetic Rationalist Society, and the film seems to express more scepticism than belief by making the two policemen comic characters.

The role of Duncan, however, is considerably expanded in *Maqbool*, mainly because of the compelling acting of Pankaj Kapur as Abbaji. He is ruthless and brutal to enemies, traitors and hapless lackeys, and he has complete power over the Mumbai police force as well as over his group. It is made fairly clear that he murdered his own way to the top, and early on he uses his sinister links to have the new, anti-corruption police chief moved away from this beat ("we're going to miss him ... no need to blow his brains out"), although the incorruptible officer returns like Macduff at the end to clean up affairs. Abbaji is self-evidently a far more dangerous and complex figure than the guileless Duncan, who is more of a pawn in the plot, a cause rather than a character. Maqbool, after the murder, is constantly haunted by hallucinations of Abbaji being still alive, conflating Duncan with Banquo. It is Abbaji's menacing presence even after his death that provides a film noir atmosphere of moody threat. Nimmi is equally the femme fatale of film noir convention, and she plays an ambiguous and complex role. Her attraction to Maqbool is intense and sensual: "My passion would consume you ... You can die for me and even kill ..." Over the image on the screen of her walking barefooted the love song intones "How glorious to have love tear your heart apart". She has the ruthless impulses of Lady Macbeth but at the same time, like Maqbool, she can be seen as vulnerable and eventually as a victim. As the discarded mistress of Abbaji she has ample cause for vindictiveness, and she also has a genuine love for Maqbool which seems to be built on a prior, strong relationship with him. In turn, her desire for revenge over Abbaji for his fickleness to some extent exonerates Maqbool of blame. His real culpability lies in being the one who actually kills Abbaji in his bed, with blood being significantly spattered over Nimmi to show her complicity, and then his murder of others to retain power once he has achieved it. The scenes at night-time – respectively with warming fire outside, delicate gauze in the bedroom – convey sensuality, mutual enjoyment, and even serenity. Amrita Sen describes these scenes as ones where the film "resorts to the familiar Bollywood *masala*, offering tangled love affairs and conflicting loyalties" (Sen 2009: 3). Later Nimmi steadily goes mad, obsessively trying to scrub imagined blood

7 *Macbeth* on Stage and Screen

from the walls, and poignantly aware of her condition: "I'm going mad, aren't I? I am going insane, aren't I?" Maqbool makes no answer but is overcome by lifeless despondence, though still attentive in his love, which remains strong to the end. Nimmi is filled with remorse and shame, repeating hypnotically "was everything a sin? Everything? Our love was chaste, wasn't it ... pure?". Her suffering is an affecting scene and very different from the estranged and despairing endings respectively of Macbeth and his wife. Finally, to make her an even more complex figure, Nimmi has been undergoing a very difficult pregnancy, bearing a child which may be Maqbool's or may be Abbaji's – Bharadwaj's solution to the question raised in Macbeth of how the couple can be childless and without heir while the woman has "given suck".

The final scenes of *Maqbool* follow fairly closely the circumstances of *Macbeth*, with Birnam Wood replaced by the sea coming to his house in the form of customs inspectors wanting to prosecute him for his involvement in smuggling. After the death of Nimmi, Maqbool is alone, isolated, and on the run from the surrounding police force, betrayed one last time by the two corrupt policemen, and finally gunned down. There is an overwhelming feeling that is absent from the end of *Macbeth*, that the protagonist despite his manifest criminality was at heart a loyal and manipulated tragic figure who had no personal inclination to violence. On the overall philosophical question raised by Shakespeare's play involving destiny and free will, the film seems finally to rest on the reading that Maqbool was essentially a relatively passive victim of circumstances; like a typical film noir protagonist he can justifiably say, "Yes. Fate or some mysterious force can put the finger on you or me, for no good reason at all". In his case the "mysterious force" is love, just as one reading of the relationship between Macbeth and his wife would suggest.

As if the twentieth-century's wheel turned full circle, the increasing tide of movie adaptations of Shakespeare's plays, especially from the 1990s onwards, to some extent reversed the longstanding tendency to give priority to language and words in discussions of Shakespeare. Instead, the new media draw on the filmic heritage from silent movies, which sought to convey a story and a vision primarily through images. Dynamic spectacle, pure bodily presence and primitive sound were used in a series of modern performance versions. Perhaps because of the play's own capacity to draw upon dark, irrational and powerful emotional states, *Macbeth* has become a common testing ground for performance art and avant-garde theatre. *The Chronicle of Macbeth* was made by the Suzuki Company of Toga (SCOT) set up by the Japanese experimental director Tadashi Suzuki (see Carruthers 2006). It exists in a televised recording shown on the Australian SBS channel in 1991. It echoes to the pounding of drum-beats and stamping feet, as a group chants the Witches' lines. The production is intensely physical and ritualised, marked by explosive but disciplined energy, and it is devoid of any attempt at naturalistic acting. Macbeth and Lady Macbeth intone – or rather shout – "anthology pieces" from the play, in a sequence which is sometimes narrative but also involves some rearrangements (the "Tomorrow, and tomorrow, and tomorrow" speech comes at the beginning instead of towards the end). "Macbeth" is delusional, and his mental state deteriorates. "Farewell to history" and "farewell to memory" are the refrains. At less than an hour in performance, it is clearly a very shorn-down, bare bones production, shot in semi-darkness with gashes of red signifying blood. In a text-over prologue, Suzuki proclaims his broader philosophy that drama such as this can bring people back to their "animal spirits", which have been submerged under modern civilisation. It is a strident experience that generates significant power in its stylised and elemental simplicity. David Williams' spectacular and athletic production in the Dolphin Theatre at the University of Western Australia in 1991 was influenced by Suzuki, and owed as much to contemporary dance effects while retaining the Shakespearian text. Again, questions of "authenticity" in the process of adaptation are raised and confounded at the same time.

Television, without the epic scope or large budgets of the big screen, often relies on reshaping plays into a more domestic setting and social environment. Not so with the BBC/Time Life *Macbeth* (1982), with its stars Nicol Williamson and a sexually explicit Jane Lapotaire, since with minimal resources the director, Jack Gold, uses large, scenic screens to give a wintry, outdoors feel at some points, and an uncomfortable, Spartan castle for indoors. Gold seems to have realised, or at least theorised, that the television screen could dangerously over-literalise some elements, and accordingly he chose to make invisible

7 *Macbeth* on Stage and Screen

the things which only Macbeth sees: the dagger, the ghost of Banquo, and the later apparitions, making them unequivocally figments of his imagination. Like many of the productions in this worthy but often dull series, most of which aimed to present largely uncut texts with period "authenticity", this *Macbeth* is subdued and studied rather than menacing.

A modernised version made in 2001, *Scotland, PA*, is set in the past (1975) at a fast-food restaurant called Duncan's Café in Scotland, Pennsylvania. The events unfold more or less as they do in the play though without Shakespeare's language, but the film seems to be intended as a particularly black comedy set in a burger café rather than a national tragedy. Duncan is disposed of in a fat-fryer chipmaker. But since the food industry seems to be a highly competitive environment, it offered ideas for others along similar but more straightforwardly tragic lines. In 2005 the BBC made a very different series under the title *ShakespearRe-told*, and in the adaptation by Peter Moffat (2005), Macbeth is turned into a Glaswegian, Joe Macbeth, who works as a sous chef with his mate Billy Banquo at a Michelin-starred restaurant under a celebrity chef, Duncan. The proximity of very sharp knives used for chopping meat, an equally sharp wife clad in black leather, and a volatile, competitive workplace involving Duncan's effete son Malcolm and the head waiter, Peter Macduff, all make murder apparently irresistible to the upwardly mobile couple. The prophetic roles of the Witches are filled by three mysterious rubbish collectors singing "Pigs Will Fly" (by the end police helicopters will be hovering overhead – get it?). *Masterchef* (and Gordon Ramsay's fiery kitchens) will never be the same again after watching this bloodstained affair. The language is again modernised, demonstrating the strength of Shakespeare's recognisable plots and character roles, and the transportability of these into different historical periods and the present day.

The most recent filmed version of *Macbeth* (2015) is directed by Justin Kurzel, who is known for his *Snowtown* (2011), based on a grisly series of murders in his home state of South Australia. The choice of subjects in both suggest he has an interest in filming evil, and in this adaptation of *Macbeth* murders are explicitly shown onstage which in Shakespeare are offstage, to accentuate the violence. At least one reviewer has detected an anti-war message, suggesting, that this

Macbeth suffers from the post-traumatic disorder of a soldier exposed to and involved in violent slaughter (Barnes 2015). Action dominates language, to the extent that even some of Shakespeare's famous passages are not used. If atmosphere is a key criterion in judging *Macbeth* movies, this one is probably the best in that department. The locations, among them the Isle of Skye, Bamburgh Castle and Ely Cathedral, shot in stormy weather and blood-red fire, at times steal the show. Michael Fassbender and Marion Cotillard are experienced star actors and their faces are able to express with some subtlety the traumas they undergo, unlike the young figures in Polanski's version. Kurzel makes clear from the opening scene what he thinks of the question "how many children has Lady Macbeth?" by showing the Macbeths grieving over the dead body of a child, and this image explains a lot about the interpretation that follows (Miller 2017). One implication is the obvious one that they are now childless and the lack of an heir is a primary motivation in Macbeth's later actions. What Kurzel does with this is carefully analysed in a review by Claire Hansen (2015). The experience also feeds into our understanding of Lady Macbeth's state of frozen emotion and transference of feelings into ambition for her husband. The Macduff family becomes especially important, not only emphasising Macduff's reaction to Malcolm's stoicism with "He has no children", but also because Lady Macbeth is witness to the deaths of Lady Macduff and her children (here burned at stakes rather than stabbed, as if to draw out the cruelty) and she is given a moment of fleeting vulnerability, breaking her usual air of profound and numbed depression. The film comes close to overdoing the imagery of children, which are at almost every stage present and highlighted. There is a child always with the Witches, and others balefully overlook the battlefield or play innocently in the background. A boy, briefly mentioned in the text, who is murdered, is set up as a surrogate son to Macbeth and continues to reappear, for example holding out the apparitional dagger. The obtrusiveness of children does perhaps become a little distracting in repetition, since although one can find ample textual references in the play, they seem more subtle and carefully placed rather than literally present so often. Nonetheless, it shows Kurzel has studied the text carefully and found his dominant theme – that it is not just gaining power which matters but keeping it in perpetuity for future generations. In a variation on Polanski's ending, Kurzel shows the boy Fleance reappearing on the battlefield, picking up Macbeth's sword, and running into the distant future. The strong implication is that the eventual accession of Banquo's line over Malcolm's will not be peaceful. Another literalism which may be implied in Shakespeare, but not shown so graphically, is the emphasis on sex between man and wife. Lady Macbeth's line, "But screw your courage to the sticking-place and we'll not fail" as she taunts his masculinity, becomes a sexual invitation to her husband, and later he strokes her under her dress to orgasm. Grim compulsion and tense frustration seem to drive these moments of relief rather than pleasure or even passion. The latter is accompanied by Macbeth's expression of regret at their apparent barrenness:

> Upon my head they placed a fruitless crown,
> And put a barren scepter in my grip,
> Thence to be wrenched with an unlineal hand,
> No son of mine succeeding. If't be so,
> For Banquo's issue have I filed my mind,
> For them the gracious Duncan have I murdered,
> Put rancours in the vessel of my peace
> Only for them, and mine eternal jewel
> Given to the common enemy of man
> To make them kings, the seeds of Banquo kings. (3.1.62-71)

It might disappoint Shakespeare enthusiasts to find some of the most memorable speeches truncated – the Witches in particular lose some of their mesmerising lines. Dropping the Porter's scene, although it is a conspicuous absence, does not seem damaging, since arguably his influence is more relevant to the stage and not so effective on screen. Much of the Porter's "humour" is lost on modern audiences anyway. Overall, it may seem unnecessary to make a short play even shorter, but the effect here is to lessen the power of words and repetition, and instead to enhance the sense of unremitting action and a relentless momentum of events carrying Macbeth to his inevitable fate. The result is a powerful movie giving new life to Shakespeare's play.

By way of summary, a point can be made here about such appropriations of Shakespeare, ways of presenting his plays as statements of a modern value system or political ideology. There is nothing new about this (as discussedd in the eighteenth century the plays were comprehensively rewritten to conform to neo-classical rules of drama), and there is nothing wrong with the practice since Shakespeare is obviously dealing with overtly political issues, especially in *Macbeth*, and plays are made for contemporary audiences rather than for scholars. But what is remarkable, and somewhat sobering, is to observe how many conflicting appropriations of the plays have been made. Shakespeare was the favourite writer of Karl Marx, co-writer of *The Communist Manifesto*, and also of Margaret Thatcher, a Conservative prime minister of England, who quoted Shakespeare in defence of her questionable war policy in the Falkland Islands. In the previous pages of this chapter I have drawn on an essay called "Macbeth on Film" by E. Pearlman (1987), which argues that Orson Welles' *Macbeth* depicts the nightmare of a right-wing dictatorship which haunted the postwar generation, that Polanski's *Macbeth* depicts a process where evil penetrates power and political institutions, and that Kurosawa's *Throne of Blood* is a parable of the masses rebelling against corrupt, feudal aristocracy. Each of these appropriations has been generated from aspects of Shakespeare's play which are identifiable and can be analysed and justified by reference to the text. The one conclusion we cannot draw, however, is the one that Pearlman unfortunately depends upon. He contrasts each of these visions against a Shakespearian text which he sees as immutable and unproblematical. The play, he asserts (but does not try to prove), "unabashedly celebrates a semi-divine monarch": Duncan is "thoroughly paternal, compassionate, and regal", Malcolm is "pure and untainted", the Witches "invade a basically healthy universe", and the moving of Birnam Wood, far from being a military stratagem by men, is "the triumph of the natural world over the human". Some of these statements will by now, I hope, strike my reader as at best debatable (for instance, the "basically healthy universe" at the beginning, despite Duncan's glimpse of the "temple-haunting martlets", is a battle zone in the middle of a bloody civil war). In these universalising and dubious flawed statements, Pearlman is himself implicitly appropriating the Shakespearian text to a set of very simple, political ideologies. This suggests Shakespeare is an apologist for conservative orthodoxy, which is only a partial option given the openness, the radical ambivalence, and the disturbing power of a play which is as thrilling and chilling today as it was in the early years of the seventeenth century.

Bibliography

Editions Consulted

The text quoted in this book is from the Oxford *Complete Works*, edited by Wells and Taylor, below, whose first two editions have been consulted. The other editions have all been used for their excellent notes and commentaries, and each provides different, valuable insights reflecting different readings, another proof that a play like *Macbeth* repays constant rethinking and a multitude of fresh views as time goes on.

Braunmuller, A.R., ed. *Macbeth: The New Cambridge Shakespeare*. Cambridge: Cambridge University Press, 1997.
Brooke, Nicholas, ed. *The Tragedy of Macbeth: The Oxford Shakespeare*. Oxford: Oxford University Press, 1990.
Clark, Sandra and Pamela Mason, eds. *Macbeth. Arden Bloomsbury Shakespeare.* London: Bloomsbury, 2015.
Hunter, G.K., ed. *Macbeth: New Penguin Edition*. Harmondsworth: Penguin Books, 1967.
Muir, Kenneth, ed. *Macbeth: The Arden Shakespeare*. London: Methuen, 9th ed., 1962.
Wells, Stanley and Gary Taylor, eds. *The Complete Works*. Oxford: The Clarendon Press, 2005.

Critical Works

Adelman, Janet. "'Born of Woman': Fantasies of Maternal Power in *Macbeth*." In *Cannibals, Witches, and Divorce: Estranging the Renaissance*, edited by Marjorie Garber, 90-121. Baltimore: Johns Hopkins University Press, 1986.
Anderson, Linda. *A Kind of Wild Justice: Revenge in Shakespeare's Comedies*. Newark: University of Delaware Press, 1987.
Arendt, Hannah. *Eichman in Jerusalem*. London: Penguin Books, 1963.
Arikha, Noga. *Passions and Tempers: A History of the Humours*. New York: Harper Collins, 2007.
Babb, Lawrence. *The Elizabethan Malady: A Study of Melancholia in English Literature from 1580 to 1642*. East Lansing: Michigan State College Press, 1951.
Bacon, Francis. *The Essayes or Counsels, Civill and Morall*. London: John Haviland, 1625.
Baker, Oliver R. "The Thanes in *Macbeth*: Fealty and obedience to *The True Lawe of Free Monarchies*." *Shakespeare* 12 (2016): 111-33.
Bambrough, J.B. *The Little World of Man*. London: Longmans, 1952.
Barnes, Henry. "Michael Fassbender: 'Macbeth Suffered from PTSD'." *The Guardian*, 23 May 2015. www.theguardian.com/film/2015/may/23/michael-fassbender-macbeth-suffered-from-ptsd.
Bartholomeusz, Dennis. *Macbeth and the Players*. Cambridge: Cambridge University Press, 1969.
Bate, Jonathan. *The Romantics on Shakespeare*. London: New Penguin Shakespeare Library, 1992.
Bayley, John. *Shakespeare and Tragedy*. London: Routledge & Kegan Paul, 1981.
BBC History: 'Macbeth' 2014. http://www.bbc.co.uk/history/historic_figures/macbeth.shtml.
Belsey, Catherine. *The Subject of Tragedy: Identity and Difference in Renaissance Drama*. London: Methuen, 1985.
Benecke, Ingrid. "The Shorter Stage Version of Shakespeare's *Macbeth* as Seen through Simon Forman's Eyes." *Notes and Queries* 61 (2014): 246-53.
Berger Jr., Harry. "The Early Scenes of *Macbeth*: Preface to a New Interpretation." *English Literary History* 47 (1980): 1-31.
Bevington, David and Eric Rasmussen, eds. *Doctor Faustus*. Manchester: Manchester University Press, 1993.
Bodleian Library. *Shakespeare Documented: Forman's Account of Seeing Plays at the Globe*: http://www.shakesparedocumented.org/exhibition/document/formans-account-seeing-plays-globe-macbeth-cymbeline-winters-tale.

Bibliography

Booth, Stephen. *King Lear, Macbeth, Indefinition, and Tragedy.* New Haven: Yale University Press, 1983.

Boyle, R. *A Disquisition about the Final Causes of Natural Things.* London: Printed by H.C. for John Taylor ..., 1688.

Bradley, A.C. *Shakespearean Tragedy.* London: Macmillan, 1904.

Bradshaw, Graham. "Operatic Macbeths: what we could still learn from Verdi." In *Macbeth: Shakespeare in Performance*, edited by Bernice Kliman, 44-61. Manchester: Manchester University Press, 2004.

Bradshaw, Graham. *Shakespeare's Scepticism.* Brighton: Harvester Press, 1981.

Brooke, Nicholas. "The Moral Tragedy of Doctor Faustus." *The Cambridge Journal* 5 (1952): 662-88.

Brooks, Cleanth. "'The Naked Babe' and the Cloak of Manliness." In *The Well-Wrought Urn*, 21-46. New York: Reynal and Hitchcock, 1947.

Bullough, Geoffrey. *Narrative and Dramatic Sources of Shakespeare: Major Tragedies: Hamlet, Othello, King Lear, Macbeth.* Vol. 7. London: Routledge Paul & Kegan, 1973.

Burnett, Mark Thornton. "*Doctor Faustus*: Dramaturgy and Disturbance." In *The Cambridge Companion to English Renaissance Tragedy*, edited by Emma Smith and Garrett A. Sullivan, 163-73. Cambridge: Cambridge University Press, 2010.

Burt, Richard, ed. *Shakespeares after Shakespeare: An Encyclopedia of the Bard in Mass Media and Popular Culture.* 2 vols. Westport, CT: Greenwood Press, 2007.

Burton, Robert. *The Anatomy of Melancholy.* London: 1621.

Calderwood, James L. *If It Were Done: Macbeth and Tragic Action.* Amherst: University of Massachusetts Press, 1986.

Callaghan, Dympna, Lorraine Helms and Jyotsna Singh, eds. *The Weyward Sisters: Shakespeare and Feminist Politics.* Oxford: Blackwell Publishers, 1994.

Carruthers, Ian, ed. *Reading Suzuki Tadashi's 'The Chronicle of Macbeth' in Australia.* University of Tsukuba: The Society of Cultural Criticism, 2006.

Clare, Janet. *'Art made tongue-tied by authority': Elizabethan and Jacobean Dramatic Censorship.* 2nd edn. Manchester: Manchester University Press, 1999.

Clarke, Mary Cowden. *The Girlhood of Shakespeare's Heroines.* London: W.H. Smith & Son, 1850-2.

Clemen, Wolfgang H. *The Development of Shakespeare's Imagery.* London: Methuen, 1951.

Cohn, Ruby. *Modern Shakespeare Offshoots.* Princeton, NJ: Princeton University Press, 1976.

Cummings, Brian. "*Metalepsis*: The Boundaries of Metaphor." In *Renaissance Figures of Speech*, edited by Sylvia Adamson, Gavin Alexander, and Katrin Ettenhuber, 217–236. Cambridge: Cambridge University Press, 2007.
Curthoys, Ned. "Hannah Arendt and the Banality of Evil." *Dialogue Australasia: Critical and Creative Ways to Teach Religion and Philosophy* 32 (2014): 25–9.
Davidson, Clifford. "Evil and Fascination in *Macbeth*." *Parergon* 34 (2017): 129–42.
De Quincey, Thomas. "On the Knocking at the Gate in *Macbeth*." *The London Magazine*, 8 October, 1823. Reprinted (without de Quincey's intended revisions) in *The Art of Conversation and Other Papers*, 1863.
De Sousa, Geraldo U. "Cookery and Witchcraft in *Macbeth*." In *Macbeth: The State of Play*, ed. Ann Thompson, 161–82. London: Bloomsbury, 2014.
Dobson, Michael, Stanley Wells, Will Sharpe and Erin Sullivan. *The Oxford Companion to Shakespeare*. 2nd edn. Oxford: Oxford University Press, 2015.
Dollimore, Jonathan. *Radical Tragedy: Religion, Ideology and Power in the Drama of Shakespeare and His Contemporaries*. Brighton: Harvester Press, 1984; 2nd edn, Hemel Hempstead: Harvester Press, 1989.
Duxfield, Andrew. "'Resolve me of all ambiguities': *Doctor Faustus* and the Failure to Unify." *Early Modern Literary Studies* 16 (October 2007): 1–21.
Empson, William. *Seven Types of Ambiguity*. London: Chatto & Windus, 1930.
Escolme, Bridget. *Talking to the Audience: Shakespeare, Performance, Self*. Abingdon, UK: Routledge, 2005.
Everett, Barbara. "Macbeth: Succeeding." In *Young Hamlet: Essays on Shakespeare's Tragedies*, 124–36. Oxford: Clarendon Press, 1989.
Fernie, Ewan. *Shame in Shakespeare*. London: Routledge, 2002.
Frow, John. *Character and Person*. Oxford: Oxford University Press, 2014.
Furphy, Joseph. *Such Is Life*. (1903) Sydney: Angus & Robertson, 1944.
Garber, Marjorie. "Macbeth: the Male Medusa." In *Shakespeare's Ghost Writers: Literature as Uncanny Causality*, 87–123. New York and London: Methuen, 1987.
Goldberg, Jonathan. "Speculations: Macbeth and source." In *Shakespeare Reproduced: The Text in History and Ideology*, edited by Jean E. Howard and Marion F. O'Connor, 242–64. New York and London: Methuen, 1987.
Goldman, Michel. *Shakespeare: The Energies of Drama*. Princeton, NJ: Princeton University Press, 1972.
Greenblatt, Stephen. "*King Lear*, a Difficult Play, Not Helped by Sloppy Analysis." *Financial Review*, 14 February 2017. http://www.afr.com/lifestyle/arts-and-entertainment/theatre-and-dance/king-lear-a-difficult-play-not-helped-by-sloppy-analysis-20170213-gubpb8.

Bibliography

Greenblatt, Stephen. "Shakespeare Bewitched." In *Shakespeare and Cultural Traditions*, edited by Tetsuo Kishi, Roger Princle and Stanley Wells, 17-42. Newark: University of Delaware Press, 1994.

Greenblatt, Stephen, gen. ed. *The Norton Shakespeare*, New York: W.W. Norton & Company, 1997.

Hansen, Claire. "Review: Justin Kurzel's *Macbeth*." *Shakespeare Reloaded*, 11 October 2015. http://www.shakespearereloaded.edu.au/review-justin-kurzels-macbeth.

Hawkins, Michael. "History, Politics and *Macbeth*." In *Focus on Macbeth*, edited by J.R. Brown, 155-88. London: Routledge and Kegan Paul, 1981.

Hazlitt, William. *Hazlitt's Criticism of Shakespeare: A Selection*. Edited by R.S. White. Lampeter: Edwin Mellen Press, 1994.

Healy, Thomas. "*Doctor Faustus*." In *The Cambridge Companion to Christopher Marlowe*, edited by Patrick Cheney. Cambridge: Cambridge University Press, 2004.

Heilman, Robert B. "The Criminal as Tragic Hero: Dramatic Methods." *Shakespeare Survey* 19 (1967): 12-24.

Helm, Caroline. *Audience as Performer: The Changing Role of Theatre Audiences in the Twenty-First Century*. Abingdon, UK: Routledge, 2016.

Hobgood, Alison P. "Feeling Fear in *Macbeth*." In *Shakespearean Sensations: Experiencing Literature in Early Modern England*, edited by Katharine A. Craik and Tanya Pollard, 29-46. Cambridge: Cambridge University Press, 2013.

Holland, Peter, ed. *Great Shakespeareans: Garrick, Kemble, Siddons, Kean*. London: Bloomsbury, 2010.

Honan, Park. *Christopher Marlowe: Poet and Spy*. Oxford: Oxford University Press, 2005.

Honigmann, E.A.J. "Macbeth: The Murderer as Victim." In *Shakespeare: Seven Tragedies*. New York: Barnes & Noble, 1976.

Hopkins, Lisa. *Christopher Marlowe: Renaissance Dramatist*. Edinburgh: Edinburgh University Press, 2008.

Hopkins, Lisa. *Shakespearean Allusions in Crime Fiction*. London: Palgrave Macmillan, 2016.

Hopkins, Lisa and Matthew Steggle. *Renaissance Literature and Culture*. London: Continuum, 2016.

Huntley, Frank. "*Macbeth* and the Background of Jesuitical Equivocation." *Publications of the Modern Language Association* 79 (1964): 390-400.

Keats, John. *John Keats: The Letters, 1814-1821*. Edited by H.E. Rollins. 2 vols. Cambridge, MA: Harvard University Press, 1958.

Keyishian, Harry. *The Shapes of Revenge: Victimization, Vengeance and Vindictivenesss in Shakespeare*. Atlantic Highlands, NJ: Humanities Press, 1995.
Kinney, Arthur F. *Lies Like Truth: Shakespeare, Macbeth, and the Cultural Moment*. Detroit, MI: Wayne State University Press, 2001.
Kliman, Bernice W. *Macbeth: Shakespeare in Performance*. 2nd edn. Manchester: Manchester University Press, 2004.
Knight, G. Wilson. *The Wheel of Fire*. (1930) London: Routledge, 1949.
Knights, L.C. "How Many Children Had Lady Macbeth?: An Essay in the Theory and Practice of Shakespeare Criticism." In *Explorations*. (1933) London: Penguin, 1946.
Kott, Jan. *Shakespeare Our Contemporary*. Garden City, NY: Anchor-Doubleday, 1966.
Lake, Peter. *How Shakespeare Put Politics on the Stage: Power and Succession in the History Plays*. New Haven and London: Yale University Press, 2016.
Leitch, Vincent B., ed. *The Norton Anthology of Theory and Criticism*. 2nd edn. New York: W.W. Norton, 2010.
Leggatt, Alexander. *William Shakespeare's Macbeth: A Casebook*. Abingdon, UK: Routledge, 2006.
Lemon, Rebecca. *Treason by Words: Literature, Law, and Rebellion in Shakespeare's England*. Ithaca, NY: Cornell University Press, 2006.
Lindfors, Bernth. *Ira Aldridge: The Last Years, 1855–1867*. Vol. 4. Suffolk, UK: Boydell & Brewer, 2015.
Logan, Robert A. *Shakespeare's Marlowe: The Influence of Christopher Marlowe on Shakespeare's Artistry*. Aldershot, UK: Ashgate, 2007.
Long, Michael. *Macbeth: Harvester New Critical Introductions to Shakespeare*. Hemel Hempstead: Harvester Wheatsheaf, 1989.
Mack, Maynard. *Killing the King: Three Studies in Shakespeare's Tragic Structure*. New Haven, CT: Yale University Press, 1973.
Marlowe, Christopher. *The Complete Plays*. Edited by J.B. Steane. London: Penguin Books, 1969.
McGillivray, Glenn. *Communities of Sentiment: Actors and Emotions in the Eighteenth Century English Theatre, 1741–1782*. Forthcoming.
Meek, Richard and Erin Sullivan, eds. *The Renaissance of Emotion: Understanding Affect in Shakespeare and His Contemporaries*. Manchester: Manchester University Press, 2015.
Miller, Gemma. "'He has no children': Changing Representations of the Child in Stage and Film Productions of *Macbeth* from Polanski to Kurzel". *Shakespeare* 12 (2016), 52–66.

Bibliography

Milton, John. *Poetical Works*. Edited by Douglas Bush. London: Oxford University Press, 1966.
Milton, John. *Selected Prose*. Edited by C. A. Patrides. Harmondsworth: Penguin English Library, 1974.
Moschovakis, Nick. *Macbeth: New Critical Essays*. New York: Routledge, 2008.
Newstok, Scott L. and Ayanna Thompson, eds. *Weyward Macbeth: Intersections of Race and Performance*. New York: Palgrave Macmillan, 2010.
Norbrook, David. "*Macbeth* and the Politics of Historiography." In *Politics of Discourse: The Literature and History of Seventeenth Century England*, edited by Kevin Sharpe and Steven Zwicker, 78-321. Berkeley: University of California Press, 1987.
Ormerod, David and Christopher Wortham, eds. *Dr Faustus: The A-Text*. Nedlands: University of Western Australia Press, 1985.
Ornstein, Robert. "Marlowe and God: The Tragic Theology of *Dr Faustus*." *Publications of the Modern Language Association* 83 (1986): 1378-85.
Paster, Gail Kern. *The Body Embarrassed: Drama and the Disciplines of Shame in Early Modern England*. Ithaca, NY: Cornell University Press, 1993.
Paster, Gail Kern. *Humoring the Body: Emotions and the Shakespearean Stage*. Chicago: University of Chicago Press, 2004.
Paster, Gail Kern, Katherine Rowe and Mary Floyd-Wilson, eds. *Reading the Early Modern Passions: Essays in the Cultural History of Emotion*. Philadelphia: University of Pennsylvania Press, 2004.
Paul, Henry N. *The Royal Play of Macbeth: When, Why, and How It Was Written by Shakespeare*. New York: Macmillan, 1950.
Pearlman, E. "Macbeth on Film: Politics." In *Shakespeare Survey 39: Shakespeare on Film and Television*, edited by Stanley Wells, 67-74. Cambridge: Cambridge University Press, 1987.
Prescott, Paul. *Reviewing Shakespeare: Journalism and Performance from the Eighteenth Century to the Present*. Cambridge: Cambridge University Press, 2013.
Prynne, William. *Histrio-Mastix*. London: Printed by E.A. and W.I. for M. Sparke, 1663.
Quintilian. *Institutio Oratoria*. Translated by H.E. Butler. Harvard: Loeb Classical Library, Harvard University Press, 1920-22.
Rabkin, Norman. *Shakespeare and the Common Understanding*. New York: Free Press, 1967.
Rabkin, Norman. *Shakespeare and the Problem of Meaning*. Chicago and London: University of Chicago Press, 1981.
Rhodes, Neil. *Shakespeare and the Origins of English*. Oxford: Oxford University Press, 2004.

Rosenberg, Marvin. *The Masks of Macbeth*. Berkeley: University of California Press, 1978.
Rossiter, A.P. *Angel with Horns and Other Shakespeare Lectures*. Edited by Graham Storey. London: Longman, 1961.
Rothwell, Kenneth S. *A History of Shakespeare on Screen: A Century of Film and Television*. Cambridge: Cambridge University Press, 1999.
Sanders, Wilbur. *The Dramatist and the Received Idea*. Cambridge: Cambridge University Press, 1968.
Schoenfeldt, Michael C. *Bodies and Selves in Early Modern England: Physiology and Inwardness in Spenser, Shakespeare, Herbert and Milton*. Cambridge: Cambridge University Press, 1999.
Semenza, Gregory M. Colon. "*The Spanish Tragedy* and Metatheatre." In *The Cambridge Companion to English Renaissance Tragedy*, edited by Emma Smith and Garrett Sullivan, 153-62. Cambridge: Cambridge University Press, 2010.
Sen, Amrita. "*Maqbool* and Bollywood Conventions." In *Borrowers and Lenders* 4 (2009): 1-63.
Shakespeare, William. *The Complete Works*. Edited by Stanley Wells and Gary Taylor. 2nd edn. Oxford: The Clarendon Press, 2005.
Sidney, Sir Philip. "The Defence of Poetry." In *Miscellaneous Prose of Sir Philip Sidney*, edited by Katherine Duncan-Jones and Jan van Dorsten. Oxford: Clarendon Press, 1973.
Simon, Joan. *Education and Society in Tudor England*. Cambridge: Cambridge University Press, 1966.
Simpson-Younger, Nancy. "Watching the Sleeper in *Macbeth*". *Shakespeare* 12 (2016): 260-73.
Sinfield, Alan, ed. *Macbeth: New Casebooks*. London: Macmillan, 1992.
Skinner, Quentin. *Forensic Shakespeare*. Cambridge University Press, 2014.
Smith, Emma. *Shakespeare's Tragedies*. Oxford: Blackwell Guides to Criticism, Blackwell Publishing, 2004.
Smith, Emma. *Macbeth: Language and Writing*. London: Bloomsbury Arden, 2013.
Spurgeon, Caroline. *Shakespeare's Imagery and What It Tells Us*. London: Macmillan, 1936.
Stern, Tiffany. "Time for Shakespeare: Hourglasses, Sundials, Clocks and Early Modern Theatre." *Journal of the British Academy* 3 (2015): 1-33.
Stuart, King James. *Basilikon Doron*. Edinburgh, 1599.
Stuart, King James. *Daemonologie, In Forme of a Dialogue, Divided into three Books: By the High and Mighty Prince, James*. (1597) London, 1603.
Sullivan, Erin. *Beyond Melancholy: Sadness and Selfhood in Renaissance England*. London: Oxford University Press, 2016.

Bibliography

Taylor, Gary. "*Macbeth* and Middleton." In *Macbeth: The Norton Critical Edition*, edited by Robert Miola, 296-305. Rev. edn. New York: Norton, 2014.
Thomas, Alfred. *Shakespeare, Dissent and the Cold War*. London: Palgrave Macmillan, 2014.
Thompson, Ann, ed. *Macbeth: The State of Play*. London: Bloomsbury, 2014.
Trawick, Buckner B. *Shakespeare and Alcohol*. Amsterdam: Rodopi, 1978.
Tredell, Nicolas. *Shakespeare: Macbeth: A Reader's Guide to Essential Criticism*. London: Palgrave, 2006.
Wells, Stanley. *Shakespeare & Co*. Harmondsworth: Penguin Books, 2006.
Wells, Stanley, ed. *Shakespeare Survey 39: Shakespeare on Film and Television*. Cambridge: Cambridge University Press, 1987.
White, R.S. *Innocent Victims: Poetic Injustice in Shakespearean Tragedy*. 2nd edn. (1986) London: Bloomsbury, 2015.
White, R.S. "Making Something Out of 'Nothing' in Shakespeare." *Shakespeare Survey* 66 (2013): 232-45.
White, R.S. "'Variable Passions': Shakespeare's Mixed Emotions." In *Conjunctions of Mind, Soul and Body from Plato to the Enlightenment*. London: Springer, 2014.
White, R.S. *Avant-Garde Hamlet: Text, Stage, Screen*. Fairleigh Dickinson Press, 2015.
White, R.S., and Ciara Rawnsley. "Discrepant Emotional Awareness in Shakespeare." In *The Renaissance of Emotion: Understanding Affect in Shakespeare and His Contemporaries*, edited by R. Meek and E. Sullivan, 241-63. London: Manchester University Press, 2015.
Wilders, John, ed. *Macbeth: Shakespeare in Production*. Cambridge: Cambridge University Press, 2004.
Wilks, John S. *The Idea of Conscience in Renaissance Tragedy*. London: Routledge, 1990.
Wills, Gary. *Verdi's Shakespeare: Men of the Theatre*. New York: Viking, 2011.
Wootton, David, ed. *Doctor Faustus with the English Faust Book*. Indianapolis, IN: Hackett Publishing Company, 2005.
Iain Wright. "All Done with Mirrors: Macbeth's Dagger Discovered." *Heat* 10 (new series, Giramondo Press: 2005): 179-200.
Wright, Thomas. *The Passions of the Minde in Generall: A Reprint Based on the 1604 Edition*. Edited by Thomas O. Sloan. Urbana: University of Illinois Press, 1971.

Index

alienation 9, 82, 133
ambition 19, 39–42, 77, 128–132
ambivalence 9, 34–49, 63, 77, 95, 130, 169; *see also* paradox
Arendt, Hannah 135
Aristotle 35, 46, 54
atheism 1, 4
audience 11, 16, 24–26, 38–43, 73–83, 106, 132, 140, 146, 168–182

Bacon, Francis 3, 123
Baker, O.R. 24
Banquo (character) 16–20, 24, 27, 49–52, 69–83, 109, 128–132, 164–166, 188–195
Blackfriars 16, 98, 171
blood 17, 29, 43, 63–67, 86–90, 161–166, 186, 190–194
Boece, Hector 20, 24
Bradley, A.C. 14, 19, 42, 88, 131, 147–148, 177
Bradshaw, Graham 38, 182
Buchanan, George 13, 20–28, 59

characterisation 62
Charles I 26, 39, 81
children 19, 41, 48, 81–95, 160–164, 185–194
Christianity 3–5, 40, 44, 118–122
Cicero 35, 45, 144
Coleridge, Samuel Taylor 131, 134, 147–152
Condell, Richard 13
consequence 54, 107, 110, 112, 123–127
Cummings, Brian 150

de Quincey, Thomas 155
Derrida, Jacques 37
dialectic *see* rhetoric and dialectic
Donalbain 22, 30, 78–82
Dostoyevsky 113, 140
Duncan, King of Scotland (character) 14, 17, 24–30, 41–42, 63–89, 106, 127–131, 153, 163, 187–196

Edward the Confessor 17, 22, 41, 78, 86
Eichmann, Adolf 135

Eliot, George 61, 174
Elizabeth I 22, 68
Elizabethan drama 15, 18, 59, 121, 145–150, 171
Empson, William 37, 147–149
equivocation*, 56, 90, 120, 126–130
Erasmus, Desiderius 45, 144
Everett, Barbara 93, 112
evil 39, 80, 118–123, 130–136, 140, 183–187

First Folio 13, 20; *see also* Shakespeare, William
Fleance (character) 16, 19, 41, 72, 74
Forman, Simon 17, 98
Foucault, Michel 36
Furphy, Joseph
  Such Is Life 96, 112

Garnet, Father Henry 127
Globe Theatre 16, 98, 171, 178
God 6, 9, 39–42, 96, 121–123
Goldberg, Jonathan 38
Greenblatt, Stephen 36, 98
Gunpowder Plot 16, 26, 127

Harvey, William 162–162
Hazlitt, William 59, 179–181
Hecate (character) 15, 97
Henry IV (character) 55, 70
Henry V (character) 67, 70
Henry VIII (character) 120
Holinshed 20–30, 65
  Chronicles of England, Scotland and Ireland 20–30, 59

Iago (character) 131–135, 178
imagery 44, 47, 143–166
  birds 159
  blood 162–166; *see also* blood

darkness and light 156
drunkenness 153–156

Jacobean drama 15, 121, 171
James I of England (VI of Scotland) 15, 22–26, 41, 71
Jonson, Ben 7, 15, 144

Keats, John 33, 150–152
Knight, G. Wilson 42, 131, 147–148
Knights, L.C. 19, 88, 147–149
Kurosawa, Akira 183–185, 196
Kurzel, Justin 149, 193–195
Kyd, Thomas 1–3, 9

Lady Macbeth (character) 19–22, 66, 86–95, 110–112, 119, 125–129, 135–140, 159–164, 169–177, 184–195
Lady Macduff (character) 83, 85–95

Macduff (character) 18, 19, 39–42, 78–93, 125–128, 154, 166, 194
Malcolm, Prince of Cumberland (character) 21–30, 39–43, 66–69, 76–88, 92, 128, 193–196
Marlowe, Christopher 1–2, 4–10, 39–40, 119–123
  Doctor Faustus 4–11, 39–42, 96, 119–123
Mary, Queen of Scots 25
Middleton, Thomas 15, 80
Milton, John 81, 120–123
  Paradise Lost 96, 120
Muir, Kenneth 21–29, 65

negative capability *see* ambivalence
numbers 49–53
  patterns of three 49–54
  philosophical significance 49

Index

Othello (character) 179
Ovid 35, 45

paradox 34–37, 107, 149, 169; *see also* ambivalence
poetry in drama 45–48, 130, 144–153, 174
Polanski, Roman 93, 184, 194
Porter, the (character) 119, 126, 154–156
power and monarchy 55–57
productions and adaptations 167–197
  music and opera 181
  screen 182–195
  stage 167–182; *see also* Blackfriars, Globe Theatre

Quintilian 46, 144, 150

Ramus, Petrus 46
redemption 77, 179
Richard III (character) 133, 136, 169, 179
rhetoric and dialectic 45–48
Rossiter, A.P. 38, 40, 122

Seneca 21, 45, 120
Shakespeare, William
  A Midsummer Night's Dream 36
  As You Like It 101–103, 147
  Hamlet 2–5, 9, 13, 120, 131, 145
  Henry IV 130
  Henry V 21, 36, 49, 147
  Henry VI 30, 135
  Julius Caesar 184
  King Lear 13, 49, 134, 146
  Love's Labour's Lost 45
  Merry Wives of Windsor, The 45
  Much Ado About Nothing 134, 189
  Othello 13, 134, 145, 183
  Pericles 15, 103
  Richard II 20, 38
  Richard III 20, 87, 135, 143

Verdi, Giuseppe 181

Witches, the (character) 15, 27, 41, 52, 69–98, 106, 108, 121–126, 129, 163, 184–187, 193